HTML5 and CSS3
Introductory
ILLUSTRATED

Second Edition

Sasha Vodnik

CENGAGE

Australia • Brazil • Canada • Mexico • Singapore • United Kingdom • United States

HTML5 and CSS3—Illustrated Introductory
Second Edition

Sasha Vodnik

Product Director: Kathleen McMahon

Senior Product Manager: Jim Gish

Senior Director of Development: Marah
Bellegarde

Product Development Manager: Leigh Hefferon

Senior Content Developer: Marjorie Hunt

Product Assistant: Abigail Pufpaff

Marketing Director: Michele McTighe

Senior Marketing Manager: Eric La Scola

Manufacturing Planner: Fola Orekoya

Developmental Editor: Pamela Conrad

Full Service Project Management: GEX Publishing
Services

Proofreader: Gail Marks

Indexer: Alexandra Nickerson

QA Manuscript Reviewers: Danielle Shaw,
Jeff Schwartz

Cover Designer: GEX Publishing Services

Cover Artist: GEX Publishing Services

Cover image: © VikaSuh/Shutterstock.com

Composition: GEX Publishing Services

For product information and technology assistance, contact us at
**Cengage Customer & Sales Support, 1-800-354-9706
or support.cengage.com.**

For permission to use material from this text or product, submit all
requests online at **www.cengage.com/permissions.**

Library of Congress Control Number: 2015933866

ISBN: 978-1-305-39405-6

Cengage
200 Pier 4 Boulevard
Boston, MA 02210
USA

Cengage is a leading provider of customized learning solutions
with employees residing in nearly 40 different countries and sales in more
than 125 countries around the world. Find your local representative at:
www.cengage.com.

To learn more about Cengage platforms and services, register or access
your online learning solution, or purchase materials for your course,
visit **www.cengage.com.**

The websites featured in this book are fictional. Names, characters,
businesses, places, are either the products of the author's imagination or
used in a fictitious manner. Any resemblance to actual websites, places, or
people is purely coincidental.

Trademarks:
Some of the product names and company names used in this book have
been used for identification purposes only and may be trademarks or
registered trademarks of their respective manufacturers and sellers.

Printed at CLDPC, USA, 10-20

Contents

Preface

Welcome to *HTML5 and CSS3—Illustrated Introductory Second Edition*. This book has a unique design: Each skill is presented on two facing pages, with steps on the left and screens on the right. The layout makes it easy to learn a skill without having to read a lot of text and flip pages to see an illustration.

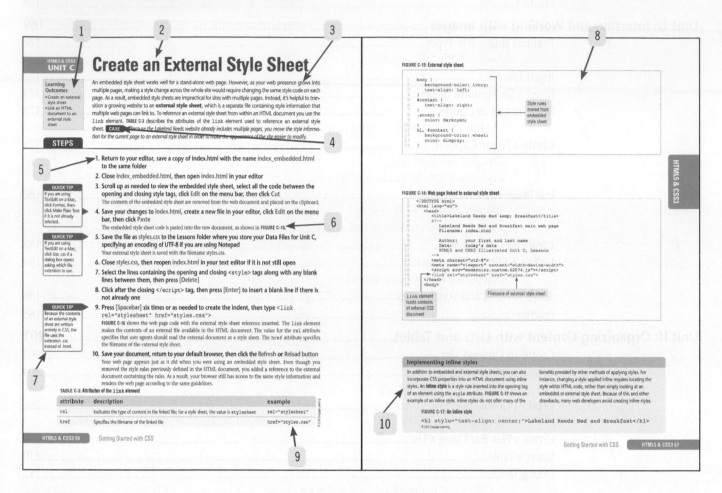

1. **New!** Learning Outcomes box lists measurable learning goals for which a student is accountable in that lesson.

2. Each two-page lesson focuses on a single skill.

3. Introduction briefly explains why the lesson skill is important.

4. A case scenario motivates the steps and puts learning in context.

5. Step-by-step instructions and brief explanations guide students through each hands-on lesson activity.

6. **New!** Figure references are now in red bold to help students refer back and forth between the steps and screenshots.

7. Tips and troubleshooting advice, right where you need it—next to the step itself.

8. **New!** Larger screen shots with green callouts and code students type shown in red.

9. Tables provide summaries of helpful information such as element and property syntax.

10. Clues to Use yellow boxes provide useful information related to the lesson skill.

This book is an ideal learning tool for a wide range of learners—the "rookies" will find the clean design easy to follow and focused with only essential information presented, and the "hotshots" will appreciate being able to move quickly through the lessons to find the information they need without reading a lot of text. The design also makes this book a great reference after the course is over! See the illustration on the left to learn more about the pedagogical and design elements of a typical lesson.

What's New in this Edition

- **Coverage** — This book covers basic concepts and skills for developing web pages and websites using HTML5 and CSS3. This new edition is fully updated with many enhancements, including new coverage of debugging using browser tools; it also now integrates mobile design and testing throughout. Designed to meet the needs of users from a broad range of experience levels, this book provides the nuts-and-bolts for beginners and allows more experienced users to brush up on the basics and quickly move on to more advanced topics.

- **New! Learning Outcomes** — Each lesson displays a green Learning Outcomes box that lists skills-based or knowledge-based learning goals for which students are accountable. Each Learning Outcome maps to a variety of learning activities and assessments.

- **New! Updated Design** — This edition features many new design Improvements to engage students — including larger lesson screenshots with green callouts and code students type formatted in red.

- **New! Independent Challenge 4: Explore** — This new case-based assessment activity allows students to explore new skills and use creativity to solve a problem or create a project.

Assignments

This book includes a wide variety of high-quality assignments you can use for practice and assessment. Assignments include

- **Concepts Review** — Multiple choice, matching, and screen identification questions.
- **Skills Review** — Step-by-step, hands-on review of every skill covered in the unit.
- **Independent Challenges 1-3** — Case projects requiring critical thinking and application of the unit skills. The Independent Challenges increase in difficulty. The first one in each unit provides the most hand-holding; the subsequent ones provide less guidance and require more critical thinking and independent problem solving.
- **Independent Challenge 4: Explore** — Case projects that let students explore new skills that are related to the core skills covered in the unit and are often more open ended, allowing students to use creativity to complete the assignment.
- **Visual Workshop** — Critical thinking exercises that require students to create a project by looking at a completed solution; they must apply the skills they've learned in the unit and use critical thinking skills to create the project from scratch.

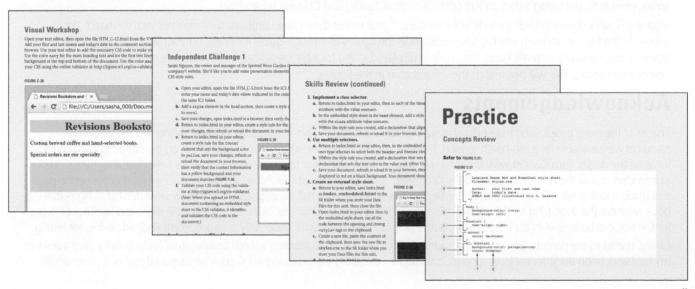

Instructor Resources

This book comes with a wide array of high-quality technology-based, teaching tools to help you teach and to help students learn. The following teaching tools are available for download at our Instructor Companion Site. Simply search for this text at *login.cengage.com*. An instructor login is required.

- **New! Learning Outcomes Map** — A grid for each unit shows the learning activities and assessments that map to each learning outcome in that unit.
- **Instructor's Manual** — Available as an electronic file, the Instructor's Manual includes lecture notes with teaching tips for each unit.
- **Data Files for Students** — To complete most units, students need Data Files, which are included as an Instructor Resource. Students can also download Data Files on cengage.com.
- **Sample Syllabus** — Prepare and customize your course easily using this sample course outline.
- **PowerPoint Presentations** — Each unit has a corresponding PowerPoint presentation covering the skills and topics in that unit.
- **Figure Files** — The figures in the text are provided on the Instructor Resources site to help you illustrate key topics or concepts.

- **Solution Files** — Solution Files are files that contain the finished project that students create or modify in the lessons or end-of-unit material.
- **Solutions Document** — This document outlines the solutions for the end-of-unit Concepts Review, Skills Review, Independent Challenges and Visual Workshops.
- **Test Banks** — Cengage Learning Testing Powered by Cognero is a full-featured, online assessment system that allows instructors to create tests from publisher-provided content as well as write new questions. With the test generator, you can

  - Create tests from publisher-provided question sets.
  - Edit publisher questions.
  - Write your own questions.
  - Tag questions with learning objectives, rubrics, and other meta-information.
  - Print tests or deliver them online through a learning management system.

Key Facts About Using This Book

Data Files are needed: To complete many of the lessons and end-of-unit assignments, you need to start from partially-completed Data Files. All Data Files are available as part of the Instructor Resources. You can also download Data Files for free at cengage.com. (For detailed instructions, go to www.cengage.com/ct/studentdownload.)

System Requirements: To complete the lessons in this book, you need 2 types of applications: an editor and one or more browsers. You can use a plain text editor such as Notepad (part of Windows) or TextEdit (part of Mac OS X), but a code editor is recommended. Free code editors include Aptana Studio 3 (Win/Mac), KomodoEdit (Win/Mac), Notepad++ (Win), and TextWrangler (Mac). You can complete the lessons with a single desktop browser, but real world web development requires testing on a wide variety of browsers and devices. If possible, you should secure access to all of the following desktop browsers: Chrome (Win and Mac), Firefox (Win and Mac), and Internet Explorer (Win). In addition, if possible, you should make arrangements to test using Safari on iOS (iPhone or iPod Touch) and Chrome on Android.

Figures: Figures showing code include line numbers. If your editor shows line numbers, they may not exactly match those shown in the figures; instead, use the line numbers in the figures as a rough guide for orienting yourself in your data files. In figures showing newly entered code, that code is displayed in red for easy identification. If your code editor highlights code in one or more colors, this will not match the color shown in the figures.

Acknowledgements

Thanks to the many people who have helped make this book a reality. Jim Gish was consistently encouraging and made sure the resources were available for a top-notch revision. Marjorie Hunt wrangled the schedule and kept her eye on the big picture so I could focus on the details. Pam Conrad went the extra mile as developmental editor to ensure the explanations were clear, the steps all worked as intended, and all the i's were dotted and the t's crossed. The great people at GEX Publishing Services laid everything out on the page and made it look great. Jeff Schwartz and Danielle Shaw meticulously tested all the steps and let me know what needed fixing before the book went out the door. John McKelvy/mackjackstudio.com and Kenji Oshima/coachkenji.com created the logos and layout prototypes for the fictitious businesses in the lessons and practice projects. Roland McGrath generously provided recent Android devices for testing.

Finally, thanks to my parents, Jim and Diana Vodnik, for helping me to see learning as both an adventure and a priority. And thanks to my husband, Jason Bucy, for his love, support, and help in navigating the balancing act that's a fundamental part of an author's life.

Getting Started with HTML

CASE You've been hired by Lakeland Reeds Bed and Breakfast to build a website. You can create your own web pages like those found on the World Wide Web using just your computer and a text editor. In this unit, you'll learn about planning and wireframing a website, creating the head and body sections of a web page, adding web page text, and testing your web page in desktop and mobile browsers.

Unit Objectives

After completing this unit, you will be able to:

- Define a project plan
- Create wireframes and a storyboard
- Create an HTML document
- Set up the document head and body
- Add text to a web page

- Add a comment to a web document
- Preview your web page on a desktop computer
- Configure web server software
- Preview your web page on mobile devices

Files You Will Need

L	0 files	IC3	0 files
SR	0 files	IC4	0 files
IC1	0 files	VW	0 files
IC2	0 files		

Define a Project Plan

Learning Outcomes
- Identify questions to ask a potential client
- Use a project plan to summarize client responses

People and organizations around the world share information using the **World Wide Web**, or **web** for short. You can make your own information available on the web by creating **web pages**, which are documents formatted to be accessible on the web, and then publishing them as **websites**, which are available to anyone with web access. Whether you intend to make a single web page or a large set of interrelated web pages, making information accessible on the web starts with careful planning. Whether you're brainstorming for a personal site or meeting with a client regarding a site you've been hired to create, your first step is to create a **project plan**, which is also known as a **design document**. A project plan summarizes your client's parameters for the site, including audience, budget, and timeline. **CASE** You held a planning meeting with Phillip Blaine, owner of Lakeland Reeds, to discuss the components he would like included in his new website. **FIGURE A-1** shows the project plan you developed based on client responses at this meeting.

DETAILS

Important questions to consider when planning a website include the following:

- **What are the goals and objectives of the website?**

  In order to understand the goals and objectives for the site, you want to ask your client a variety of questions. For example, "What is the mission of the organization? Why do you want a website? What are the short-term goals of the website? What are the long-term goals of the website? What do you hope to gain by having a web presence? Who is your target audience? Do your objectives support the needs of your target audience?" The more thorough you are in asking questions of the client, the better prepared you will be to design the website.

- **Who is the target audience?**

  It can be helpful to know the target audience for a website when choosing a layout and design. Websites should look different based upon who will be visiting the site and why they are interested in the content. Some potential questions to ask about the target audience might be, "Who are the typical members of your audience? What is the mix of genders? What is the age range? What professions are they in? What is the average education level? Why will people visit this website? Will your desktop visitors be using Microsoft Windows, Apple OS X, or another operating system? Which web browsers will they use to view the website? How common is mobile device use among your audience members? Which types of mobile devices do they use?" While your client may not have ready answers to all of these questions, getting even a few answers can help prepare you for the design phase.

QUICK TIP

Listing exclusions in the project plan will help reduce the potential for scope creep, which is the expansion of a project beyond the original goals and objectives.

- **What type of website is it?**

  Identifying the type of website the owner wants can help to focus the scope of the project. A website usually has one of a small number of main functions: providing a web presence that serves as an online informational brochure, providing important information for special interest groups and nonprofit organizations, showcasing examples of different types of works and designs commonly used by web design individuals and agencies, providing multiple levels of information with page templates, extracting information from databases, or conducting the sale of products or services and other business transactions through the Internet. It is important to clearly define what the site will include, as well as what the site won't include.

- **What is the budget for the project?**

  Every website design project should include a budget that is presented to the client prior to completing any work. The budget should be included in the project plan, which becomes part of the contract.

- **What is the timeline for the project?**

  You should always provide the website owner with a timeline that includes the delivery date of the final website, along with various implementation milestones along the way. The timeline should always identify who is responsible for which tasks.

Project plan for Lakeland Reeds Bed and Breakfast

Objectives:

- Make general info about the facility and contact info available online
- Enable prospective guests to view the accommodations and grounds
- Allow prospective guests to book a stay online

Target audience:

- 35+
- Live in southern Canada and the upper Midwest U.S.
- Want to "get away from it all"
- Not sure about technical details of users, but it's assumed most will have some web experience

Site type:

- Billboard (while the client wants some e-commerce functionality, they will accomplish this by linking to another site that takes reservations; thus, no advanced functionality is required for this site)

Budget:

- Hien is preparing a few detailed options for the client; this section will be updated when the budget is finalized and the contract is signed

Timeline:

Milestone	Date	Who's responsible
Design mockup submitted for approval	April 1, 2018	Project manager
Draft site published to testing server	April 15, 2018	Project manager
Feedback received from client	April 22, 2018	Phillip Blaine
Client feedback incorporated	May 1, 2018	Project manager
Final feedback from client	May 8, 2018	Phillip Blaine
Final feedback incorporated	May 22, 2018	Project manager
Final signoff from client	June 5, 2018	Phillip Blaine
Site goes live	June 5, 2018	Project manager

Client contact info:

Phillip Blaine
Lakeland Reeds Bed and Breakfast
45 Marsh Grass Ln.
Marble, MN 55764
(218) 555-5253

Deciding how much to charge

Estimating the amount of time a project will take can be difficult, especially for new web designers. If you work for a web design agency, the budget will typically be developed by your supervisors. If you are a freelance web designer, you must place a value on your time that takes many things into consideration, such as the cost of computer equipment and software, supplying your own insurance, advertising, and other expenses. There really is no set hourly or project fee in this industry, as it varies dramatically depending upon the geographic market, competition, and experience level of the web designer. New web designers often barter, or trade, their skills for products or services offered by a website owner as a means of building a portfolio.

Create Wireframes and a Storyboard

Learning
Outcomes
• Define wireframes
  and storyboards
• Identify wireframe
  and storyboard
  components

When you create a web page or a website, it can be helpful to start by getting a clear idea of what you're trying to build. Web designers typically accomplish this by creating a **wireframe**, which is a sketch that outlines the components of each web page and their place in the layout. A designer usually creates one wireframe for each web page or web page type. For a website containing multiple pages, they also create a **storyboard**, which illustrates links among the pages. When there is a web design team working on a project, the people responsible for art or design often create the wireframes and storyboard, and then they hand off these documents to the developers, who use these documents to create a web page or website. **CASE** ▶ *You work with Karl Dixon, one of your colleagues in the art department, to create a wireframe and a storyboard for the Lakeland Reeds website based on the project plan.*

DETAILS

When you create a wireframe and a storyboard for a website, be sure to include these main steps:

- **Identify components to include**

  Before you start sketching, it's important to get a firm handle on all the elements that the website you're working on must include. A good place to start is your project plan, which should include a thorough inventory of items that must be part of the website; for instance, an existing logo and color scheme that a client already uses in all of its printed materials. You should augment this list with any other essential design elements based on your understanding of the site's target audience and functionality; for example, most multipage websites need a standardized navigation section that provides links to each of the pages.

- **Sketch possible layouts and then select one**

  The next step is to place the elements in a layout that's functional, usable, and, ideally, aesthetically pleasing. This step is often the job of a graphic designer; however, it's a skill that many web developers without artistic backgrounds have obtained with study and practice. Whoever does this step, it often involves a series of sketches that either lays out a set of choices or progressively fine-tunes a theme. For a simple website, a single layout should suffice for all the site's pages; however, if some pages have requirements that are best served by distinct layouts, these layouts need to be finalized in this step as well. The wireframe in **FIGURE A-2** shows the layout for the main page of the Lakeland Reeds website.

- **Map the relationships among web pages**

  Any time you're creating a website or a single web page with links to other websites, it's helpful to map out the relationships between pages. This map is a crucial tool when you create the navigation system for the website. The storyboard in **FIGURE A-3** lists the pages of the Lakeland Reeds website and illustrates the relationships among them, as well as links to external pages.

FIGURE A-2: Wireframe for Lakeland Reeds main web page

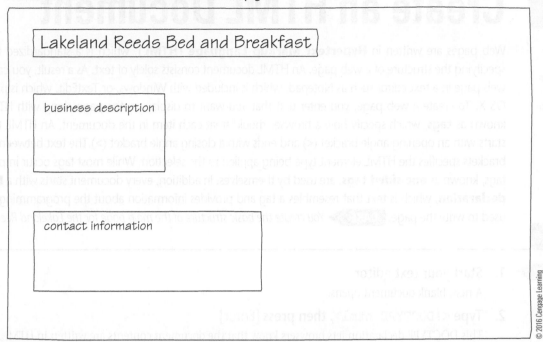

Lakeland Reeds Bed and Breakfast

business description

contact information

FIGURE A-3: Storyboard for Lakeland Reeds website

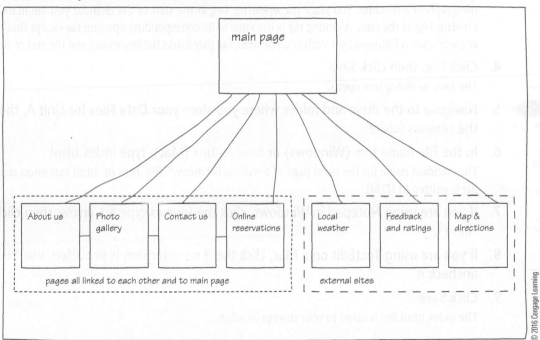

main page

About us

Photo gallery

Contact us

Online reservations

Local weather

Feedback and ratings

Map & directions

pages all linked to each other and to main page

external sites

Creating a website from a template

An alternative to creating a layout for your website is to download a **template**, which is a generic layout that includes a color scheme and element positions but which uses placeholder images and text. Some templates are available to download and use for free, while others must be purchased from the designer. A web developer can simply replace the placeholder items with elements specific to the website being developed. While a template is not as specifically tailored to the companies or topics of the websites where it is used, it can save time in the web development process and can be an invaluable tool when a site needs to be up right away.

Create an HTML Document

Learning Outcomes
• Enter a DOCTYPE declaration
• Add basic tags to an HTML document
• Save an HTML document

Web pages are written in **Hypertext Markup Language (HTML)**, which is a standardized format for specifying the structure of a web page. An HTML document consists solely of text. As a result, you can create a web page in a text editor such as Notepad, which is included with Windows, or TextEdit, which is part of Mac OS X. To create a web page, you enter text that you want to display on the page along with HTML codes known as **tags**, which specify how a browser should treat each item in the document. An HTML tag always starts with an opening angle bracket (<) and ends with a closing angle bracket (>).The text between the angle brackets specifies the HTML element type being applied to the selection. While most tags occur in pairs, some tags, known as **one-sided tags**, are used by themselves. In addition, every document starts with a **DOCTYPE declaration**, which is text that resembles a tag and provides information about the programming language used to write the page. **CASE** *You create the basic structure of the main page for the Lakeland Reeds website.*

STEPS

1. **Start your text editor**
   A new, blank document opens.

2. **Type** `<!DOCTYPE html>`, **then press [Enter]**
   This DOCTYPE declaration lets browsers know that the document contents are written in HTML.

3. **Type** `<html>`, **press [Enter] twice, then type** `</html>`, **as shown in FIGURE A-4**
   A tag pair assigns meaning to a web page **element**, which is a specific component of the page, such as a paragraph or a heading. You place the **opening tag** at the start of the element you are marking and the **closing tag** at the end. A closing tag is the same as its corresponding opening tag except that the opening angle bracket is followed by a slash (/). The `html` tag pair marks the beginning and the end of the web page.

4. **Click** File, **then click** Save
   The Save As dialog box opens.

5. **Navigate to the drive and folder where you store your Data Files for Unit A, then open the** Lessons **folder**

6. **In the** File name box (Windows) **or** Save As box (Mac), **type** index.html
   The standard name for the main page of a website is "index." The .htm or .html extension signifies that a file is written in HTML.

7. **If you are using Notepad in Windows, click the** Save as type list arrow, **then click** All Files (*.*)

8. **If you are using TextEdit on a Mac, click the** If no extension is provided, use ".txt" box **to uncheck it**

9. **Click** Save
   The index.html file is saved to your storage location.

Using other web page creation software

Many other programs are available that allow you to create web pages visually by clicking buttons and using drag-and-drop to place items on a page. However, creating your first web pages by entering HTML directly—sometimes referred to as **hand-coding**— is one of the best ways to become familiar with HTML and the underlying structure of a web page. Many professional developers use a **code editor**, which is a text editor that is optimized for writing code in a programming language. **FIGURE A-5** shows the web page in Notepad++, a free code editor available for Windows, and points out some features common to code editors. Other popular free code editors include Aptana Studio 3 (Win and Mac), Komodo Edit (Win and Mac), and TextWrangler (Mac).

FIGURE A-4: The basic structure of the web page

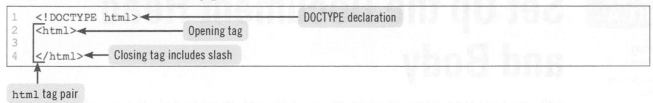

```
1    <!DOCTYPE html>          DOCTYPE declaration
2    <html>                   Opening tag
3
4    </html>                  Closing tag includes slash
```

html tag pair

FIGURE A-5: The basic structure of the web page in Notepad++

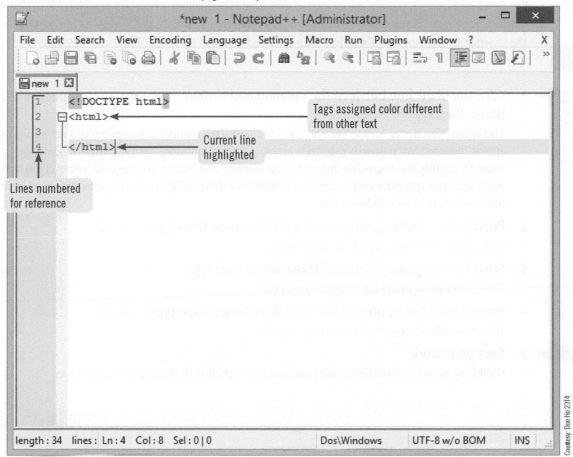

```
*new 1 - Notepad++ [Administrator]

File   Edit   Search   View   Encoding   Language   Settings   Macro   Run   Plugins   Window   ?                    X

new 1

1    <!DOCTYPE html>
2    <html>                              Tags assigned color different
3                                        from other text
4    </html>                             Current line
                                         highlighted
```

Lines numbered for reference

length : 34   lines :   Ln : 4   Col : 8   Sel : 0 | 0   Dos\Windows   UTF-8 w/o BOM   INS

Courtesy: Don Ho 2014

Understanding the difference between HTML and XHTML

Extensible Hypertext Markup Language (XHTML) is a version of HTML that conforms to the rules of Extensible Markup Language (XML). Although most modern web documents are written in HTML, some organizations require XML-compatible code, and therefore use XHTML instead of HTML. HTML and XHTML have only a handful of differences, and utilities are available that can automatically convert code from one to the other. In general, HTML syntax is less strict than XHTML code, and some aspects of code that you can omit in HTML are required in XHTML code. Except where otherwise stated, all the code you write in this book will conform to the rules of HTML.

Set Up the Document Head and Body

Learning
Outcomes
• Define element
nesting
• Add a head
section to an
HTML document
• Add a body
section to an
HTML document

Within the `html` tag pair for a web page, the document contents are divided into two sections. The **head section** contains elements that specify information about the web page but are not displayed in the browser window, such as the page title that appears in a browser tab. The contents of the **body section** are visible in the main window of a web browser and include elements like headings and paragraphs. Both the `head` and `body` tag pairs are located within, or **nested** within, the `html` tag pair. Most elements in the code for a web page are nested within one or more other elements. **CASE** ▶ *As you continue creating the structure for the Lakeland Reeds web page, you add the head and body sections to the page.*

STEPS

QUICK TIP
To read more about
any HTML tag used
in this book, see
Appendix A.

1. **Click the blank line between the opening and closing `html` tags, press [Spacebar] three times, then type** `<head>`

   This is the opening tag for the `head` tag pair. Adding a fixed number of spaces before a nested tag makes it appear indented. As your web page code becomes longer and more complex, these indentations make it easier to identify the beginning and end of an element at a glance. For the code you enter in this book, you'll use three spaces for each indent level. **FIGURE A-6** shows HTML code with several layers of nested tags that are formatted with indentations.

2. **Press [Enter] twice, press [Spacebar] three times, then type** `</head>`

   This creates the closing tag for the `head` tag pair.

3. **Press [Enter], press [Spacebar] three times, then type** `<body>`

   This creates the opening tag for the `body` tag pair.

4. **Press [Enter] twice, press [Spacebar] three times, then type** `</body>`

   This creates the closing tag for the `body` tag pair.

QUICK TIP
To save your work
without using the
menus, you can press
[Ctrl][S] (Windows) or
[command][S] (Mac).

5. **Save your work**

   FIGURE A-7 shows the completed web page structure including the head and body sections.

FIGURE A-6: HTML code containing multiple layers of nested elements

```
1    <!DOCTYPE html>
2    <html>
3       <head>
4          <title>Comparing HTML and XHTML</title>
5       </head>
6       <body>
7          <p>HTML vs. XHTML</p>
8          <table>
9             <tr>
10               <th>Aspect</th>
11               <th>HTML</th>
12               <th>XHTML</th>
13            </tr>
14            <tr>
15               <td>Tag nesting</td>
16               <td>Tags may be closed out of order</td>
17               <td>Tags must be closed in the order opened</td>
18            </tr>
19            <tr>
20               <td>Tag case</td>
21               <td>Tags may be written in upper or lower case</td>
22               <td>Tags must be written in lower case</td>
23            </tr>
24         </table>
25      </body>
26   </html>
```

Indentations indicate sections of code visually

FIGURE A-7: Completed web page structure

```
1    <!DOCTYPE html>
2    <html>
3       <head>
4
5       </head>
6       <body>
7
8       </body>
9    </html>
```

Head section

Body section

Describing nesting relationships

An element nested within another element is called a **child element** of the enclosing element, and the enclosing element is known as the **parent element**. In the code shown in **FIGURE A-6**, the head element is both a child of the html element and the parent of the title element. In addition, the html element is the **grandparent**

element of the title element, which can be referred to as a **grandchild element** of the html element. Two elements that are both children of the same parent element are known as **sibling elements**. The head element and the body element are sibling elements, because they are both children of the html element.

Add Text to a Web Page

Learning Outcomes
- Add a title element
- Add an h1 element
- Add paragraphs with the p element

Because an HTML document is simply a plain text document that includes HTML codes, entering text for your web pages is as simple as typing it. You add the appropriate HTML tags to specify the element type for each text item on the page as you type that text. **CASE** *You enter the page title that will appear in the tab or title bar of a viewer's browser, along with the basic information about Lakeland Reeds.* **FIGURE A-8** *shows an updated wireframe of the main Lakeland Reeds web page that includes the specific text content.*

STEPS

TROUBLE

If your code editor indents automatically, you may not need to add spaces. Just be sure that your insertion point is indented six spaces before entering the `title` element.

1. **Click the blank line above the closing** `</head>` **tag, press [Spacebar] six times, then type** `<title>Lakeland Reeds Bed and Breakfast</title>`

   The `title` element specifies text that appears in the tab or title bar of the web browser opening the page. This element is part of the document's head section because the text does not appear in the main browser window. This line is indented six spaces because it is nested within the `head` element, which is nested within the `html` element.

2. **Click the blank line between the opening and closing** `<body>` **tags, press [Spacebar] six times, then type** `<h1>Lakeland Reeds Bed and Breakfast</h1>`

   The h1 element represents the highest-level heading on the page. **TABLE A-1** compares this element to the 5 other heading elements in HTML.

TROUBLE

If you're using Notepad and can't see all the text in the window at once, click Format on the Menu bar, then click Word Wrap.

3. **Press [Enter], press [Spacebar] six times, then type** `<p>A country getaway perfect for fishing, boating, biking, or just watching the day go by.</p>`

   The p element marks a paragraph of text.

4. **Press [Enter], press [Spacebar] six times, then type** `<p>(218) 555-5253</p>`

   Your document should look like the one shown in **FIGURE A-9**. Not all editors wrap text in the same way, so your editor may show line 9 starting at the far left, rather than indenting it. This does not affect the meaning of the code, however.

5. **Save your work**

Understanding the complementary roles of HTML and CSS

Browsers generally display the content of HTML elements such as h1 and p in ways that visually distinguish the content. However, at its core, HTML is intended to indicate only the meanings of elements such as headings and paragraphs in a web page, but not to tell web browsers how the elements should appear. Instead, HTML has a companion language, **Cascading Style Sheets (CSS)**, which is designed for describing the appearance of items. As you write HTML, you should keep in mind that your only goal in marking content with HTML elements is to describe to browsers and to user agents the type of content a page includes. When you learn to write CSS code, you'll use that language to specify visual display properties such as fonts, colors, borders, and placement within a browser window.

FIGURE A-8: Updated wireframe

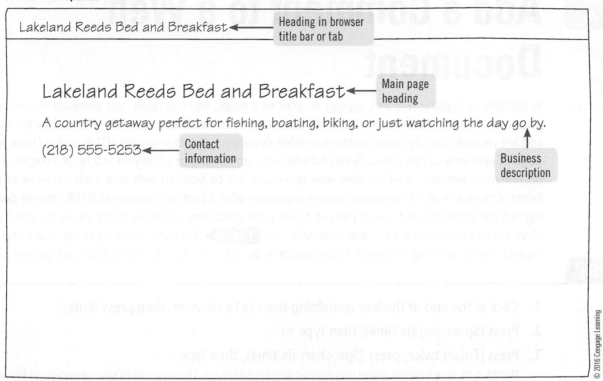

FIGURE A-9: title, h1, and p elements entered

```
1    <!DOCTYPE html>
2    <html>                        title element
3       <head>
4          <title>Lakeland Reeds Bed and Breakfast</title>
5       </head>          h1 element
6       <body>
7          <h1>Lakeland Reeds Bed and Breakfast</h1>
8          <p>A country getaway perfect for fishing, boating, biking, or just watching the day
9          go by.</p>
10         <p>(218) 555-5253</p>
11      </body>
12   </html>
```

p element for business description

p element for contact information

TABLE A-1: HTML heading elements

element	sample code	default rendering in browsers
h1	`<h1>Heading 1</h1>`	**Heading 1**
h2	`<h2>Heading 2</h2>`	**Heading 2**
h3	`<h3>Heading 3</h3>`	**Heading 3**
h4	`<h4>Heading 4</h4>`	**Heading 4**
h5	`<h5>Heading 5</h5>`	**Heading 5**
h6	`<h6>Heading 6</h6>`	**Heading 6**

Add a Comment to a Web Document

Learning Outcomes
• Add comment tags
• Add comment text

In addition to marking text that appears on your web pages, you can create text elements in your web page code that browsers ignore. These elements, known as **comments**, are not rendered by browsers and are viewable only by team members or other developers who examine the HTML code of your web pages. Comments can be especially helpful when you are creating or adding on to a large, complex web document or website, or when other web developers will be working with your code—now or in the future. Common uses for comments include explaining what a particular section of HTML does or pointing out the beginning and end of parts of a web page containing numerous HTML elements. The comment tag pair begins with `<!--` and ends with `-->`. **CASE** *You add a comment to the head section of your document describing its content, listing yourself as the author, and indicating the date it was last modified.*

STEPS

1. **Click at the end of the line containing the** `title` **element, then press [Enter]**

2. **Press [Spacebar] six times, then type** `<!--`

3. **Press [Enter] twice, press [Spacebar] six times, then type** `-->`
   FIGURE A-10 shows the comment tags entered in your document. The contents of your comment go between the opening `<!--` and closing `-->` tags. **TABLE A-2** describes the tags used to create a comment element, along with tags for all the other elements you've created in this unit.

4. **Click the blank line between the opening and closing comment tags, press [Spacebar] nine times, type** Lakeland Reeds Bed and Breakfast main web page, **then press [Enter]**

5. **Press [Spacebar] nine times, type** Filename: index.html, **then press [Enter] twice**
   You can include blank lines within a comment to improve readability.

QUICK TIP
Adding extra spaces after the colon lines up your name with the filename in the previous line of text, making the information easier to read.

6. **Press [Spacebar] nine times, type** Author:, **press [Spacebar] three times, type your first and last name, then press [Enter]**

7. **Press [Spacebar] nine times, type** Date:, **press [Spacebar] five times, type today's date, then press [Enter]**

8. **Press [Spacebar] nine times, then type** HTML5 and CSS3 Illustrated Unit A, Lessons
   Your completed comment should match the one shown in **FIGURE A-11**.

9. **Save your work**

Understanding single-line and multi-line comments

An HTML comment can be either single-line or multi-line. A **single-line comment** includes the opening tag, comment text, and closing tag on a single line. For instance, the following comment is a single-line comment:
`<!-- This page last updated 5/26/2018 -->`
By contrast, a **multi-line comment** occupies multiple lines. In a multi-line comment, the opening and closing tags are often on their own lines, and the content may occupy one or more additional lines, like the comment you created in the steps in this lesson. The choice to use a single-line comment or a multi-line comment is generally based on the amount of comment text you want to add to your document. A single-line comment makes sense for a word or phrase, while using a multi-line comment can make it easier to read a longer comment by breaking it up over multiple lines.

FIGURE A-10: Comment tags added to an HTML document

```
1   <!DOCTYPE html>
2   <html>
3     <head>
4       <title>Lakeland Reeds Bed and Breakfast</title>
5       <!--                     Opening comment tag
6
7       -->                      Closing comment tag
8     </head>
9     <body>
10      <h1>Lakeland Reeds Bed and Breakfast</h1>
11      <p>A country getaway perfect for fishing, boating, biking, or just watching the day
12      go by.</p>
13      <p>(218) 555-5253</p>
14    </body>
15  </html>
```

FIGURE A-11: Comment text added to an HTML document

```
1   <!DOCTYPE html>
2   <html>
3     <head>
4       <title>Lakeland Reeds Bed and Breakfast</title>
5       <!--
6       Lakeland Reeds Bed and Breakfast main web page        Comment text
7       Filename: index.html                                  entered between
8                                                             opening and closing
9       Author:    Faduma Egal                                comment tags
10      Date:      9/26/2018
11      HTML5 and CSS3 Illustrated Unit A, Lessons
12      -->
13    </head>
14    <body>
15      <h1>Lakeland Reeds Bed and Breakfast</h1>
16      <p>A country getaway perfect for fishing, boating, biking, or just watching the day
17      go by.</p>
18      <p>(218) 555-5253</p>
19    </body>
20  </html>
```

TABLE A-2: Basic web page elements

element	function	code sample
comment	adds text viewable only by team members or other developers who examine the HTML code of your web pages	`<!-- This page last updated 5/26/2018 -->`

html	marks the beginning and the end of the web page	`<html>`
		web page contents
		`</html>`

head	contains elements that are not part of the web page shown in the browser window	`<head>`
		head contents, such as title and meta elements
		`</head>`

title	specifies text that appears in the title bar of the web browser opening the page	`<title>Lakeland Reeds</title>`

body	includes contents that are visible in the main window of a web browser	`<body>`
		body contents, such as p and h1 elements
		`</body>`

p	marks a paragraph of text	`<p>Escape to the lake!</p>`
h1	represents the highest-level heading on the page	`<h1>Lakeland Reeds</h1>`

Preview Your Web Page on a Desktop Computer

Learning Outcomes
• Open an HTML document in a web browser
• Compare how HTML documents are rendered by different browsers

An important step in the process of creating a web page is to **preview** it, which involves opening it in one or more browsers and examining the result. When a web page isn't interpreted as expected by a browser, you can research the problem and make corrections to the code before publishing the page. In addition, because different browsers can interpret the same page with slight differences, it's good practice to test your pages with multiple browsers. While many desktop browsers and versions exist, a good place to start is the current versions of Google Chrome, Mozilla Firefox, and Microsoft Internet Explorer (IE). **CASE** ➤ *You preview your Lakeland Reeds web page in the three most commonly used desktop web browsers.*

STEPS

1. **Navigate to the drive and folder where you store your Data Files for Unit A using your file manager, open the** Lessons folder, **then double-click** index.html

   The web page opens in your system's default web browser. **FIGURE A-12** shows the file open in Chrome.

2. **Return to your file manager, right-click (Windows) or press [control] and click (Mac)** index.html, **point to** Open with, **then click another browser name in the list**

   The web page opens in another browser.

3. **Note any differences between the two browsers in the way the page is displayed**

   Often differences in the way each browser displays, or **renders**, a web page are subtle, such as slight variations in the space between lines. **FIGURE A-13** shows a web page displayed in different browsers.

4. **Repeat Steps 2 and 3 until you have viewed your page in the current versions of Chrome, Firefox, and Internet Explorer**

Understanding the effect of browser extensions on page rendering

Modern browsers are highly customizable, allowing users to install new features and modify default settings. One common way of customizing a browser is to install an **extension**, which is a small application that changes the way web pages are rendered or integrates features with the content of a web page. Some of the most common extensions stop video or audio from loading and playing automatically on a web page, or enable web developers to examine or change the code of a web document. Some extensions may highlight or underline text or add icons to web page text rendered in the browser window. It's important to understand that these changes are not part of the web page code you're opening, but they are added by extensions. For instance, if you have an extension installed for an Internet calling service such as Skype, you may see formatting changes to any phone number displayed on a web page you open. Extensions can be disabled, which stops them from functioning but keeps them installed on your system. As you're testing web documents that you create, you should disable any extensions installed on each browser you're using. You can find instructions to disable extensions on each major browser by using a search engine to perform a search on the words "disable extensions" and the name of the browser.

FIGURE A-12: Web page in Google Chrome

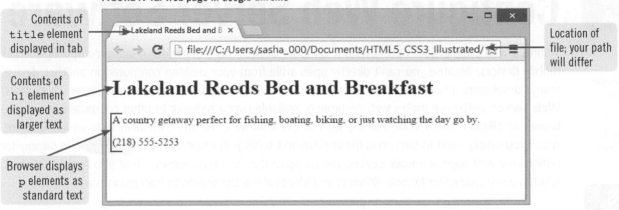

Contents of `title` element displayed in tab

Location of file; your path will differ

Contents of `h1` element displayed as larger text

Browser displays `p` elements as standard text

Lakeland Reeds Bed and Breakfast

A country getaway perfect for fishing, boating, biking, or just watching the day go by.

(218) 555-5253

FIGURE A-13: HTML document rendered in different browsers

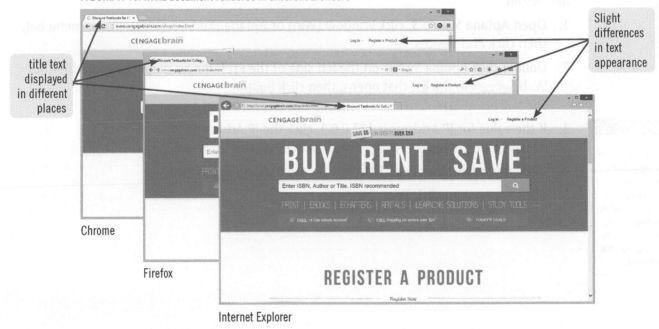

Slight differences in text appearance

title text displayed in different places

Chrome

Firefox

Internet Explorer

Understanding why browsers display web pages differently

The display of web pages in HTML5 starts with the specifications maintained by groups such as the **World Wide Web Consortium (W3C)**, an organization that helps build consensus around changes and additions to the language, and publishes descriptions of the current standards. The standards list and describe all the available elements, along with parameters for how browsers should handle them. Browsers are built around software known as **rendering engines** that translate web page elements into visual, auditory, or tactile representations based on these standards. Because the standards require some interpretation, no two engines render the same HTML code in exactly the same way. In addition, the creators of rendering engines do not always implement all of the current standards in their software. Because the audience for your web pages will almost always be using a number of different browsers, it's important to test your code in a variety of popular desktop browsers and on multiple desktop operating systems (such as Windows 8, Windows 7, and Mac OS X).

Configure Web Server Software

Learning
Outcomes
• Describe the role
  of web server
  software in
  website testing
• Enable the web
  server in a code
  editor

Testing a web page includes previewing it on some devices other than your desktop computer, such as mobile devices. Because you can't directly open a file from your desktop computer on another device, many developers install software known as web server software on their desktop computers. **Web server software** makes web documents available over a network to other computers, which are known as **clients**. Many code editors, such as Dreamweaver, include their own web server software, which you simply need to turn on in the application's settings in order to use it. **CASE** ➤ *To prepare for testing your web page on mobile devices, you configure the web server software built into Aptana Studio 3, which is a free code editor for both Windows and Mac that you can download from aptana.com.*

STEPS

Note: The following steps use Aptana Studio 3, which is a free code editor for both Windows and Mac, and which integrates by default with Firefox. If you're using a different code editor with a built-in web server, use the editor's documentation to enable its web server, then proceed to the next lesson.

1. **Open Aptana Studio 3, click Window (Win) or Aptana Studio 3 (Mac) on the menu bar, then click Preferences**

2. **Double-click Aptana Studio on the left side of the Preferences dialog box, double-click Web Servers in the list that opens, then click Built-in**
   The Built-in Web Server Preferences are displayed as shown in **FIGURE A-14**.

QUICK TIP
The IP address
127.0.0.1 is a
special value that's
accessible only
on the current
computer. Any other
value in the list will
also be accessible to
other devices on the
same network.

3. **If the value for IP Address is 127.0.0.1, click the IP Address arrow**
   A list of possible IP addresses is displayed as shown in **FIGURE A-15**.

4. **Click any value other than 127.0.0.1 on the IP Address menu**

5. **Click Apply, then click OK**

Understanding web servers

Creating and saving a web page on your computer is not sufficient to make it available to all web users. Every web page accessible on the web is located on a **web server**, which is a computer that is running web server software and that is always connected to the Internet. Although someone who's technologically proficient can configure a personal web server in their home or business, most public websites are made available on dedicated web servers that are maintained by teams of professionals and connected to the Internet with high-capacity connections. Many companies run web servers and sell space on them for a monthly fee. When you create a web page that you want to make publicly available on the web, you must first secure space on a web server and upload your files to that web server.

FIGURE A-14: Aptana Studio 3 Built-in Web Server Preferences

FIGURE A-15: Aptana Studio 3 IP Address options

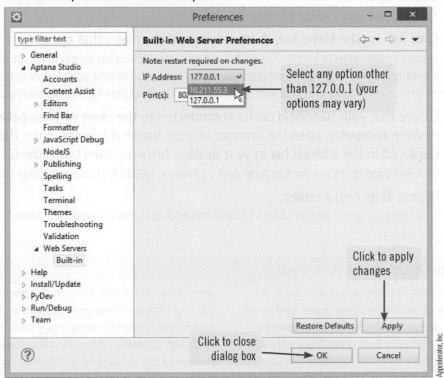

Preview Your Web Page on Mobile Devices

Previewing a web page on multiple desktop browsers is a good start for getting an idea of how it will look for users. However, a significant share of web access happens on mobile devices rather than on desktop computers. For this reason, it's important to see how an HTML document is rendered on web browsers on devices such as smartphones and tablets. You can use web server software running on your desktop computer to view a web page on mobile devices connected to the same wireless network. **CASE** ▸ *You test your web page on a smartphone and on a tablet using the web server built into Aptana Studio 3.*

STEPS

Note: The following steps use Aptana Studio 3, which is a free code editor for both Windows and Mac, and Firefox. If you're using a different code editor with a built-in web server, use the editor's web server to open your web page in a browser, and start with Step 7.

1. **Close Aptana Studio 3, then restart Aptana Studio 3**

2. **Click File on the menu bar, click Import, double-click General if necessary to view the options beneath it, then double-click Existing Folder as New Project**

3. **Click Browse, navigate to the drive and folder where you store your Data Files for this unit, click OK (Win) or Open (Mac), then click Finish**

4. **Click Window on the menu bar, point to Show View, then click Project Explorer**
   The Project Explorer pane is displayed, with the location of your data files listed.

5. **Click the triangle ▷ to the left of the folder containing your Data Files for this unit in the Project Explorer pane, click the triangle ▷ next to the Lessons folder, then double-click index.html**
   Your web page opens in Aptana Studio 3.

6. **Click Run on the Menu bar, then click Run on the menu that opens**
   Your web page opens in Firefox. Notice the address in the Address bar shown in **FIGURE A-16**. Because you are accessing the web page via the Aptana Studio 3 web server, the address starts with a series of numbers, which is the numerical address of your web server. The numerical address varies from computer to computer.

7. **Ensure that your handheld device is connected to the same wireless network as your desktop computer, open the browser on your handheld device, enter the address displayed in the address bar in your desktop browser, then touch the Go button**
   Your web page opens in your handheld device's browser. **FIGURE A-17** shows the page on a smartphone.

8. **Repeat Step 7 on a tablet**
   Your web page opens in your tablet's browser. **FIGURE A-18** shows the page on a tablet.

Testing web documents on mobile devices

As people increasingly access the web using mobile devices, it's important to test your content on the mobile devices used by your audience. Most users accessing the web on a mobile device use either Safari (on Apple iOS devices such as the iPhone and iPad) or Chrome (on Google Android devices such as Nexus and Galaxy series phones and tablets). Although it's unlikely that you'll physically own every device that your audience may use to access your content, you can start by testing on any mobile devices you have. In addition, by sharing devices with fellow students and colleagues, you may be able to access many of the most common devices.

FIGURE A-16: Web page address in a desktop browser

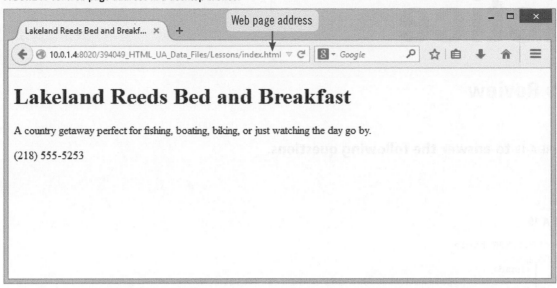

FIGURE A-17: Web page in Chrome on an Android smartphone

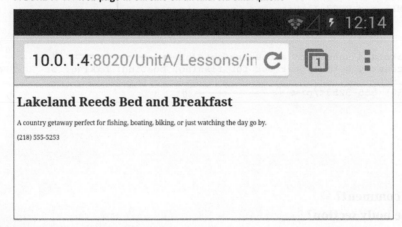

FIGURE A-18: Web page in Safari on an iPad tablet

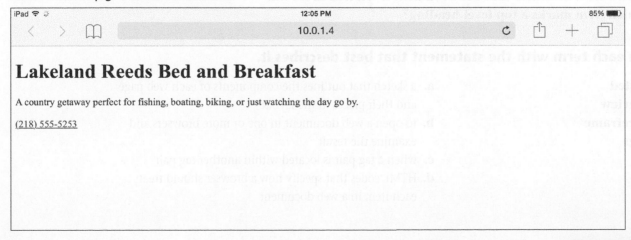

Practice

Concepts Review

Refer to FIGURE A-19 to answer the following questions.

FIGURE A-19

```
a  →  1 →<!DOCTYPE html>
      2  <html>
      3    <head>
      4      <title>Lakeland Reeds Bed and Breakfast</title>←        g
      5      <!--
      6        Lakeland Reeds Bed and Breakfast main web page
      7        Filename: index.html
b  →  8
      9      Author:    Faduma Egal
     10      Date:      9/26/2018                                    f
     11      HTML5 and CSS3 Illustrated Unit A, Lessons
     12      -->
     13    </head>
     14    <body>
     15      <h1>Lakeland Reeds Bed and Breakfast</h1>←              e
     16      <p>A country getaway perfect for fishing, boating, biking, or just watching the day
c  →  17      go by.</p>
     18      <p>(218) 555-5253</p>←                    d
     19    </body>
     20  </html>
```

1. Which item creates a comment?
2. Which item marks the body section?
3. Which item marks text that is displayed in the browser tab?
4. Which item marks the head section?
5. Which item specifies a paragraph of text?
6. Which item indicates that the document is written in HTML?
7. Which item marks a top-level heading?

Match each term with the statement that best describes it.

8. nested
9. preview
10. wireframe
11. tags

   a. a sketch that outlines the components of each web page and their places in the layout

   b. to open a web document in one or more browsers and examine the result

   c. when a tag pair is located within another tag pair

   d. HTML codes that specify how a browser should treat each item in a web document

Select the best answer from the list of choices.

12. The process of identifying the goals and objectives, as well as the target audience, of the website is summed up in the _____ .
    a. web server
    b. wireframe
    c. project plan
    d. storyboard

13. A text editor that's optimized for writing code in a programming language is known as a _____ .
    a. hand coder
    b. code editor
    c. web browser
    d. visual editor

14. What code in an HTML document lets browsers know that the document contents are written in HTML?
    a. `title` element
    b. head element
    c. body element
    d. DOCTYPE declaration

15. Which type of tag do you place at the end of an element?
    a. deprecated
    b. closing
    c. one-sided
    d. opening

16. A _____ makes web documents available over a network to other computers.
    a. browser
    b. DOCTYPE declaration
    c. web server
    d. client

Skills Review

1. **Create an HTML document.**
   a. Open a new document in your text editor.
   b. Enter a DOCTYPE declaration.
   c. Enter tags to create the `html` element.
   d. Save the file as **index.html** to the Review folder in the drive and folder where you store your Data Files for this unit.

2. **Set up the document head and body.**
   a. Enter tags to create the document's head section.
   b. Enter tags to create the document's body section.
   c. Save your work.

3. **Add text to a web page.**
   a. Within the head section, add a `title` element containing the text **Big J's Deep Dish Pizza**.
   b. Within the body section, add an `h1` element containing the text **Big J's Deep Dish Pizza**.
   c. Below the `h1` element and within the body section, enter a `p` element containing the text **Authentic Chicago-style deep dish pizza—eat in, carry out, or call for delivery**.
   d. Below the existing `p` element, add another `p` element containing the text **(416) 555-3337**.
   e. Save your work.

4. **Add a comment to a web page.**
   a. Within the head section, add tags to create a comment.
   b. Within the comment, enter the following text:
      Big J's Deep Dish Pizza main web page
      Filename: index.html
      Author: your first and last name
      Date: today's date
      HTML5 and CSS3 Illustrated Unit A, Skills Review
   c. Save your work.

Skills Review (continued)

5. Preview your web page on a desktop computer.

a. Open index.html from the Review folder in your Data Files folder for this unit using your default browser. Compare your screen to **FIGURE A-20**

b. Repeat Step 5a using other browsers until you have viewed the document in current versions of Chrome, Firefox, and Internet Explorer.

Big J's Deep Dish Pizza

Authentic Chicago-style deep dish pizza--eat in, carry out, or call for delivery.

(416) 555-3337

6. Preview your web page on mobile devices.

a. Open index.html from the Review folder in your Data Files folder for this unit using Aptana Studio 3 or another code editor with a built-in web server.

b. Use your code editor to open index.html in a desktop browser using the built-in web server.

c. Use the web address displayed in the desktop browser to open index.html on a smartphone, then repeat to open index.html on a tablet.

Independent Challenge 1

Spotted Wren Garden Center, a local garden shop and plant store, has hired you to create a website for its business. Sarah Nguyen, the shop's owner and manager, would like you to create a web presence as a new avenue of marketing, as well as a means to keep regular customers up to date on seasonal specials and new products.

a. Open a new document in your text editor, then create a DOCTYPE declaration by typing **<!DOCTYPE html>**

b. Type **<html>** and **</html>** on separate lines to create the html element.

c. Within the html element, type <head> and </head> on separate lines to create the head element.

d. After the head tags, type <body> and </body> on separate lines to create the body element.

e. Save the file as **index.html** to the UnitA/IC1 folder.

f. Within the head section, add a title element containing the text **Spotted Wren Garden Center**. (*Hint*: Type <title> as the opening tag and </title> as the closing tag.)

g. Within the body section, add an h1 element containing the text **Spotted Wren Garden Center**. (*Hint*: Type <h1> as the opening tag and </h1> as the closing tag.)

h. Below the h1 element and within the body section, enter a p element containing the text **For your year-round garden and yard needs, with a focus on the unusual and hard to find.** (*Hint*: Type <p> as the opening tab and </p> as the closing tag.)

i. Below the existing p element, add another p element containing the text **(402) 555-9736**. (*Hint*: Be sure to use the opening and closing tags for the p element.)

j. Within the head section, add a comment using <!-- as the opening tag and --> as the closing tag that contains the following text:

Spotted Wren Garden Center main web page
Filename: index.html
Author: your first and last name
Date: today's date
HTML5 and CSS3 Illustrated
Unit A, Independent Challenge 1

Spotted Wren Garden Center

For your year-round garden and yard needs, with a focus on the unusual and hard to find.

(402) 555-9736

k. Save your work.

l. Open index.html from the IC1 folder in your Data Files folder for this unit using your default browser. Compare your screen to **FIGURE A-21**. Repeat using other browsers until you have viewed the document in current versions of Chrome, Firefox, and Internet Explorer.

m. Use a code editor with a built-in web server to view index.html on a smartphone and on a tablet.

Independent Challenge 2

To help build your web design skills, you have volunteered to create a website for the Murfreesboro Regional Soccer League (MRSL). The league organizes recreational leagues every summer and fall for local, nonprofessional soccer players to get exercise and have fun. You start your work on the site by creating a web page with a basic description of the league along with contact information.

a. Open a new document in your text editor, then create a DOCTYPE declaration.

b. Enter tags to create the html element.

c. Within the html element, enter tags to create the head and body elements.

d. Save the file as **index.html** to the UnitA/IC2 folder.

e. Within the head section, add a title element containing the text **Murfreesboro Regional Soccer League**.

f. Within the body section, add an h1 element containing the text **Murfreesboro Regional Soccer League**.

g. Below the h1 element and within the body section, enter a p element containing the text **Get exercise, have fun, and build your soccer skills playing with us. Teams for beginners as well as experienced players.**

h. Below the existing p element, add another p element containing the text **(615) 555-2255**.

i. Within the head section, add a comment containing the following text:
   Murfreesboro Regional Soccer League main web page
   Filename: index.html
   Author: your first and last name
   Date: today's date
   HTML5 and CSS3 Illustrated Unit A, Independent Challenge 2

j. Save your work.

k. Open index.html from the IC2 folder in your Data Files folder for this unit using your default browser. Compare your screen to **FIGURE A-22**. Repeat using other browsers until you have viewed the document in current versions of Chrome, Firefox, and Internet Explorer.

l. Use a code editor with a built-in web server to view index.html on a smartphone and on a tablet.

FIGURE A-22

Murfreesboro Regional Soccer League

Get exercise, have fun, and build your soccer skills playing with us. Teams for beginners as well as experienced players.

(615) 555-2255

Independent Challenge 3

In your new job creating sites for a web design firm, you've been assigned a new client, Hotel Natoma. The hotel's business manager, Diego Merckx, wants to use the web to showcase the facility and its amenities.

a. Open a new document in your text editor, then create a DOCTYPE declaration.

b. Enter tags to create the html element.

c. Within the html element, enter tags to create the head and body elements.

d. Save the file as **index.html** to the UnitA/IC3 folder.

e. Within the head section, add a title element containing the text **Hotel Natoma**.

f. Within the body section, add an h1 element containing the text **Hotel Natoma**.

Independent Challenge 3 (continued)

g. Below the h1 element and within the body section, enter a p element containing the text **A low-impact, Earth-friendly home base in the center of everything San Francisco has to offer**.

h. Below the existing p element, add another p element containing the text **(415) 555-8378**.

i. Within the head section, add a comment containing the following text:

Hotel Natoma main web page

Filename: index.html

Author: your first and last name

Date: today's date

HTML5 and CSS3 Illustrated Unit A, Independent Challenge 3

j. Save your work.

k. Open index.html from the UnitA/IC3 folder using your default browser. Compare your screen to **FIGURE A-23**. Repeat using other browsers until you have viewed the document in current versions of Chrome, Firefox, and Internet Explorer.

l. Use a code editor with a built-in web server to view index.html on a smartphone and on a tablet.

FIGURE A-23

Hotel Natoma

A low-impact, Earth-friendly home base in the center of everything San Francisco has to offer.

(415) 555-8378

Independent Challenge 4: Explore

You've been hired to create a website for Eating Well in Season (EWIS), a business in Glover, Vermont, that delivers produce from local farms to its customers. You'll start by creating a basic web page that describes the business and provides contact information.

a. Draw a wireframe for the main web page of the EWIS website. Include title and heading elements containing the name of the business. Below the main heading, include three subheadings: Meals, Sources, and Scheduling. Include a paragraph of text below each subheading. At the bottom of the page, include contact information.

b. Open a new document in your text editor, then add a DOCTYPE declaration and all structuring elements necessary to create the sections of an HTML document. Save the file as **index.html** to the Unit A/IC4 folder.

c. Add a title element containing the text **Eating Well in Season**.

d. Within the body section, add an h1 element containing the text **Eating Well in Season**.

e. Below the h1 heading, use an <h2></h2> tag pair to create a subheading containing the text **Meals**. Below the h2 heading, add a paragraph containing the text **Meals prepared fresh daily using local ingredients.** Add a second h2 heading containing the text **Sources**, and a paragraph below it containing the text **Produce and meats supplied by New England farmers and gardeners.** Add a third h2 heading containing the text **Scheduling**, and a paragraph below it containing the text **Deliveries on your schedule, any time of the afternoon or evening.**

f. Below the final paragraph, add a paragraph containing the text **(802) 525-3947**.

g. Within the head section, add single-line comments containing the name of the business, the filename, your first and last name, today's date, and the text **HTML5 and CSS3 Illustrated Unit A, Independent Challenge 4**.

Independent Challenge 4: Explore (continued)

h. Save your work.

i. Open index.html from the IC4 folder in the Data Files folder for this unit using your default browser. Compare your screen to **FIGURE A-24**. Repeat using other browsers until you have viewed the document in current versions of Chrome, Firefox, and Internet Explorer.

j. Use a code editor with a built-in web server to view index.html on a smartphone running Apple iOS, on a smartphone running Google Android, on a tablet running Apple iOS, and on a tablet running Google Android. (*Hint*: Ask classmates, friends, and family members about using their devices to preview your document.)

FIGURE A-24

Eating Well in Season

Meals

Meals prepared fresh daily using local ingredients.

Sources

Produce and meats supplied by New England farmers and gardeners.

Schedule

Deliveries on your schedule, any time of the afternoon or evening.

(802) 525-3947

Visual Workshop

Use a text editor to create the web page shown in **FIGURE A-25**. Include a comment that contains the business name, filename, your first and last name, today's date, and the text **HTML5 and CSS3 Illustrated Unit A, Visual Workshop**. When you are finished, save the file as **index.html** to the UnitA/VW folder. Preview the web page in all three major desktop browsers, as well as on a smartphone and a tablet.

FIGURE A-25

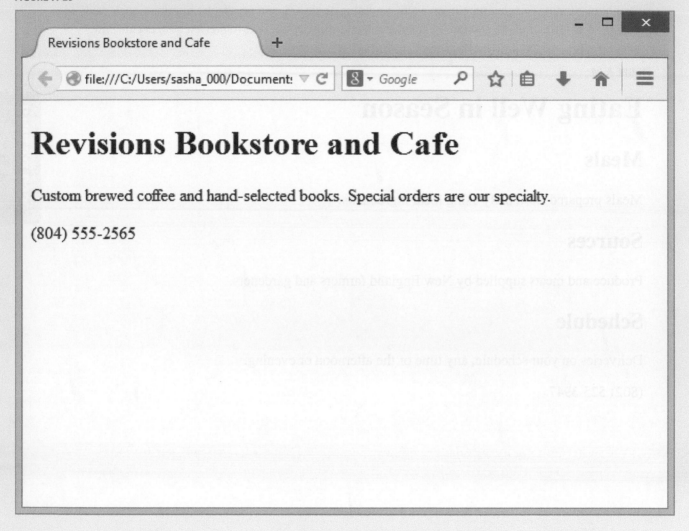

Getting Started with HTML

Structuring Content in a Web Document

CASE You are building a web page for Lakeland Reeds Bed and Breakfast that contains basic information about the business. In this unit, you will use HTML elements and attributes to structure the page contents, incorporate information for browsers, and validate and debug your work.

Unit Objectives

After completing this unit, you will be able to:

- Evaluate web accessibility standards
- Incorporate attributes
- Implement the `div` element
- Add HTML5 semantic elements
- Use special characters
- Specify the viewport
- Debug your HTML code
- Validate your HTML code
- Create an XHTML document

Files You Will Need

 L 3 files   IC3 3 files

 SR 3 files   IC4 2 files

 IC1 2 files   VW 2 files

 IC2 3 files

For specific filenames, see Filenames_B.pdf in the Unit B Data Files folder.

Evaluate Web Accessibility Standards

Learning
Outcomes
• Identify guidelines
  for creating
  accessible web
  pages

Once you make a web page publicly available on the Internet, users can access it using a wide variety of **user agents**, which are programs and devices that interpret web documents. Many web users view pages with the default settings in modern desktop and mobile browsers such as Google Chrome, Apple Safari, Mozilla Firefox, and Microsoft Internet Explorer (IE). Some users with disabilities may use custom browser settings, or even specialized software or hardware, to access the web. While laws in many countries spell out mandatory accessibility standards for government websites, building a high level of accessibility into any web pages you create widens the potential audience for your work, as illustrated in FIGURE B-1. Thus, as a web developer, it's important that you understand and implement web accessibility standards as you create your web pages in order to make them adaptable to the needs of different users and the capabilities of different user agents. A widely used reference for implementing web accessibility is the **Web Content Accessibility Guidelines (WCAG)** maintained by the World Wide Web Consortium (W3C). **CASE** *To help ensure that the Lakeland Reeds website is widely accessible, you review the main tenets of web accessibility standards.*

DETAILS

The WCAG describes techniques for helping your web content meet the following goals as broadly as possible:

QUICK TIP

As you learn to create web page elements for specific types of content, be sure to study the best practices for accessibility related to those elements. You can read about the WCAG at w3.org/WAI/intro/wcag.

- **Perceivable**

  All your web page content needs to be accessible in whatever format a given user needs to access it. This includes ensuring that any information that you convey visually is also available by non-visual means, such as text descriptions for images and videos. Many people with visual impairments access the web using devices called **screen readers** that read aloud web page content, such as text and descriptions that a user selects. In addition, any audio content should be accompanied by transcripts or written descriptions, which can substitute for many users with auditory impairments.

- **Operable**

  Users interface with computers in different ways. While many users scroll web pages and click links using a mouse, ensuring that no elements of your web pages rely on the use of a mouse makes your web pages more accessible to people with some physical impairments. Web pages need to allow users to explore and read the web page content at the users' pace. Web pages should allow scrolling or self-updating features to be paused, stopped, or hidden. Designs should not include elements known to cause seizures, such as certain frequencies of flashing. Finally, navigation within the site and to external pages should be clearly indicated, easy to understand, and, ideally, redundant.

- **Understandable**

  The language that a web page is written in should be indicated, and ways for users to understand any specialized vocabulary used in the web page should be included. Links should not make unexpected or drastic changes to the way a web page is displayed; some warning should be given if clicking a link will result in a non-standard change. When possible, forms that accept user input should include means for identifying common errors and allowing users to correct them.

- **Robust**

  Web pages should be coded according to web standards, ensuring that they can be accessed by the widest possible variety of programs and devices.

Be sure you understand and use these techniques when designing web pages in order to maximize accessibility.

Revisions Bookstore and Cafe

Custom brewed coffee and hand-selected books.

Special orders are our specialty.

Learn about our <u>store history</u>, look at our <u>upcoming events</u>, and see <u>where we're located</u>.

412 N. 25th St.
Richmond, VA 23223
(804) 555-2565

Background darkened for improved text contrast

Navigation bar added to facilitate moving around site and to make site organization viewable at a glance

Revisions Bookstore and Cafe

<u>Home</u> | <u>Store History</u> | <u>Upcoming Events</u> | <u>Location</u>

Custom brewed coffee and hand-selected books.

Special orders are our specialty.

412 N. 25th St.
Richmond, VA 23223
(804) 555-2565

Understanding your role in web accessibility

In addition to a web developer's work creating a site, other factors significantly influence web accessibility. The developers of user agents make decisions that affect how their software and devices interact with web content, which impacts whether users can access content in specific ways. In addition, some web content is produced using software that automates the web development process, and the accessibility choices of the makers of these packages affects the accessibility of the content produced using them. Thus, while web developers have a crucial role to play in building and maintaining a web page that's available to everyone, it can be useful to see your role as part of a larger team and to recognize when you run against a limitation that can't easily be fixed.

Incorporate Attributes

Learning
Outcomes
• Add an attribute
name
• Add an attribute
value

Many, but not all, HTML elements allow you to set attributes. An **attribute** is additional code within an opening element tag that specifies information about that element. To use an attribute, you provide two pieces of information: an attribute name and the value you are assigning to the attribute. Within an element's opening tag and following the tag name, you insert a space, followed by the attribute name, an equal sign (=), and the attribute value enclosed in quotes. **CASE** *You add attributes to two elements in your document to give browsers information about the document's content.*

STEPS

QUICK TIP

For most editors, you press [Ctrl][Shift][S] (Win) or [command] [shift][S] (Mac), type the new filename, then press [Enter].

1. **In your editor, open the HTM_B-1.html file from the Lessons folder where you store your Data Files for this unit**

2. **Below the** `title` **element, insert the comment shown in FIGURE B-2, substituting your name and today's date where indicated**

3. **Save a copy of the file to the Lessons folder with the name** aboutus.html

   As shown in **FIGURE B-2**, the body section of the document contains an h1 element, an h2 element, and two p elements.

TROUBLE

Be sure to click in the <html> tag and not at the end of the DOCTYPE statement.

4. **Open** aboutus.html **in a browser**

   The document is displayed with a large heading, a smaller heading, and two paragraphs of text.

5. **Return to your editor, then click just to the left of the closing > in the opening <html> tag**

6. **Press [Spacebar], then type** `lang="en"`

   The `lang` attribute specifies the language in which a document's content is written. The value en specifies English as the language. **TABLE B-1** lists the `lang` values for several other languages. **FIGURE B-3** shows the `lang` attribute and value inserted in the opening <html> tag.

TROUBLE

Because some code editors indent automatically, you may not need to press [Spacebar] to indent. Use the figures to check for and match indenting.

7. **Click after the closing comment tag (-->), press [Enter], then press [Spacebar] six times or as needed to create the indent**

   Because you want the new element nested within two other elements (html and head), you indent six spaces—three for each level of indentation.

QUICK TIP

The <meta> tag is a one-sided tag, so it does not require a closing tag.

8. **Type** `<meta charset="utf-8">`

   FIGURE B-4 shows the `meta` element and the `charset` attribute and value in the head section of the document. The `meta` element enables you to pass information about a web page to user agents that open it. The `charset` attribute specifies the **character encoding**, which is the system user agents should employ to translate the electronic information representing the page into human-recognizable symbols, such as letters and numbers.

9. **Save your document, return to your browser, then click the** Refresh **or** Reload **button to view the changes to your web document**

   The appearance of the page in the browser does not change. In general, `meta` elements and attributes of the html element do not change how a document is rendered.

FIGURE B-2: Starting code for About Us page

```
1    <!DOCTYPE html>
2    <html>
3        <head>
4            <title>Lakeland Reeds Bed and Breakfast - About Us</title>
5            <!--
6                Lakeland Reeds Bed and Breakfast
7                Filename: aboutus.html
8
9                Author:    your first and last name
10               Date:      today's date
11               HTML5 and CSS3 Illustrated Unit B, Lessons
12           -->
13       </head>
14       <body>
15           <h1>Lakeland Reeds Bed and Breakfast</h1>
16           <h2>About Us</h2>
17           <p>Lakeland Reeds is an ideal place to unplug from your daily routine. We're here
18           to help you get the most out of your time with us, from canoes and life vests for a
19           day out on the lake, to DVDs and popcorn for a quiet evening in. We look forward to
20           welcoming you!</p>
21           <p>45 Marsh Grass Ln. - Marble, MN 55764 - (218) 555-5253</p>
22       </body>
23   </html>
```

Comment → (lines 5–12)

h1 element → (line 15)

h2 element → (line 16)

First p element → (lines 17–20)

Second p element → (line 21)

FIGURE B-3: lang attribute inserted in opening <html> tag

```
1    <!DOCTYPE html>
2    <html lang="en">
3        <head>
4            <title>Lakeland Reeds Bed and Breakfast - About Us</title>
                keland Reeds Bed and Breakfast
                  ilename: aboutus.html
```

Attribute name

Attribute value enclosed in quotes

Attribute placed within opening <html> tag

FIGURE B-4: meta element with charset attribute

```
1    <!DOCTYPE html>
2    <html lang="en">
3        <head>
4            <title>Lakeland Reeds Bed and Breakfast - About Us</title>
5            <!--
                Lakeland Reeds Bed and Breakfast
                Filename: aboutus.html

                Author:    Faduma Egal
10              Date:      10/13/18
11              HTML5 and CSS3 Illustrated Unit B, Lessons
12          -->
13          <meta charset="utf-8">
14      </head>
            dy>
            <h1>Lakeland Reeds Bed and Breakfast</h1>
            <h2>About Us</h2>
```

meta element added to head section

closing tag for head section

Attribute name

Attribute value enclosed in quotes

TABLE B-1: Basic lang attribute values

lang value	language	lang value	language	lang value	language
ar	Arabic	fr	French	pt	Portugese
de	German	he	Hebrew	ru	Russian
el	Greek	hi	Hindi	sa	Sanskrit
en	English	it	Italian	ur	Urdu
es	Spanish	ja	Japanese	zh	Chinese

Implement the `div` Element

Learning Outcomes
• Use the HTML `div` element
• Add a parent element to existing elements

To create the basic structure of a web page, you use the `html`, `head`, and `body` elements. In addition, you can add content to the body section with elements such as `h1` and `p`. It can be useful to group content within the body section to help keep the code organized, especially in larger web documents. The `div` element is used as a parent element for other elements on your page that function together. For instance, you could use a `div` element to mark a heading element and its related paragraph elements as a group. **CASE** *The code for the Lakeland Reeds About Us page includes content specific to this page. You organize the code by adding a `div` element enclosing the content specific to this page, which includes the `h2` heading and the first `p` element.*

STEPS

1. **Return to aboutus.html in your editor, click after the closing </h1> tag, then press [Enter] to add a new line**

QUICK TIP
If your code editor indents new elements automatically, you may not need to press [Spacebar] at all. Remember to compare your code to the figures to confirm indents.

2. **Press [Spacebar] six times or as needed to create an indent that matches the indent for the preceding </h1> tag, then type <div>**

   The `<div>` tag is the opening tag for the `div` element and should be indented 3 spaces more than the opening `<body>` tag.

3. **Click after the first closing </p> tag, then press [Enter]**

4. **Press [Spacebar] six times or as needed to create an indent that matches the indent for the opening <div> tag, then type </div>**

   The `div` element contains both the `h2` element and the first `p` element between its opening and closing tags.

QUICK TIP
The h2 element marks a heading that's at the second-highest heading level in the document.

5. **Click before the opening <h2> tag, press [Spacebar] three times or as needed to create an indent, click before the first opening <p> tag, then press [Spacebar] three times or as needed to create an indent**

   Because you are adding a parent element, you increase the indentation of tags for child elements to keep your code readable. Compare your code to **FIGURE B-5**, which shows the code containing the new `div` element.

6. **Save your document, return to your browser, then refresh or reload aboutus.html in your browser**

   As shown in **FIGURE B-6**, the appearance of the page in the browser does not change. Because the `div` element is used for structuring code, adding the `div` element to the document does not change the way the document is rendered. The document looks the same after the `div` element is added as it did before.

Writing for the web

Many users want a process of finding and consuming web content that is dynamic and fast-paced. When you write content for the web, you should keep this in mind. Web content should generally be brief and scannable. A user should be able to get the gist of what your page contains with a quick glance. This allows users to quickly decide to stay on the page if the page contains the information they're looking for, or to navigate elsewhere and keep looking. You can make content scannable by including a short, descriptive heading at the top, and by breaking the content itself into sections with headings. After writing the actual content, it can be useful to revise it with the goal of removing half the words. This helps focus your writing and reduces the content of your web page to the essentials, which makes it easier for web users to scan and read.

After you publish content online, it's crucial to keep it up to date—out of date information makes your website's content seem unreliable. You can minimize the amount of regular updating you need to do by reducing or eliminating relative references to dates (such as "5 years ago" or "in 18 months") or labeling specific dates as being in the future (such as "The building will be completed in 2013.")

FIGURE B-5: Code containing new `div` element

```
1   <!DOCTYPE html>
2   <html lang="en">
3      <head>
4         <title>Lakeland Reeds Bed and Breakfast - About Us</title>
        <!--
           Lakeland Reeds Bed and Breakfast
           Filename: aboutus.html

           Author:    your first and last name
           Date:      today's date
           HTML5 and CSS3 Illustrated Unit B, Lessons
        -->
13        <meta charset="utf-8">
14     </head>
15     <body>
16        <h1>Lakeland Reeds Bed and Breakfast</h1>
17        <div>
18           <h2>About Us</h2>
19           <p>Lakeland Reeds is an ideal place to unplug from your daily routine. We're
20           here to help you get the most out of your time with us, from canoes and life
21           vests for a day out on the lake, to DVDs and popcorn for a quiet evening in. We
22           look forward to welcoming you!</p>
23        </div>
24        <p>45 Marsh Grass Ln. - Marble, MN 55764 - (218) 555-5253</p>
25     </body>
26  </html>
```

Children of new div element indented three additional spaces

Opening `<div>` tag added

Closing `</div>` tag added

FIGURE B-6: About Us page in a browser

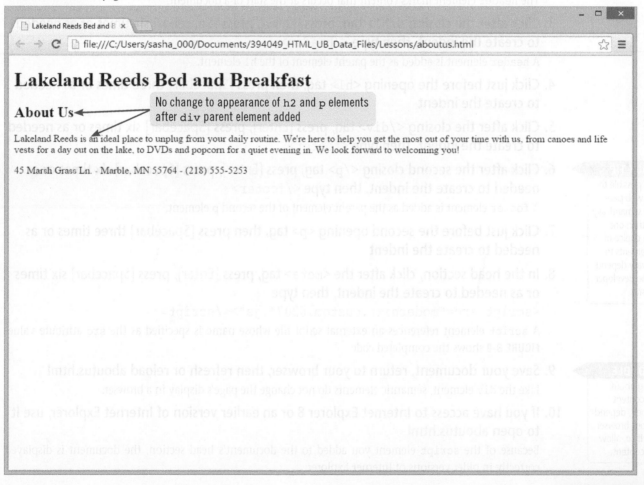

No change to appearance of `h2` and `p` elements after `div` parent element added

Lakeland Reeds Bed and B ✕

file:///C:/Users/sasha_000/Documents/394049_HTML_UB_Data_Files/Lessons/aboutus.html

Lakeland Reeds Bed and Breakfast

About Us

Lakeland Reeds is an ideal place to unplug from your daily routine. We're here to help you get the most out of your time with us, from canoes and life vests for a day out on the lake, to DVDs and popcorn for a quiet evening in. We look forward to welcoming you!

45 Marsh Grass Ln. - Marble, MN 55764 - (218) 555-5253

Add HTML5 Semantic Elements

Learning Outcomes
• Use the HTML5 header, article, and footer elements
• Make semantic elements work for IE8 users.

All HTML elements have **semantic** value—that is, they indicate the meaning of their content. For instance, the h1 element marks text as a top-level heading, and the p element marks a paragraph of text. The div element has limited semantic meaning—it groups elements but adds no information about what type of information it contains. However, the most recent version of HTML, known as **HTML5**, includes a number of grouping elements, known as **semantic elements** that indicate the role of their content. Search engines can use this semantic information to provide more accurate search results. This means that using semantic elements can make it easier for people using a search engine to find information about your business or organization. **TABLE B-2** lists several semantic elements. Because older versions of Internet Explorer can't interpret semantic elements, you also include a script element in the head section, which instructs older browsers how to interpret the semantic elements. The script element references code in an external file that browsers can use to help them interpret the elements. **CASE** *You add the* header *and* footer *elements to indicate the content at the start and end of the page, and you add a* script *element referencing a file that makes it possible for users of older versions of Internet Explorer to view the document.* **FIGURE B-7** *shows a wireframe of the About Us page with each section marked.*

STEPS

1. **Return to aboutus.html in your editor**

2. **Click after the opening `<body>` tag, press [Enter], press [Spacebar] six times or as needed to create the indent, then type `<header>`**
   The header element marks content that occurs at the start of a document.

3. **Click after the closing `</h1>` tag, press [Enter], press [Spacebar] six times or as needed to create the indent, then type `</header>`**
   A header element is added as the parent element of the h1 element.

4. **Click just before the opening `<h1>` tag, then press [Spacebar] three times or as needed to create the indent**

5. **Click after the closing `</div>` tag, press [Enter], press [Spacebar] six times or as needed to create the indent, then type `<footer>`**

QUICK TIP
It's often possible to mark up web page contents semantically in more than one way. The choice of which elements to use can vary depending on the developer and the site.

6. **Click after the second closing `</p>` tag, press [Enter], press [Spacebar] six times or as needed to create the indent, then type `</footer>`**
   A footer element is added as the parent element of the second p element.

7. **Click just before the second opening `<p>` tag, then press [Spacebar] three times or as needed to create the indent**

8. **In the head section, click after the `<meta>` tag, press [Enter], press [Spacebar] six times or as needed to create the indent, then type**
   `<script src="modernizr.custom.62074.js"></script>`
   A script element references an external script file whose name is specified as the src attribute value. **FIGURE B-8** shows the completed code.

TROUBLE
A warning about blocked content might open, depending on your browser settings. If so, allow blocked content.

9. **Save your document, return to your browser, then refresh or reload aboutus.html**
   Like the div element, semantic elements do not change the page's display in a browser.

10. **If you have access to Internet Explorer 8 or an earlier version of Internet Explorer, use it to open aboutus.html**
    Because of the script element you added to the document's head section, the document is displayed correctly in older versions of Internet Explorer.

FIGURE B-7: Wireframe for Lakeland Reeds About Us page

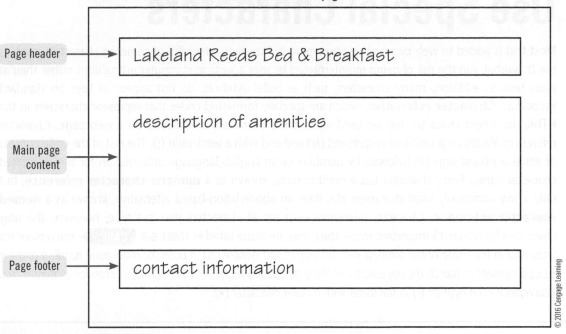

Page header → Lakeland Reeds Bed & Breakfast

Main page content → description of amenities

Page footer → contact information

© 2016 Cengage Learning

FIGURE B-8: Code with semantic elements and `script` element

```
10              Date:        today's date
11              HTML5 and CSS3 Illustrated Unit B,
12      -->
13      <meta charset="utf-8">
14      <script src="modernizr.custom.62074.js"></script>
15      </head>
16      <body>
17          <header>
18              <h1>Lakeland Reeds Bed and Breakfast</h1>
19          </header>
20          <div>
21              <h2>About Us</h2>
22              <p>Lakeland Reeds is an ideal place to unplug from your daily routine. We're
23              elp you get the most out of your time with us, from canoes and life
24              a day out on the lake, to DVDs and popcorn for a quiet evening in. We
25              ard to welcoming you!</p>
26          </div>
27          <footer>
28              <p>45 Marsh Grass Ln. - Marble, MN 55764 - (218) 555-5253</p>
29          </footer>
30      </body>
31  </html>
```

Attribute value enclosed in quotes

script element added for IE8 compatibility

Attribute name

header element added as parent of h1 element

footer element added as parent of second p element

TABLE B-2: Selected HTML5 semantic elements

element	intended use
article	stand-alone piece of work, such as a single entry in a blog
aside	part of a page that's tangential to the main page content, such as a sidebar or pull quote
footer	information about a section or document that usually appears at the end, such as contact information, attributions, and/or footnotes
header	information about a section or document that usually appears at the beginning, such as a heading, logo, and/or table of contents
nav	main elements of site and page navigation
section	section of content focused on a common theme, such as a chapter of a larger work

© 2016 Cengage Learning

Use Special Characters

Learning Outcomes
- Use a named character reference
- Use a numeric character reference

Most text is added to web pages simply by typing it. However, a handful of common characters, such as the & symbol, run the risk of being misinterpreted by user agents as computer instructions rather than as plain text. In addition, many characters, such as bullet symbols, do not appear as keys on standard keyboards. **Character references**, which are specially formatted codes that represent characters in the HTML document character set, are used when these characters are needed on a web page. Character references always begin with an ampersand (&) and end with a semicolon (;). The rest of the code consists of either a pound sign (#) followed by numbers or an English language abbreviation for the associated character name. Every character has a number code, known as a **numeric character reference**, but only a few commonly used characters also have an abbreviation-based alternative, known as a **named character reference**. Character references exist for all characters you can type; however, the only characters for which it's important to use the codes are those listed in **TABLE B-3**. **CASE** ▶ *You replace the word* and *in the name of the business with an ampersand symbol (&) in both the main page heading and the* title *element to match the appearance of the organization name on signs and other branded materials. You also replace each hyphen (-) in the footer with a bullet character (•).*

STEPS

1. **Return to** aboutus.html **in your editor, then locate the** title **element**

2. **Delete the word** and **in the name Lakeland Reeds Bed and Breakfast, type** &**, then be sure there is a space before and after the character reference**

3. **Locate the** h1 **element**

4. **Delete the word** and **in the name Lakeland Reeds Bed and Breakfast, type** &**, then be sure there is a space before and after the character reference**

5. **Delete the first hyphen (-) within the** footer **element, type** •**, then be sure there is a space before and after the character reference**

6. **Delete the second hyphen (-) within the** footer **element, type** •**, then be sure there is a space before and after the character reference**

   FIGURE B-9 shows the special characters inserted in the code for the web page.

7. **Save your work, then refresh or reload aboutus.html in your browser**

   As shown in **FIGURE B-10**, the word *and* in the browser title bar and in the main web page heading is replaced with the ampersand (&) symbol, and each hyphen in the final line of text is replaced with the bullet (•) character.

Finding codes for other characters

UTF-8 is the most commonly used character encoding on the web today. This encoding supports character references for thousands of characters. These symbols may include characters in different writing systems and international currency symbols, as well as icons and pictograms for a variety of themes. You can go to unicode.org/charts or fileformat.info to browse supported characters by subject. Note that not all symbols are displayed in every browser or operating system. This is because browsers and operating systems use different default fonts, and a given font may contain character descriptions for some, but not all, UTF-8 characters. For this reason, it's important to test a page containing a less-common special character in all browsers that you anticipate your audience will use to view the page. This lets you confirm that the character is recognized and displayed when the page is rendered in a browser, or make adjustments if the character is not recognized.

FIGURE B-9: Codes for special characters inserted in web page

```
1    <!DOCTYPE html>
2    <html lang="en">
3        <head>
4            <title>Lakeland Reeds Bed &amp; Breakfast - About Us</title>
5            <!--
6                Lakeland Reeds Bed and Breakfast
7                Filename: aboutus.html
8
9                Author:    your first and last name
10               Date:      today's date
11               HTML5 and CSS3 Illustrated Unit B, Lessons
12           -->
13           <meta charset="utf-8">
14           <script src="modernizr.custom.62074.js"></script>
15       </head>
16       <body>
17           <header>
18               <h1>Lakeland Reeds Bed &amp; Breakfast</h1>
19           </header>
20           <div>
21               <h2>About Us</h2>
22               <p>Lakeland Reeds is an ideal place to unplug from your daily routine. We're
23               here to help you get the most out of your time with us, from canoes and life
24               vests for a day out on the lake, to DVDs and popcorn for a quiet evening in. We
25               look forward to welcoming you!</p>
26           </div>
27           <footer>
28               <p>45 Marsh Grass Ln. &#8226; Marble, MN 55764 &#8226; (218) 555-5253</p>
29           </footer>
30       </body>
31   </html>
```

Named character references for the ampersand (&) character

Numeric character references for the bullet (•) character

HTML5 & CSS3

FIGURE B-10: About Us page incorporating special characters

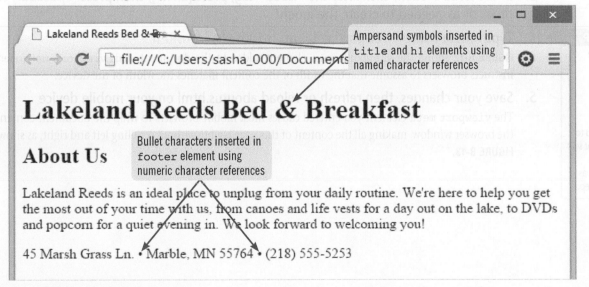

Ampersand symbols inserted in title and h1 elements using named character references

Lakeland Reeds Bed & Breakfast

About Us

Bullet characters inserted in footer element using numeric character references

Lakeland Reeds is an ideal place to unplug from your daily routine. We're here to help you get the most out of your time with us, from canoes and life vests for a day out on the lake, to DVDs and popcorn for a quiet evening in. We look forward to welcoming you!

45 Marsh Grass Ln. • Marble, MN 55764 • (218) 555-5253

TABLE B-3: Important character references

character	character name	numeric character reference	named character reference
&	ampersand	&	&
'	apostrophe	'	' (does not work in older versions of Internet Explorer)
>	greater-than sign	>	>
<	less-than sign	<	<
"	quotation mark	"	"

© 2016 Cengage Learning

Specify the Viewport

Learning Outcomes
- Add viewport meta element
- Set content attribute value

When the browser on a mobile device opens a web page, it needs to figure out how the document should be displayed on its small screen. Some web pages can scale to fit any browser, no matter the screen size. For other web pages, though, displaying the whole page at once would make its content too small to read. For this reason, most mobile browsers by default display only a portion of the page but at a legible size. These browsers display the page as if looking through an imaginary window, which is known as the **viewport**. To instruct browsers to display a page at the width of the browser window without zooming in, you change the browser's viewport settings using a `viewport meta` **element**, which is a meta element with the `name` attribute set to a value of `viewport`. As part of the `viewport meta` element, you also include a second attribute, `content`, whose value specifies one or more pairs of properties and values **TABLE B-4** lists `viewport` properties. To scale the page to fit the browser window, you use a `content` value of `width=device-width` **CASE** ▶ *You add a* `viewport meta` *element to the About Us page to ensure that it is displayed at the width of the browser window on mobile devices.*

STEPS

1. **Using your web server, open aboutus.html on a smartphone or other handheld mobile device**

   As shown in **FIGURE B-11**, most mobile devices zoom the web page, displaying it as if viewing only a portion of a much larger screen and cutting off some of the content. To see all of the content at once would require zooming out, at which point most content would be illegible.

2. **Return to aboutus.html in your editor**

3. **In the head section, click after the `<meta>` tag, press [Enter], then press [Spacebar] six times or as needed to create the indent**

4. **Type `<meta name="viewport" content="width=device-width">`**

   FIGURE B-12 shows the `viewport meta` element added to the document. This `viewport meta` element instructs browsers to assume that the width of the content matches the width of the device.

5. **Save your changes, then refresh or reload aboutus.html on your mobile device**

   The `viewport meta` element you entered causes most mobile browsers to wrap the document contents to the browser window, making all the content of this page legible without scrolling left and right, as shown in **FIGURE B-13**.

TABLE B-4: `viewport` attribute properties

property	description	allowable values
width	The width of the viewport	device-width or a value in pixels
height	The height of the viewport	device-height or a value in pixels
initial-scale	The scale of the viewport when the document opens	a number representing the scale, with 1.0 equal to 100%
minimum-scale	The lower limit on the scale of the viewport	a number representing the scale, with 1.0 equal to 100%
maximum-scale	The upper limit on the scale of the viewport	a number representing the scale, with 1.0 equal to 100%
user-scalable	Whether a user is allowed to zoom the page or not	yes or no

FIGURE B-11: Web page without a `meta` `viewport` element on a mobile device

FIGURE B-12: `meta` `viewport` element added to document

```
1   <!DOCTYPE html>
2   <html lang="en">
3     <head>
4       <title>Lakeland Reeds Bed &amp; Breakfast - About Us</title>
5       <!--
6           Lakeland Reeds Bed and Breakfast
7           Filename: aboutus.html
8
9           Author:   your first and last name
10          Date:     today's date
11          HTML5 and CSS3 Illustrated Unit B, Lessons
12      -->
13      <meta charset="utf-8">
14      <meta name="viewport" content="width=device-width">
15      <script src="modernizr.custom.62074.js"></script>
16    </head>
```

FIGURE B-13: Web page with a `meta` `viewport` element on a mobile device

Mobile devices commonly mark a phone number as a link so users can touch it to call the number

Debug your HTML Code

**Learning
Outcomes**
• Identify bugs
  based on coding
  errors
• Correct coding
  errors

Even the most careful developer writes code from time to time that doesn't work. A problem that results from incorrectly written code is known as a **bug**, and the process of finding and removing bugs from code is called **debugging**. Simply viewing a document in one or more browsers can sometimes help illuminate bugs and narrow down where in the code the errors causing the problems might be located. **TABLE B-5** lists some common bugs in HTML code along with what often causes them. �**CASE** ▶ *You practice debugging by introducing errors in the code for the About Us page, viewing the document in a desktop browser, and then examining the effects of the errors.*

STEPS

1. **Return to aboutus.html in your editor**

2. **Delete the opening `<h1>` tag within the `header` element**

3. **Delete the & at the start of the first character reference within the `footer` element**
   FIGURE B-14 shows the code with the two errors introduced.

4. **Save your changes, then refresh or reload aboutus.html in a browser**
   As shown in **FIGURE B-15**, the text of the first heading is no longer large, and the first bullet in the footer is replaced by the text of the character code that follows the &.

5. **Return to aboutus.html in your editor, click just before the word Lakeland within the `header` element, then type `<h1>`**

6. **Save your changes, then refresh or reload aboutus.html in a browser**
   The first heading is now displayed in larger text than the second heading, as it was previously.

7. **Return to aboutus.html in your editor, click just before the first # within the `footer` element, then type &**
   Your code should match **FIGURE B-16**.

TROUBLE
If your page does not
display as expected,
be sure your
corrected code
matches
FIGURE B-16.

8. **Save your changes, then refresh or reload aboutus.html in a browser**
   The first bullet character is once again displayed in the footer. Your web page should once again match **FIGURE B-10**.

TABLE B-5: Common bugs and causes

bug	common causes
Element appearance different than expected	Missing tags around content
	Element enclosed by tags for a different element
	Opening tag missing
	Closing > omitted from a tag
Special character not displayed correctly	Invalid character code specified
	& omitted from start of character code
	Code for a different character specified

© 2016 Cengage Learning

```
17        <body>
18          <header>
19       ▶Lakeland Reeds Bed &amp; Breakfast</h1>
20          </header>
21          <div>
22            <h2>About Us</h2>
            <p>Lakeland Reeds is an ideal place to unplug from your daily routine. We're
            here to help you get the most out of your time with us, from canoes and life
            vests for a day out on the lake, to DVDs and popcorn for a quiet evening in. We
26          look forward to welcoming you!</p>
27          </div>
28          <footer>
29            <p>45 Marsh Grass Ln. #8226; Marble, MN 55764 &#8226; (218) 555-5253</p>
30          </footer>
31        </body>
32      </html>
```

Opening <h1> tag removed

Opening & deleted from character code

Opening & still part of character code

FIGURE B-15: Web page with errors in browser

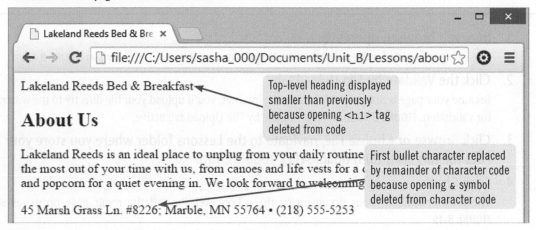

Lakeland Reeds Bed & Bre ×

file:///C:/Users/sasha_000/Documents/Unit_B/Lessons/about

Lakeland Reeds Bed & Breakfast

Top-level heading displayed smaller than previously because opening <h1> tag deleted from code

About Us

Lakeland Reeds is an ideal place to unplug from your daily routine the most out of your time with us, from canoes and life vests for a and popcorn for a quiet evening in. We look forward to welcoming

First bullet character replaced by remainder of character code because opening & symbol deleted from character code

45 Marsh Grass Ln. #8226; Marble, MN 55764 • (218) 555-5253

FIGURE B-16: Web page code after debugging

```
1   <!DOCTYPE html>
2   <html lang="en">
3     <head>
4       <title>Lakeland Reeds Bed &amp; Breakfast - About Us</title>
5       <!--
6         Lakeland Reeds Bed and Breakfast
7         Filename: aboutus.html
8
9         Author:   your first and last name
10        Date:     today's date
11        HTML5 and CSS3 Illustrated Unit B, Lessons
12      -->
13      <meta charset="utf-8">
14      <meta name="viewport" content="width=device-width">
15      <script src="modernizr.custom.62074.js"></script>
16    </head>
17    <body>
18      <header>
19        <h1>Lakeland Reeds Bed &amp; Breakfast</h1>
20      </header>
21      <div>
22        <h2>About Us</h2>
23        <p>Lakeland Reeds is an ideal place to unplug from your daily routine. We're
24        here to help you get the most out of your time with us, from canoes and life
25        vests for a day out on the lake, to DVDs and popcorn for a quiet evening in. We
26        look forward to welcoming you!</p>
27      </div>
28      <footer>
29        <p>45 Marsh Grass Ln. &#8226; Marble, MN 55764 &#8226; (218) 555-5253</p>
30      </footer>
31    </body>
32  </html>
```

Validate your HTML Code

Previewing web pages in a variety of browsers can be useful for spotting problems with code and making sure that web pages display as expected for users. Another tool is **validation**, which is an automated process of comparing code you've written against the HTML5 coding standards. When previewing a page reveals an error in your code that is difficult to track down, validation can sometimes be useful in identifying the specific source of the problem. In addition, sometimes a user agent can interpret a web page as expected in spite of code that doesn't conform to specifications. In this case, validating code and correcting errors can help to ensure that the code will continue to work with future versions of both user agents and HTML standards, which may not continue to deal seamlessly with erroneous coding. The W3C offers a free online validator for web documents at validator.w3.org. **CASE** ▶ *Before sharing your work with your contacts at Lakeland Reeds, you validate your code.*

STEPS

1. **In a web browser, open** http://validator.w3.org

   The web page opens for the validation service provided by the W3C, as shown in **FIGURE B-17**.

2. **Click the Validate by File Upload tab**

   Because your page is not yet published on the Internet, you'll upload your file directly to the w3.org website for validation. **FIGURE B-18** shows the Validate by File Upload tab active.

3. **Click Browse or Choose File, navigate to the Lessons folder where you store your Data Files for this unit, then double-click aboutus.html**

4. **Click Check**

   The browser uploads your document to the w3.org website and the result page opens, as shown in **FIGURE B-19**.

QUICK TIP
Errors listed by the validator always specify the line and character ("column") numbers where it encountered the error. This is sometimes, but not always, the location of the code you need to fix.

5. **Scroll down to read the validation results, including any notes or warnings**

   Notes and warnings provide additional information about aspects of your document that you may want to change. However, they do not prevent your document from validating. **TABLE B-6** lists and explains some common validation errors as well as two common validation warnings.

6. **If your document does not successfully validate as HTML5, return to your text editor, compare your document to FIGURE B-12 and make any necessary changes, save your work, then repeat Steps 1–4 to revalidate your file**

TABLE B-6: Common validation errors and warnings

error message	common cause
"End tag for body seen, but there were unclosed elements."	
"End of file seen when expecting text or an end tag."	You entered the opening tag for an element but left out its closing tag.
"Unclosed element *element*."	
"End of file reached when inside an attribute value. Ignoring tag."	You forgot the closing quotes (") after an attribute value.
"Named character reference was not terminated by a semicolon. (Or & should have been escaped as &.)"	You forgot the closing semicolon (;) after a character reference.
"Character reference was not terminated by a semicolon."	

warning message	explanation
"Using experimental feature: *HTML5 Conformance Checker.*"	The w3.org validator does not consider its HTML5 validation service 100% accurate because the language is constantly being updated.
"Byte-Order Mark found in a UTF-8 file."	Your editor saved your document based on a standard that is not universally supported by older editors or browsers.

FIGURE B-17: W3C Markup Validation Service web page

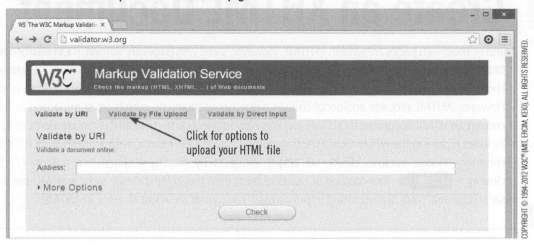

Click for options to upload your HTML file

FIGURE B-18: Validate by File Upload tab

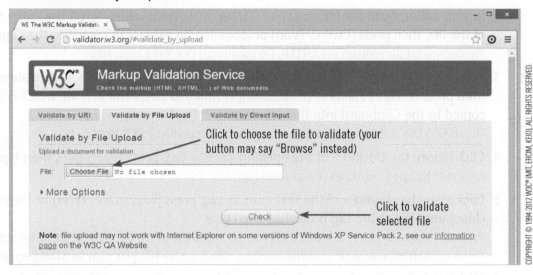

Click to choose the file to validate (your button may say "Browse" instead)

Click to validate selected file

FIGURE B-19: Validation results for aboutus.html

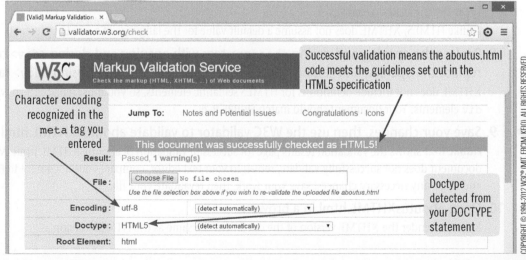

Successful validation means the aboutus.html code meets the guidelines set out in the HTML5 specification

Character encoding recognized in the meta tag you entered

Doctype detected from your DOCTYPE statement

Create an XHTML Document

Learning Outcomes
- Create a document that conforms to XHTML rules
- Validate an XHTML document

Today, most web pages are written in HTML. However, some web pages are written in **Extensible Hypertext Markup Language (XHTML)**, which is a version of HTML that conforms to the rules of another language known as **Extensible Markup Language (XML)**. The way HTML and XHTML are written is very similar. However, XHTML requires additional code in a number of situations, which are summarized in TABLE B-7. To convert an HTML document to XHTML requires editing the code to meet all the requirements of XHTML. This includes replacing the HTML DOCTYPE statement, `<!DOCTYPE html>`, with an XHTML DOCTYPE. Another common change involves closing all empty elements by placing a space and a slash (/) before the closing >. **CASE** ▶ *Your contacts at Lakeland Reeds think they'd like their site to be in HTML, but they'd like to see a page in XHTML before making a final decision. You convert the About Us page to XHTML.*

STEPS

1. **Return to** aboutus.html **in your editor, save a copy of the file to the Lessons folder with the name** aboutusXHTML.html, **then in the comment in the head section, change the filename listed to** aboutusXHTML.html

2. **In your editor, open the file** doctype.txt **from the Lessons folder, select the entire contents of the file, then press [Ctrl][C] (Win) or [command][C] (Mac) to copy it to the Clipboard**
   The doctype.txt file contains the XHTML 1.0 Transitional DOCTYPE declaration.

QUICK TIP
Because an XHTML DOCTYPE is so complex, developers generally either copy them from an online resource and paste them into their code, or rely on a code editor to generate the DOCTYPE for them.

3. **Return to** aboutusXHTML.html **in your editor, delete the entire DOCTYPE statement, then press [Ctrl][V] (Win) or [command][V] (Mac) to paste the XHTML DOCTYPE you copied to the Clipboard into the document**
   The HTML5 DOCTYPE is replaced with the XHTML 1.0 Transitional DOCTYPE.

4. **Click before the closing > of the opening** `<html>` **tag, press [Spacebar], then type** `xmlns="http://www.w3.org/1999/xhtml"`

5. **Click after the closing > of the first** `<meta>` **tag, press [Backspace] (Win) or [delete] (Mac) until the entire tag is deleted, then type**
   `<meta http-equiv="Content-Type" content="text/html; charset=utf-8" />`
   This is the XHTML statement to specify encoding, which is more complex than its HTML5 equivalent.

6. **Click just before the closing > for the second** `<meta>` **tag, press [Spacebar], then type** /
   Adding a / before the closing > of a one-sided tag is necessary to close that element in XHTML.

7. **Click just before the closing > for the opening** `<script>` **tag, press [Spacebar], then type** type="text/javascript"
   Unlike HTML5, XHTML does not assume a default value for the language of a `script` element.

8. **Replace the opening and closing** `<header>` **tags with opening and closing** `<div>` **tags, then replace the opening and closing** `<footer>` **tags with opening and closing** `<div>` **tags**
   XHTML does not include definitions for HTML5 semantic elements, so you must replace them with generic div elements. Your document should match FIGURE B-20.

TROUBLE
Refer to the steps in the previous lesson "Validate your HTML Code" as needed to complete Step 9.

9. **Save your changes, then use the W3C validator to validate** aboutusXHTML.html
   FIGURE B-21 shows the validation results page for successful validation of aboutusXHTML.html. *Note*: If your document does not successfully validate, return to your text editor, compare your document to FIGURE B-20 and make any necessary changes, save your work, then revalidate your file.

10. **Open** aboutusXHTML.html **in a browser**
    Browsers render the XHTML version of the document the same as the HTML5 version.

FIGURE B-20: About Us document converted to XHTML

```
1    <!DOCTYPE html PUBLIC "-//W3C//DTD XHTML 1.0 Transitional//EN"
2        "http://www.w3.org/TR/xhtml1/DTD/xhtml1-transitional.dtd">
3    <html lang="en" xmlns="http://www.w3.org/1999/xhtml">
4        <head>
5            <title>Lakeland Reeds Bed &amp; Breakfast - About Us</title>
        meta element        eland Reeds Bed and Breakfast
           specifying       lename: aboutus.html
     character encoding
        replaced with    hor:    your first and last name
          XHTML version   e:       today's date
12            TML5 and CSS3 Illustrated Unit B, Lessons
13        -->
14        <meta http-equiv="Content-Type" content="text/html; charset=utf-8" />
15        <meta name="viewport" content="width=device-width" />
16        <script src="modernizr.custom.62074.js" type="text/javascript"></script>
17    </head>
18    <body>
19        <div>
20            <h1>Lakeland Reeds Bed &amp; Breakfast</h1>
21        </div>
22        <div>
23            <h2>Al
24            <p>La      header and     an ideal place to unplug from your daily routine. We're
25            here      footer tag pairs  the most out of your time with us, from canoes and life
26            vests     replaced by div    n the lake, to DVDs and popcorn for a quiet evening in. We
27            look      tag pairs          ming you!</p>
28        </div>
29        <div>
30            <p>45 Marsh Grass Ln. &#8226; Marble, MN 55764 &#8226; (218) 555-5253</p>
31        </div>
32    </body>
33    </html>
```

HTML5 DOCTYPE statement replaced with XHTML Transitional version

xmlns attribute and value in quotes added to opening `<html>` tag

Space and closing / added to one-sided tag

type attribute and value in quotes added to script element

FIGURE B-21: Validation results for aboutusXHTML.html

This document was successfully checked as XHTML 1.0 Transitional!

Result:	Passed
File :	Choose File No file chosen
	Use the file selection box above if you wish to re-validate the uplo...
Encoding :	utf-8 (detect automatic...)
Doctype :	XHTML 1.0 Transitional (detect automatically) ▼
Root Element:	html
Root Namespace:	http://www.w3.org/1999/xhtml

Character encoding recognized in the updated meta tag you entered

Successful validation means the aboutusXHTML.html code meets the guidelines set out in the XHTML Transitional specification

Doctype detected from your updated DOCTYPE statement

TABLE B-7: Differences between HTML and XHTML

aspect	HTML	XHTML
Tag nesting	Tags may be closed out of order	Tags must be closed in the order opened
Tag case	Tags may be written in upper or lower case	Tags must be written in lower case
Tag closure	Closing tags may be omitted for some elements	All opening tags must be matched with closing tags
Attribute-value pairs	Certain attribute names may be specified without values	Values required for all attributes
One-sided tags	One-sided tags do not need to be closed	One-sided tags must be closed
`script` and `style` elements	Element content requires no special formatting	Element content must be marked with code identifying it as CDATA
Attribute values	Values may be enclosed within quotes	Values must be enclosed within quotes
`id` and `name` attributes	Either attribute may be used	`id` attribute may be used, but `name` attribute prohibited
Character codes for certain special characters	Codes recommended	Codes required

Practice

Concepts Review

Refer to FIGURE B-22 **to answer the following questions.**

FIGURE B-22

```
a    1    <!DOCTYPE html>
     2    <html lang="en">                            f
     3      <head>
     4        <title>Lakeland Reeds Bed &amp; Breakfast - About Us</title>
     5        <!--
     6          Lakeland Reeds Bed and Breakfast
     7          Filename: aboutus.html
     8
     9          Author:   your first and last name
     10         Date:     today's date
     11         HTML5 and CSS3 Illustrated Unit B, Lessons
     12       -->
b    13      <meta charset="utf-8">
     14      <meta name="viewport" content="width=device-width">
c    15      <script src="modernizr.custom.62074.js"></script>
     16      </head>
     17    <body>
     18      <header>
d    19        <h1>Lakeland Reeds Bed &amp; Breakfast</h1>
     20      </header>
     21      <div>
     22        <h2>About Us</h2>
     23        <p>Lakeland Reeds is an ideal place to unplug from your daily routine. We're
     24        here to help you get the most out of your time with us, from canoes and life
     25        vests for a day out on the lake, to DVDs and popcorn for a quiet evening in. We
     26        look forward to welcoming you!</p>
     27      </div>
     28      <footer>
     29        <p>45 Marsh Grass Ln. &#8226; Marble, MN 55764 &#8226; (218) 555-5253</p>
     30      </footer>                                    e
     31    </body>
     32    </html>
```

1. **Which item is a semantic element?**
2. **Which item tells mobile browsers how to display the document?**
3. **Which item is a named character reference?**
4. **Which item is an attribute name and value?**
5. **Which item is a numeric character reference?**
6. **Which item specifies the character encoding for the document?**

Match each term with the statement that best describes it.

7. **WCAG**
8. **attribute**
9. **character reference**
10. **viewport meta element**
11. **debugging**
12. **validation**
13. **XHTML**

   a. the process of finding and removing incorrectly written code

   b. a version of HTML that complies with the rules of XML

   c. an automated process of comparing code you've written against the HTML5 coding standards

   d. a specially formatted code that represents a character in the HTML document character set

   e. code you can use to instruct mobile browsers to display a page at the width of the browser window without zooming in

   f. additional code within an opening tag that specifies information about an element

   g. a widely used reference for implementing web accessibility

Select the best answer from the list of choices.

14. According to WCAG, to make your web pages _____ you should ensure that no elements rely on the use of a mouse.
    - **a.** perceivable
    - **b.** operable
    - **c.** understandable
    - **d.** robust

15. Where are an attribute's name and value placed in your code?
    - **a.** In the DOCTYPE
    - **b.** In an element's opening tag
    - **c.** In an element's closing tag
    - **d.** In an external file

16. The `header` and `footer` elements are known as _____ elements.
    - **a.** presentational
    - **b.** structural
    - **c.** semantic
    - **d.** mandatory

17. Character references always begin with an ampersand (&) and end with a _____.
    - **a.** quote (")
    - **b.** hyphen (-)
    - **c.** colon (:)
    - **d.** semicolon (;)

18. Simply viewing your document in one or more browsers can sometimes help you recognize _____.
    - **a.** bugs
    - **b.** semantic elements
    - **c.** attributes
    - **d.** character references

Skills Review

1. **Incorporate attributes.**
   - **a.** In your editor, open the HTM_B-2.html file from the SR folder where you store your Data Files for this unit, then save it as **history.html**.
   - **b.** Below the `title` element, insert the following comment, substituting your name and today's date where indicated:

     ```
     <!--
         Big J's Deep Dish Pizza History web page
         Filename: history.html
         Author:    your name
         Date:      today's date
         HTML5 and CSS3 Illustrated Unit B, Skills Review
     -->
     ```
   - **c.** Preview history.html in a browser.
   - **d.** Return to your editor, then in the opening `<html>` tag, insert the attribute and value **lang="en"**.
   - **e.** Below the comment add a `meta` element with an attribute and value that specifies the character encoding as utf-8.
   - **f.** Save your document, then view the revised document in a browser.

2. **Implement the `div` element.**
   - **a.** Return to history.html in your editor.
   - **b.** Add a `div` element as the parent element of the h2 element and the first two p elements.
   - **c.** Indent all three child elements of the new `div` element.
   - **d.** Save your document, then view the revised document in a browser.

3. **Add HTML5 semantic elements.**
   - **a.** Return to history.html in your editor.
   - **b.** Add a `header` element as the parent element of the h1 element.
   - **c.** Add a `footer` element as the parent element of the last p element.
   - **d.** Indent the child elements of the new `header` and `footer` elements.
   - **e.** Below the `<meta>` tag in the head section, add the following `script` element:

     ```
     <script src="modernizr.custom.62074.js"></script>
     ```

f. Save your document, then view the revised document in a browser.

g. If you have access to Internet Explorer 8 or an earlier version of Internet Explorer, use it to open history.html.

4. Use special characters.

a. Return to history.html in your editor.

b. In the content of the `title` element, replace the apostrophe (') with `&#39;`.

c. In the content of the `h1` element, replace the apostrophe (') with `&#39;`.

d. In the `footer` element, replace each instance of a hyphen (–) with `&#8226;`.

e. Save your document, then view the revised document in a browser. Your document should match **FIGURE B-23**.

5. Specify the viewport.

a. Using your web server, open history.html on a smartphone or other handheld mobile device.

b. Return to history.html in your editor.

c. In the head section, below the `<meta>` tag, enter the following `viewport meta` tag:

`<meta name="viewport" content="width=device-width">`

d. Save your changes, then view the revised document on your mobile device. Your document should match **FIGURE B-24**.

6. Debug your HTML code.

a. Return to history.html in your editor.

b. Within the `div` element, delete the opening `<h2>` tag.

c. Within the `footer` element, delete the & at the start of the second character reference.

d. Save your changes, refresh or reload history.html in a browser, then identify the rendering errors.

e. Return to history.html in your editor, click just before the word History within the `div` element, then type `<h2>`.

f. Save your changes, then refresh or reload history.html in a browser.

g. Return to history.html in your editor, click just before the second # within the `footer` element, then type `&`.

h. Save your changes, refresh or reload history.html in a browser, then verify that no errors remain.

7. Validate your HTML code.

a. In a web browser, open http://validator.w3.org.

b. Use the Validate by File Upload tab to upload and validate history.html from the SR folder where you store your Data Files for this unit.

c. Scroll down to read the validation results, including any notes or warnings.

d. If your document does not successfully validate as HTML5, examine the error messages, return to your text editor, make any necessary changes, save your work, then revalidate your file

8. Create an XHTML document.

a. Return to history.html in your editor, save a copy of history.html to the SR folder with the name **historyXHTML.html**, then in the comment in the head section, change the filename listed to **historyXHTML.html**.

b. Delete the DOCTYPE, open doctype.txt from the SR folder, copy the contents of the file, then paste it at the start of historyXHTML.html.

FIGURE B-23

FIGURE B-24

Skills Review (continued)

c. In the opening `<html>` tag, add the attribute and value **xmlns="http://www.w3.org/1999/xhtml"**.

d. Replace the meta tag that specifies the character encoding for the document with **<meta http-equiv= "Content-Type" content="text/html; charset=utf-8" />**.

e. Add a closing / to the viewport `<meta>` tag.

f. Within the opening `<script>` tag, add the attribute and value **type="text/javascript"**.

f. Replace the `header` and `footer` elements with `div` elements.

g. Use http://validator.w3.org to validate historyXHTML.html.

h. Open historyXHTML.html in a browser and verify that its appearance matches that of history.html.

Independent Challenge 1

Spotted Wren Garden Center, a local garden shop and plant store, has hired you to create a website for their business. Sarah Nguyen, the shop's owner and manager, would like you to create a web presence as a new avenue of marketing, as well as a means to keep regular customers up to date on seasonal specials and new products. You continue building the site by structuring a page listing the store's summer hours.

a. In your editor, open the HTM_B-3.html file from the IC1 folder where you store your Data Files for this unit, then save it as **hours.html**.

b. In the head section, insert a comment containing the text **Spotted Wren Garden Center Summer Hours web page**, the filename **hours.html**, your first and last name, today's date, and the text **HTML5 and CSS3 Illustrated Unit B, Independent Challenge 1**, then save the file.

c. Preview hours.html in a browser.

d. Return to hours.html in your text editor, add an attribute specifying that the document contents are in English, then add an element that specifies the character encoding as utf-8. (*Hint*: Use the `charset` `meta` element.)

e. Add a `header` element as the parent of the h1 element and the first p element, then add a `div` element as the parent of the h2 element and the next seven p elements (*Note*: This includes all but the last p element).

f. Add a `footer` element as the parent of the final p element, then indent all child elements of the newly added `header`, `div`, and `footer` elements.

g. Add the following `script` element in the head section of your document:
<script src="modernizr.custom.62074.js"></script>

h. Replace the hyphen (-) in each p element within the `div` element with the named character reference **–**, then replace each hyphen within the `footer` element with the numeric character reference **•**. (*Hint*: Be sure your named character reference starts with & and ends with a semicolon (;).)

i. Save your changes and preview the document in a browser. Your document should match **FIGURE B-25**.

j. Add the following viewport `meta` tag to your document:
<meta name="viewport" content="width=device-width">

k. Save your changes and view the document on a handheld device such as a smartphone. Your document should match **FIGURE B-26**.

FIGURE B-25

Independent Challenge 1 (continued)

l. Make intentional coding errors by deleting the third opening `<p>` tag within the `div` element and deleting the `&` at the start of the named character reference in the last p element within the `div` element, save your changes, view the document in a browser, then examine the results of the errors you introduced.

m. Fix the errors you introduced and use your browser to verify that the page is once again rendered as it was before. (*Hint*: Add back the opening `<p>` tag and the `&` as noted in step l.)

n. Use http://validator.w3.org to validate your document. If necessary, fix any errors in your document until it validates.

FIGURE B-26

10.0.1.4   ↻

Spotted Wren Garden Center

For your year-round garden and yard needs

Summer Hours

Mon: 8am – 8pm

Tue: 8am – 8pm

Wed: 8am – 5pm

Thu: 8am – 8pm

Fri: 8am – 8pm

Sat: 9am – 6pm

Sun: 11am – 6pm

548 N. 58th St. • Omaha, NE 68132 • (402) 555-9736

‹   ›   ⬆   ▢   ▢

Independent Challenge 2

To help build your web design skills, you have volunteered to create a website for the Murfreesboro Regional Soccer League (MRSL). The league organizes recreational leagues every summer and fall for local, nonprofessional soccer players to get exercise and have fun. You continue working on the site by adding structure to the page that provides information for prospective participants.

a. In your editor, open the HTM_B-4.html file from the IC2 folder where you store your Data Files for this unit, then save it as **started.html**.

b. In the head section, insert a comment containing the text **Murfreesboro Regional Soccer League Getting Started web page**, the filename **started.html**, your first and last name, today's date, and the text **HTML5 and CSS3 Illustrated Unit B, Independent Challenge 2**, then save the file.

c. Preview started.html in a browser.

d. Add an attribute specifying that the document contents are in English in the opening `html` tag, then add a `meta` element after the closing comment tag that specifies the character encoding as **utf-8**.

e. Add a `header` element as the parent of the h1 element and the first p element. Add a `div` element as the parent of the next two p elements. Add a `footer` element as the parent of the final p element. Indent all child elements of the newly added `header`, `div`, and `footer` elements.

f. Add the following `script` element in the head section of your document:
`<script src="modernizr.custom.62074.js"></script>`

g. Within the `footer` element, replace each hyphen with the numeric character reference **•**. Save your changes and preview the document in a browser. Your document should match **FIGURE B-27**.

h. Add the following `viewport` `meta` tag to your document:
`<meta name="viewport" content="width=device-width">`

i. Save your changes and view the document on a handheld device such as a smartphone. Your document should match **FIGURE B-28**.

j. Introduce errors into your code by deleting one of the opening `<p>` tags and deleting the # within one of the character references. Save your changes, view the document in a browser, then identify the errors you introduced. Fix the errors you introduced and verify that the page is once again rendered as it was before.

FIGURE B-27

Murfreesboro Regional Soccer League

Part of the North American Recreational Soccer Association

The MRSL is open to players of all levels who want to play soccer in a relaxed, friendly environment. Even if you've never played soccer before, the MRSL is a great place to start.

To get a feel for our league, we recommend you call us at the number below or stop by Davies Sporting Goods to talk to one of our coordinators and get the details on our next all-team practice or workshop day. Then come kick around the ball with us and meet other players in the league.

MRSL • c/o Davies Sporting Goods • 418 N. Sartoris St. • Murfreesboro, TN 37130 • (615) 555-2255

Independent Challenge 2 (continued)

k. Use http://validator.w3.org to validate your document. If necessary, fix any errors in your document until it validates.

l. Save a copy of your document as **startedXHTML.html** to the IC2 folder, changing the filename listed in the comment in the head section, then replace the DOCTYPE with the contents of doctype.txt in the IC2 folder.

m. In the opening `<html>` tag, add the attribute and value **xmlns=http://www.w3.org/1999/xhtml**, then replace the `meta` element that specifies the character encoding for the document with **<meta http-equiv="Content-Type" content="text/html; charset=utf-8" />**.

n. Add a closing / to the viewport `<meta>` tag, then in the opening `<script>` tag add **type="text/javascript"**.

o. Replace the `header` and `footer` elements with `div` elements.

p. Use http://validator.w3.org to validate startedXHTML.html. If necessary, fix any errors in your document until it validates.

Independent Challenge 3

In your new job creating sites for a web design firm, you've been assigned Hotel Natoma as a client. The hotel's business manager, Diego Merckx, wants to use the web to showcase the facility and its amenities. As you continue your work on the site, you work with the structure of the code for the page listing attractions near the hotel.

a. In your editor, open the HTM_B-5.html file from the IC3 folder where you store your Data Files for this unit, then save it as **nearby.html**.

b. In the head section, insert a comment containing the text **Hotel Natoma What's Nearby web page**, the filename **nearby.html**, your first and last name, today's date, and the text **HTML5 and CSS3 Illustrated Unit B, Independent Challenge 3**. Save the file, then preview it in a browser.

c. Add an attribute specifying that the document contents are in English. Add an element that specifies the character encoding as utf-8.

d. Add a `header` element as the parent of the h1 element. Add a `div` element as the parent of the h2 element and the next six p elements. Add a `footer` element as the parent of the final p element. Indent all child elements of the newly added `header`, `div`, and `footer` elements.

e. Add the following script element in the head section of your document:

```
<script src="modernizr.cus-tom.62074.js"></script>
```

f. Within the `title` element and the h2 element, replace the apostrophe with the numeric character reference **'**. Within the `footer` element, replace each pipe character (|) with the numeric character reference **•**. Save your changes and preview the document in a browser. Your document should match **FIGURE B-29**.

HTML5 & CSS3

Independent Challenge 3 (continued)

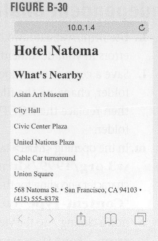

g. Add the following viewport `meta` tag to your document:

<meta name="viewport" content="width=device-width">

Save your changes and view the document on a handheld device such as a smartphone. Your document should match **FIGURE B-30**.

h. Introduce errors into your code by deleting one of the opening `<p>` tags, deleting the # within one of the character references, and deleting the & within a different character reference. Save your changes, view the document in a browser, then identify the errors you introduced. Without fixing the errors you introduced, use http://validator.w3.org to validate your document. Examine the error messages generated by the validator, then use the messages to track down and fix the errors in your document. Fix all errors in your document until it validates. Preview the document in a browser, then verify that the page is once again rendered as it was in **FIGURE B-29**.

i. Save a copy of your document as **nearbyXHTML.html** to the IC3 folder, changing the filename listed in the comment in the head section. Replace the DOCTYPE with the contents of doctype.txt in the IC3 folder. Without making any other changes to the document, use http://validator.w3.org to validate startedXHTML.html. Examine the error messages generated by the validator, then make the following changes one at a time, validating after each change, and noticing the differences in the error message list after each change:

- In the opening `<html>` tag, add the attribute and value **xmlns="http://www.w3.org/1999/xhtml"**.
- Replace the `meta` element that specifies the character encoding for the document with **<meta http-equiv="Content-Type" content="text/html; charset=utf-8" />**.
- Add a closing / to the `viewport` `<meta>` tag.
- In the opening `<script>` tag, add the attribute and value **type="text/javascript"**.
- Replace the `header` and `footer` elements with `div` elements.

Independent Challenge 4—Explore

You've been hired to create a website for Eating Well in Season (EWIS), a business in Glover, Vermont, that delivers produce from local farms to its customers. You'll continue your work on the site by enhancing the structure of a page that explains delivery options.

a. In your editor, open the HTM_B-6.html file from the IC4 folder where you store your Data Files for this unit, then save it as **delivery.html**.

b. In the head section, insert a comment containing the text **Eating Well in Season Delivery Options web page**, the filename **delivery.html**, your first and last name, today's date, and the text **HTML5 and CSS3 Illustrated Unit B, Independent Challenge 4**. Save the file.

c. The document's code contains two errors. Using the debugging tools you learned in this unit, locate and fix the errors.

d. Add an attribute specifying that the document contents are in English. Add an element that specifies the character encoding as utf-8.

e. Add a `header` element as the parent of the h1 element. Use **TABLE B-2** to choose an appropriate semantic element to use as the parent of the h2 element and the next two p elements. Add a `footer` element as the parent of the final p element. Indent all child elements of the three newly added semantic elements.

f. Add the following `script` element in the head section of your document:

<script src="modernizr.custom.62074.js"></script>

Independent Challenge 4—Explore (continued)

g. Browse the characters at fileformat.info for an appropriate character to replace the asterisks (*) in the footer element. (*Hint*: Many of the punctuation characters at http://www.fileformat.info/info/unicode/block/general_punctuation/list.htm are suited to the task. When you identify an appropriate character, click the link on the same line starting with U, then on the page that opens, locate the value labeled "HTML Entity (decimal)".) Use the value for your new symbol to replace the * three times in the footer. Save your changes and preview the document in current versions of all three modern browsers on both Windows and Mac (Chrome for Windows and Mac, Firefox for Windows and Mac, and Internet Explorer for Windows), noting any differences between them. If the character does not display consistently among browsers, choose a different character and test it, repeating until you identify a character that all three browsers display consistently under both operating systems. **FIGURE B-31** shows one possibility.

h. Add the following viewport `meta` tag to your document:

`<meta name="viewport"`
`content="width=device-width">`

Save your changes and view the document on a handheld device such as a smartphone. Your document should resemble **FIGURE B-32**.

i. If you are using a code editor, introduce some errors by deleting one of the opening <p> tags and deleting the # symbol within one of the character references. Notice any changes to the formatting of the code in your editor after you introduce the errors, such as underlining or changes in color. Use the documentation for your code editor to identify whether it includes features that suggest fixes to detected coding errors. Fix the errors you introduced and verify that the page is once again rendered as shown in **FIGURE B-31**.

j. If you are using a code editor, use the editor's documentation to learn whether it can validate HTML documents. If so, use your editor to validate your document. If not, use http://validator.w3.org to validate your file. If necessary, fix any errors in your document until it validates.

FIGURE B-31

FIGURE B-32

Visual Workshop

In your editor, open the HTM_B-7.html file from the VW folder where you store your Data Files for this unit, then save it as **events.html**. In the head section, insert a comment containing a description of the page content, the filename **events.html**, your first and last name, today's date, and the text **HTML5 and CSS3 Illustrated Unit B, Visual Workshop**. Structure the web page to specify the following: the document contents are in English; the character encoding is utf-8; the main heading is the page header; the second-level heading and the four events are the main page content; and the contact information is the page footer. Ensure that Internet Explorer 8 correctly parses the page. Replace the word "and" in the browser tab and the main page heading with a character reference for the ampersand (&) symbol. Replace each hyphen in the contact information with a bullet character (•). The structured page should match **FIGURE B-33**. Also add code to ensure that smartphone browsers display the page as shown in **FIGURE B-34**. Validate your document, then if necessary, fix any errors until it validates successfully.

FIGURE B-33

FIGURE B-34

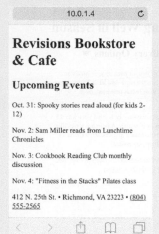

Getting Started with CSS

CASE As you continue your work on the Lakeland Reeds Bed & Breakfast website, your supervisor, Faduma Egal, has asked you to change the appearance of some web page content. In this unit, you learn about Cascading Style Sheets (CSS) and you use CSS code to style your web documents.

Unit Objectives

After completing this unit, you will be able to:

- Assess style rules
- Create an embedded style sheet
- Implement an ID selector
- Implement a class selector
- Use multiple selectors
- Create an external style sheet
- Link to an external style sheet
- Add a comment to a style sheet
- Debug and validate CSS code

Files You Will Need

L	3 files	IC3	3 files
SR	3 files	IC4	3 files
IC1	2 files	VW	2 files
IC2	3 files		

For specific filenames, see Filenames_C.pdf in the Unit C Data Files folder.

Assess Style Rules

Learning
Outcomes
• Describe the parts
of a style rule
• Identify proper
syntax for a style
rule

Cascading Style Sheets (CSS) is a language used to specify how web page elements should be rendered in a browser. CSS is a separate language from HTML but the two languages are complementary—HTML code specifies the content of each web page element, and CSS code indicates how that content should be displayed. Because CSS is a separate language, it uses its own syntax. You create CSS code for an HTML document by writing **style rules**, which are lines or blocks of CSS code that specify the presentation of web page elements. The most recent version of CSS is known as **CSS3**. While CSS3 supports some features not available in previous versions, it uses the same syntax as previous versions. **CASE** ▶ *As you prepare to integrate CSS into the Lakeland Reeds website, you review style rule structure and syntax.*

DETAILS

CSS code builds on a few basic concepts:

- **Properties**

  A CSS **property** is an aspect of the appearance of a web page element that can be modified. For instance, you can change the background color or text alignment of an element. CSS property names do not include spaces but they may include hyphens to make them more readable. For instance, to change text alignment, you use the text-align property. **TABLE C-1** lists CSS properties that you will use in this unit.

QUICK TIP
Appendix B provides a reference for many commonly used CSS properties and their values.

- **Declarations**

  The basic building block of CSS code is the **declaration**, which is a combination of a property name and a value. When you specify a property name in CSS code, it is followed by a colon, the value, and a semicolon. Allowable values are specific to each property and vary widely, including keywords such as center and numerical values expressed in percentages or units of measurement. In addition, some properties take multiple values, separated by spaces. The following declaration specifies the text-align property and sets its value to center:

  ```
  text-align: center;
  ```

  The space after the colon is not required. However, because this space does not change the meaning of the code, it's common practice to include it to make the code easier to read at a glance.

- **Selectors**

  To associate declarations with a web page element, you use **selectors**, which identify the HTML element or elements to which the declarations apply. CSS supports several different types of selectors. The most general selectors are the names of HTML elements, such as h1 or p, which are known as **type selectors**. Type selectors apply associated declarations to every instance of the specified element in a web document. They also apply the declarations to all descendant elements of selected elements, a process known as **inheritance**. To apply declarations to all p elements in a document and their descendant elements, you would use the following selector:

  ```
  p
  ```

  You can specify multiple type selectors for a single set of declarations by separating the type selectors with commas. For instance, the following type selector applies declarations to all p elements and their descendants in a document, as well as to all h1 elements and their descendants in that document:

  ```
  p, h1
  ```

QUICK TIP
To learn more about a specific CSS property, you can look it up in an online CSS reference such as the one at developer.mozilla.org/en-US/docs/Web/CSS/Reference.

- **Style rules**

  You create a style rule by combining a selector and one or more declarations. The declarations are enclosed within curly braces ({ }). For readability purposes, each declaration is usually entered on its own line. In addition, the opening curly brace is placed after the selector, and the closing curly brace is placed on its own line after the final declaration. For instance, the style rule shown in **FIGURE C-1** centers text within all p elements and their descendants and also applies a background color of ivory to these elements and their descendants. You may also see style rules written on a single line, as shown in **FIGURE C-2**.

FIGURE C-1: A style rule

Selector

Opening curly brace placed after the selector

Style rule composed of a selector and declarations

```
p {
    text-align: center;
    background-color: ivory;
}
```

Declarations

Closing curly brace on its own line after final declaration

© 2016 Cengage Learning

FIGURE C-2: A style rule entered on a single line

Selectors

Semicolon marks end of each declaration

```
p, h1 {text-align:center; width:960px;}
```

Opening curly brace placed after the selectors

Declarations

Closing curly brace after final declaration

© 2016 Cengage Learning

TABLE C-1: CSS properties and values

property	affects	allowable values	example
background-color	an element's fill color, behind any content such as text	name from a list of supported colors, or code using one of several systems for specifying color using numeric values	background-color: ivory;
color	an element's foreground color; for elements containing text, this is the text color	name from a list of supported colors, or code using one of several systems for specifying color using numeric values	color: wheat;
text-align	the horizontal alignment of text within the element that contains it	left, right, center, justify, inherit (same value as enclosing element)	text-align: center;

© 2016 Cengage Learning

Spacing your CSS code

Web page rendering engines recognize declarations after a selector as starting after an opening curly brace ({) and ending with the closing curly brace (}). As long as a semicolon follows each value, any number of spaces, tabs, and new lines can occur within a set of declarations. As a result, the appearance of CSS code can vary widely. Most developers prefer to give each declaration its own line, often indented beneath its selector, as shown in **FIGURE C-1**, to make the code easier to read. Others prefer to keep all declarations on the same line as the selector, as shown in **FIGURE C-2**, to keep their code compact and make it obvious which pairs are associated with which selector. While the code shown in this book uses the format shown in **FIGURE C-1**, don't be surprised to see the single-line format shown in **FIGURE C-2**—as well as other variations—in other examples of CSS that you may encounter. While you may be required to follow a given code format by an employer or a client, such formatting is most often a matter of personal taste.

Create an Embedded Style Sheet

Learning Outcomes
• Add an embedded style sheet to an HTML document
• Create a style rule using a type selector

To affect the presentation of elements in a single web page, you can create an **embedded style sheet**, which consists of CSS style rules entered in the `head` element of an HTML document. When you add the CSS style rules to the `head` element, you indicate to user agents that your style rules are written in CSS by nesting them within an HTML `style` element. **CASE** > *You specify the background color for the body element and center the `h1` text of the main web page for Lakeland Reeds B&B by adding an embedded style sheet to the document.*

1. **Open your editor, open the HTM_C-1.html file from the Lessons folder where you store your Data Files for Unit C, then save the file as index.html to the same location**

2. **In the comment in the head section, enter your name and today's date where indicated, then save the file**

3. **Open index.html in your browser**

   The web page contains a level 1 heading and three paragraphs, as shown in **FIGURE C-3**.

4. **Return to your editor, click at the end of the line containing the `script` element, then press [Enter]**

5. **Press [Spacebar] six times or as needed to create the indent, type `<style>`, press [Enter] twice, press [Spacebar] six times or as needed to create the indent, then type `</style>`**

6. **Click the blank line between the opening and closing style tags, press [Spacebar] nine times or as needed to create the indent, type `body {`, press [Enter] twice, press [Spacebar] nine times or as needed to create the indent, then type `}`**

   You enter CSS code between the opening and closing tags for the `style` element. Styles specified for the `body` element are inherited by all elements in the web document.

7. **Click the blank line between the opening and closing curly braces, press [Spacebar] twelve times or as needed to create the indent, type `background-color: ivory;`, press [Enter], press [Spacebar] twelve times or as needed to create the indent, then type `text-align: left;`**

   The `background-color` property sets the color behind page content, and the `text-align` property determines the horizontal alignment of text. This style rule sets the background color of the entire page (the `body` element) to `ivory`, and left-aligns all text within the `body` element. Compare your document to **FIGURE C-4**.

8. **Save your document, return to your default browser, then click the Refresh or Reload button to view changes to your web document**

   As **FIGURE C-5** shows, the background of the entire document is now ivory. Because major browsers left-align text by default, the text alignment is unchanged from **FIGURE C-3**.

FIGURE C-3: Default appearance of index.html in a browser

h1 element ⟶ **Lakeland Reeds Bed & Breakfast**

A country getaway perfect for fishing, boating, biking, or just watching the day go by.

p elements ⟶ Reserve your perfect weekend today.

45 Marsh Grass Ln. :: Marble, MN 55764 :: (218) 555-5253

FIGURE C-4: Embedded style sheet added to HTML document

```
14    <meta name="      body selector applies declarations  vice-width">
15    <script src       to the body element             ></script>
16    <style>                                                          background-color
17      body {                                                         property sets the color
18        background-color: ivory;                                     behind content
19        text-align: left;
20      }                              text-align property
21    </style>                         sets the horizontal
22  </head>                            alignment of text
23  <body>
        r>
Style rules contained    >Lakeland Reeds Bed &amp; Breakfast</h1>
within a style           er>
element for an           ountry getaway perfect for fishing, boating, biking, or just watching the day
embedded style sheet
```

FIGURE C-5: Web page styled by embedded style sheet

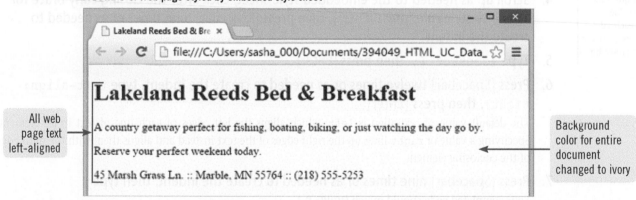

All web page text left-aligned ⟶ **Lakeland Reeds Bed & Breakfast**

A country getaway perfect for fishing, boating, biking, or just watching the day go by.

Reserve your perfect weekend today.

45 Marsh Grass Ln. :: Marble, MN 55764 :: (218) 555-5253

Background color for entire document changed to ivory

HTML5 & CSS3

Understanding the `type` attribute of the `style` element

XHTML and older versions of HTML require an attribute in the opening `<style>` tag to specify the language of the code the element contains. When style sheets were first developed, this attribute was incorporated into web standards to allow for multiple style languages to be used with web pages. To specify that a style sheet contained CSS code, you would use the value `text/css` for the `type` attribute, as in the following opening tag:

`<style type="text/css">`

CSS has emerged as the standard for providing style information for web documents. For this reason, when parsing an HTML5 document, modern browsers assume that the contents of a `style` element are written in CSS. Therefore, you do not need to specify the `type` attribute when using the HTML5 DOCTYPE (`<DOCTYPE html>`).

Implement an ID Selector

Learning Outcomes
- Add an id attribute to an HTML element
- Create a style rule using an ID selector

Sometimes instead of affecting the presentation of all the elements of a certain type, you want to make changes that affect only a single element. For instance, maybe a certain p element requires a different alignment from all the other p elements in a document. HTML allows you to add the id attribute to the opening tag for an element to give the element a unique identifier. You can then create a special type of selector known as an **ID selector** to create CSS code that applies to that element alone. An ID selector is simply a pound sign (#) followed by the value of the id attribute for the element, as shown in **FIGURE C-6**. The declarations in a style rule that uses an ID selector apply only to the element with the specified id attribute value. Although all descendant elements of a selected element inherit the same declarations, creating a style rule for a descendant element with different values for the same properties overrides the inherited values. For instance, setting a value for the text-align property using the p selector would override a text-align value set using the body selector. Likewise, setting this property using an id selector on a p element would override the inherited value. **CASE** *The main Lakeland Reeds web page contains several paragraph elements. The visual style for the page calls for the paragraph element containing the contact information to be right-aligned. You use an id attribute and ID selector to change the alignment of the contact information.*

STEPS

1. **Return to your editor, scroll down as needed to the** p **element within the** footer **element**

2. **In the opening** <p> **tag, position the insertion point between the** p **and the** > **, then press [Spacebar]**

QUICK TIP

Only one element in a document can have any given id attribute value because each id attribute value in a document must be unique.

3. **Type** id="contact"
   The paragraph containing the contact information is assigned the unique id value contact.

4. **Scroll up as needed to the embedded style sheet, click after the closing curly brace for the** body **style rule, press [Enter], then press [Spacebar] nine times or as needed to create the indent**

5. **Type** #contact { **, then press [Enter]**

6. **Press [Spacebar] twelve times or as needed to create the indent, type** text-align: right; **, then press [Enter]**
   The default value of text-align is left, which aligns the left edges of each line of text in an element. Specifying a value of right lines up the right edges of the text instead and aligns them with the right edge of the enclosing element.

7. **Press [Spacebar] nine times or as needed to create the indent, then type** }
   Your completed code should match **FIGURE C-7**.

8. **Save your document, return to your default browser, then click the** Refresh **or** Reload **button to view changes to your web document**
   As **FIGURE C-8** shows, the contact information at the bottom of the page is right-aligned.

FIGURE C-6: A style rule using an ID selector

The pound sign indicates this is an ID selector →

```
#contact {
    text-align: right;
}
```

This ID selector applies to the element with the `id` attribute value `contact`

FIGURE C-7: `id` attribute and style rule with ID selector added

```
16    <style>
17        body {
18            background-color: ivory;
19            text-align: left;
20        }
21        #contact {
22            text-align: right;
23        }
24    </style>
25    </head>
26    <body>
27        <header>
28            <h1>Lakeland Reeds Bed &amp; Breakfast</h1>
29        </header>
30        <p>A country getaway perfect for fishing, boating, biking, or just watching the day
31        go by.</p>
32        <p>Reserve your perfect weekend today.</p>
33        <footer>
34            <p id="contact">45 Marsh Grass Ln. :: Marble, MN 55764 :: (218) 555-5253</p>
35        </footer>
36    </body>
37    </html>
```

New style rule using an ID selector

id attribute with value of `contact` added to opening `<p>` tag

FIGURE C-8: `p` element right-aligned using ID selector

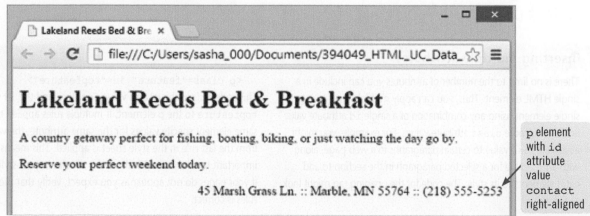

p element with `id` attribute value `contact` right-aligned

Implement a Class Selector

Learning
Outcomes
• Add a class
  attribute to an
  HTML element
• Create a style rule
  using a class
  selector

Sometimes you want to apply a style rule to multiple elements in a web document without adding an additional layer of HTML code. While the `id` attribute limits a given value to a single instance in a web page, you can create a selector that applies to any number of elements on a page using the HTML `class` attribute, which does not have this limit. A **class selector** creates a style rule based on values assigned to elements using the HTML `class` attribute. This allows you to apply a style rule to an unlimited number of separate elements. As **FIGURE C-9** shows, a class selector consists of a period followed by a class attribute value. **CASE** ▸ *The next step in implementing the visual design for the Lakeland Reeds web page is to change the text color of the two paragraphs that appear before the contact information. You add a `class` attribute to the two elements containing these paragraphs and then add a style rule using a class selector and the `color` property to modify their presentation.*

STEPS

QUICK TIP
Developers generally
use class names that
describe the goal of
the formatting, such
as accent, rather
than describing the
content, like blue.

1. **Return to your text editor, scroll down if necessary to the opening tag for the first p element, position the insertion point between the p and the >, press [Spacebar], then type** `class="accent"`

2. **In the opening tag for the second p element, position the insertion point between the p and the >, press [Spacebar], then type** `class="accent"`

   The first two p elements are both assigned the class value accent.

3. **Scroll up as needed to view the embedded style sheet, click after the closing curly brace for the #contact style rule, press [Enter], then press [Spacebar] nine times or as needed to create the indent**

4. **Type** `.accent {`**, then press [Enter]**

5. **Press [Spacebar] twelve times or as needed to create the indent, type** `color: darkcyan;`**, then press [Enter]**

   The `color` property sets the color of text in an element that contains text.

6. **Press [Spacebar] nine times or as needed to create the indent, then type** `}`

   Compare your completed code to **FIGURE C-10**.

7. **Save your document, return to your default browser, then click the Refresh or Reload button to view changes to your web document**

   As **FIGURE C-11** shows, the text of the first two p elements in the document is bluish rather than black.

Inserting multiple attributes

There is no limit to the number of attributes you can include in a single HTML element. Thus, you can apply multiple style rules to a single element using any combination of a single `id` attribute value and one or more `class` attribute values. For example, you might assign a `class` value to certain paragraphs in a web page, along with an `id` value for a selected paragraph in the section to add extra elements to its style. The code for the opening tag might look as follows:

```
<p class="feature" id="topfeature">
```
This code assigns the `class` value `feature` and the `id` value `topfeature` to the p element. If multiple rules applied to the same element specify values for the same attribute, the value from the last rule in the style sheet is applied. This means it's important to take care with the order of rules in your style sheets. If your pages do not appear as you expect, verify that the order of rules is correct.

FIGURE C-9: A style rule using a class selector

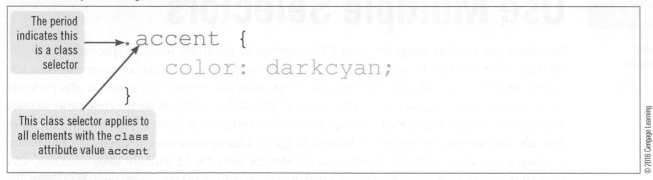

The period indicates this is a class selector

```
.accent {
    color: darkcyan;
}
```

This class selector applies to all elements with the `class` attribute value `accent`

FIGURE C-10: `class` attributes and style rule with class selector added

```
16      <style>
17          body {
18              background-color: ivory;
19              text-align: left;
20          }
21          #contact {
22              text-align: right;
23          }
24          .accent {
25              color: darkcyan;
26          }
27      </style>
28  </head>
29  <body>
30      <header>
31          <h1>Lakeland Reeds Bed &amp; Breakfast</h1>
32      </header>
33      <p class="accent">A country getaway perfect for fishing, boating, biking, or just
34      watching the day go by.</p>
35      <p class="accent">Reserve your perfect weekend today.</p>
36      <footer>
37          <p id="contact">45 Marsh Grass Ln. :: Marble, MN 55764 :: (218) 555-5253</p>
```

New style rule using a class selector

`class` attribute with value of `accent` added to opening `<p>` tags for two elements

FIGURE C-11: Text color of `p` elements changed using a class selector

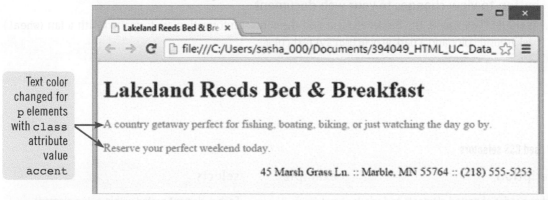

Text color changed for `p` elements with `class` attribute value `accent`

Lakeland Reeds Bed & Breakfast

A country getaway perfect for fishing, boating, biking, or just watching the day go by.

Reserve your perfect weekend today.

45 Marsh Grass Ln. :: Marble, MN 55764 :: (218) 555-5253

Deciding whether to use an ID or class selector

The fact that only one element in a web document can have a given `id` attribute value can cause problems, especially in large documents. If you inadvertently add the same `id` attribute value to multiple elements on a page, the results in the browser may not be what you expected. In addition, changes to your HTML code may expose problems that weren't previously apparent and that are caused by duplicate `id` values. For this reason, many designers avoid using ID selectors at all, preferring to do all element-specific styling with the `class` attribute. The same `class` attribute value can be assigned to one element or to multiple elements, which provides designers with more flexibility. In addition, the `class` attribute accepts multiple values, separated by spaces, so there's no danger of running out of class values for an element.

Use Multiple Selectors

Learning Outcomes
• Create a style rule using multiple selectors

Sometimes you want to assign the same CSS properties to the HTML elements specified by multiple selectors. While you could create a style rule and duplicate it for each selector, an easier way is to add multiple selectors to a single rule. To do this, you simply enter the selectors with a comma after each one except the last. Adding a space after each comma is optional, but it helps make the code easier to read. After the final selector, you type an opening curly brace and enter declarations as you would for any other style rule. For example, the style rule in **FIGURE C-12** applies a background color of wheat and a text color of dimgray to all h1 elements as well as to the element with the id attribute value contact. CSS supports many other selectors, and **TABLE C-2** describes some of the most commonly used. **CASE** ▶ *The page design calls for the background of the h1 element and the element with the ID contact to be set to the color wheat, and the text color of both to be dimgray. You use a single style rule to apply these declarations to both elements.*

STEPS

1. **Return to your text editor, click after the closing curly brace for the body style rule, then press [Enter]**

2. **Press [Spacebar] nine times or as needed to create the indent, type h1, #contact {, then press [Enter]**

QUICK TIP
For more information about color names that you can use in HTML documents, see www.w3.org/TR/css3-color/#svg-color.

3. **Press [Spacebar] twelve times or as needed to create the indent, type background-color: wheat;, then press [Enter]**

4. **Press [Spacebar] twelve times or as needed to create the indent, type color: dimgray;, then press [Enter]**

5. **Press [Spacebar] nine times or as needed to create the indent, then type }**
   Compare your completed code to **FIGURE C-13**.

6. **Save your document, return to your default browser, then click the Refresh or Reload button to view changes to your web document**
   As **FIGURE C-14** shows, the header element and the contact information are formatted with a tan (wheat) background color and a dark gray (dimgray) text color.

TABLE C-2: Commonly used CSS selectors

selector	description	example	selects
Descendant	Specifies a series of nested elements and selects the final, most deeply nested element	article div p	Each p element nested within a div element that is itself nested within an article element
Direct child	Selects an element that is a child (but not grandchild, etc.) of another specified element	div > p	Each p element whose parent element is a div element
Direct next sibling	Selects an element that is a sibling of another specified element and *directly* follows that element	h1 + p	Each p element that is a sibling of an h1 element and *directly* follows that h1 element
Next sibling	Selects an element that is a sibling of another specified element and follows that element (potentially with other siblings between them)	h1 ~ p	Each p element that is a sibling of an h1 element and follows that h1 element

© 2016 Cengage Learning

FIGURE C-12: A style rule that uses multiple selectors

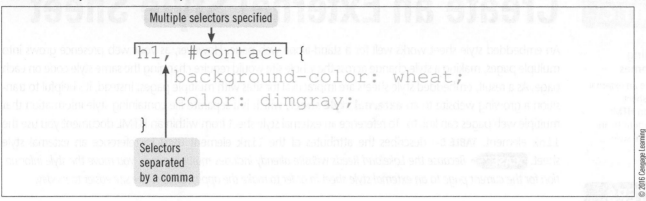

Multiple selectors specified

```
h1, #contact {
    background-color: wheat;
    color: dimgray;
}
```

Selectors separated by a comma

© 2016 Cengage Learning

FIGURE C-13: Style rule with multiple selectors added

```
16      <style>
17          body {
18              background-color: ivory;
19              text-align: left;
20          }
21          #contact {
22              text-align: right;
23          }
24          .accent {
25              color: darkcyan;
26          }
27          h1, #contact {
28              background-color: wheat;
29              color: dimgray;
30          }
31      </style>
```

New style rule using multiple selectors

FIGURE C-14: Text and background colors of two elements changed using multiple selectors

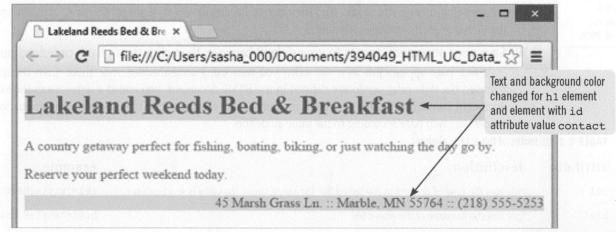

Lakeland Reeds Bed & Bre ✕

file:///C:/Users/sasha_000/Documents/394049_HTML_UC_Data_

Lakeland Reeds Bed & Breakfast

A country getaway perfect for fishing, boating, biking, or just watching the day go by.

Reserve your perfect weekend today.

45 Marsh Grass Ln. :: Marble, MN 55764 :: (218) 555-5253

Text and background color changed for h1 element and element with id attribute value contact

Create an External Style Sheet

Learning Outcomes
• Create an external style sheet
• Link an HTML document to an external style sheet

An embedded style sheet works well for a stand-alone web page. However, as your web presence grows into multiple pages, making a style change across the whole site would require changing the same style code on each page. As a result, embedded style sheets are impractical for sites with multiple pages. Instead, it's helpful to transition a growing website to an **external style sheet**, which is a separate file containing style information that multiple web pages can link to. To reference an external style sheet from within an HTML document you use the `link` element. **TABLE C-3** describes the attributes of the `link` element used to reference an external style sheet. **CASE** ▸ *Because the Lakeland Reeds website already includes multiple pages, you move the style information for the current page to an external style sheet in order to make the appearance of the site easier to modify.*

STEPS

1. **Return to your editor, save a copy of index.html with the name** index_embedded.html **to the same folder**

2. **Close** index_embedded.html, **then open** index.html **in your editor**

QUICK TIP
If you are using TextEdit on a Mac, click Format, then click Make Plain Text if it is not already selected.

3. **Scroll up as needed to view the embedded style sheet, select all the code between the opening and closing style tags, click** Edit **on the menu bar, then click** Cut
   The contents of the embedded style sheet are removed from the web document and placed on the clipboard.

4. **Save your changes to** index.html, **create a new file in your editor, click** Edit **on the menu bar, then click** Paste
   The embedded style sheet code is pasted into the new document, as shown in **FIGURE C-15**.

QUICK TIP
If you are using TextEdit on a Mac, click Use .css if a dialog box opens asking which file extension to use.

5. **Save the file as** styles.css **to the Lessons folder where you store your Data Files for Unit C, specifying an encoding of UTF-8 if you are using Notepad**
   Your external style sheet is saved with the filename styles.css.

6. **Close** styles.css, **then reopen** index.html **in your text editor if it is not still open**

7. **Select the lines containing the opening and closing** <style> **tags along with any blank lines between them, then press** [Delete]

8. **Click after the closing** </script> **tag, then press** [Enter] **to insert a blank line if there is not already one**

QUICK TIP
Because the contents of an external style sheet are written entirely in CSS, the file uses the extension .css instead of .html.

9. **Press** [Spacebar] **six times or as needed to create the indent, then type** <link rel="stylesheet" href="styles.css">
   FIGURE C-16 shows the web page code with the external style sheet reference inserted. The `link` element makes the contents of an external file available in the HTML document. The value for the `rel` attribute specifies that user agents should read the external document as a style sheet. The `href` attribute specifies the filename of the external style sheet.

10. **Save your document, return to your default browser, then click the** Refresh **or** Reload **button**
    Your web page appears just as it did when you were using an embedded style sheet. Even though you removed the style rules previously defined in the HTML document, you added a reference to the external document containing the rules. As a result, your browser still has access to the same style information and renders the web page according to the same guidelines.

TABLE C-3: Attributes of the `link` element

attribute	description	example
rel	Indicates the type of content in the linked file; for a style sheet, the value is `stylesheet`	`rel="stylesheet"`
href	Specifies the filename of the linked file	`href="styles.css"`

FIGURE C-15: External style sheet

```
1    body {
2        background-color: ivory;
3        text-align: left;
4    }
5    #contact {
6        text-align: right;
7    }
8    .accent {
9        color: darkcyan;
10   }
11   h1, #contact {
12       background-color: wheat;
13       color: dimgray;
14   }
```

Style rules moved from embedded style sheet

FIGURE C-16: Web page linked to external style sheet

```
1    <!DOCTYPE html>
2    <html lang="en">
3        <head>
4            <title>Lakeland Reeds Bed &amp; Breakfast</title>
5            <!--
6            Lakeland Reeds Bed and Breakfast main web page
7            Filename: index.html
8
9            Author:   your first and last name
10           Date:     today's date
11           HTML5 and CSS3 Illustrated Unit C, Lessons
12           -->
13           <meta charset="utf-8">
14           <meta name="viewport" content="width=device-width">
15           <script src="modernizr.custom.62074.js"></script>
16           <link rel="stylesheet" href="styles.css">
17       </head>
18       <body>
```

`link` element loads contents of external CSS document

Filename of external style sheet

Implementing inline styles

In addition to embedded and external style sheets, you can also incorporate CSS properties into an HTML document using inline styles. An **inline style** is a style rule inserted into the opening tag of an element using the `style` attribute. **FIGURE C-17** shows an example of an inline style. Inline styles do not offer many of the benefits provided by other methods of applying styles. For instance, changing a style applied inline requires locating the style within HTML code, rather than simply looking at an embedded or external style sheet. Because of this and other drawbacks, many web developers avoid creating inline styles.

FIGURE C-17: An inline style

```
<h1 style="text-align: center;">Lakeland Reeds Bed and Breakfast</h1>
```

© 2016 Cengage Learning

Link to an External Style Sheet

Once you create an external style sheet for a website, you can apply the style rules it contains to every page on the site simply by adding a `link` element referencing the style sheet file to each HTML document. If you later decide to make changes to the appearance of your website, any change you make to the external style sheet is reflected immediately on all the pages that link to it. **FIGURE C-18** illustrates the relationship between the HTML documents that make up a website and an external style sheet. **CASE** *The class and id attributes that correspond to the code you added to the main web page have been added to the Lakeland Reeds B&B About Us page. You add a link in the About Us document to the external style sheet file you created in order to apply the style rules from the external style sheet to the About Us page as well.*

STEPS

1. **Return to your text editor, open the file HTM C-2.html from the Lessons folder where you store your Data Files for Unit C, then save it as aboutus.html**

   The file contains multiple elements with the `class` attribute value of `accent` and an element with an `id` attribute value of `contact`.

2. **In the comment within the head section, enter your name and today's date where indicated, then save your changes**

3. **Open aboutus.html in your browser**

   All the page elements are left-aligned and all text is black on a white background, resembling the appearance of the main Lakeland Reeds page at the beginning of the unit.

4. **Return to your editor, click at the end of the line containing the `script` element, then press [Enter]**

5. **Press [Spacebar] six times or as needed to create the indent, then type `<link rel="stylesheet" href="styles.css">`**

   This is the same `link` element you inserted into index.html. **FIGURE C-19** shows the completed code.

6. **Save your document, return to your default browser, then click the Refresh or Reload button to view the changes to the About Us page**

   The browser now renders the web page with a layout similar to the main page of the website.

7. **Return to your editor, open styles.css, then in the `h1, #contact` style rule, change the value for the `background-color` property from `wheat` to `palegoldenrod`**

8. **Save your document, return to your default browser, then click the Refresh or Reload button to view the changes to the About Us page**

   As **FIGURE C-20** shows, the background of the main heading and the contact information is now a different shade.

9. **Reopen index.html in your default browser**

   As shown in **FIGURE C-20**, the changes in the main page match the changes in the About Us page because the presentation of both documents is based on the external style sheet in styles.css.

FIGURE C-18: Relationship between web pages and external style sheet

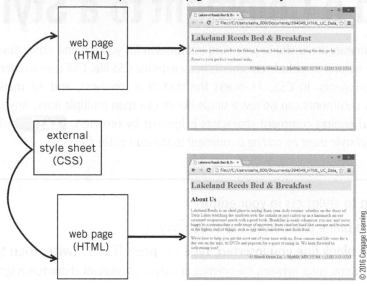

© 2016 Cengage Learning

FIGURE C-19: About Us page with link to external style sheet

```
15        <script src="modernizr.custom.62074.js"></script>
16        <link rel="stylesheet" href="styles.css">

          Reeds Bed &amp; Breakfast</h1>
21        </header>
22        <h2>About Us</h2>
23        <p class="accent">Lakeland Reeds is an ideal place to unplug from your daily
24        routine, whether on the shore of Twin Lakes watching the sundown over the cattails
25        or just curled up in a hammock on our screened wraparound porch with a good book.
26        Breakfast is ready whenever you are, and we're happy to accommodate a wide range of
27        appetites, from comfort food like sausage and biscuits to the lighter end of
28        things, such as egg white omelettes and fresh fruit.</p>
29        <p class="accent">We're here to help you get the most out of your time with us,
30        from canoes and life vests for a day out on the lake, to DVDs and popcorn for a
31        quiet evening in. We look forward to welcoming you!</p>
32        <footer>
33            <p id="contact">45 Marsh Grass Ln. :: Marble, MN 55764 :: (218) 555-5253</p>
34        </footer>
35        </body>
36   </html>
```

Every document linking to an external style sheet uses the same code for the `link` element

Document contains class and ID values corresponding to selectors in external style sheet

FIGURE C-20: Multiple pages styled with a single style sheet

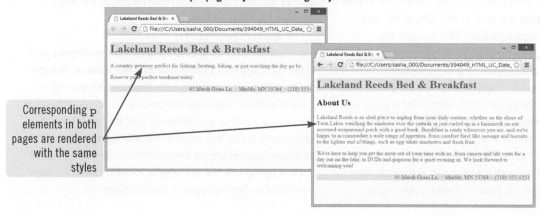

Corresponding p elements in both pages are rendered with the same styles

Add a Comment to a Style Sheet

Learning Outcomes
- Add CSS comment characters to a style sheet
- Add text to a CSS comment

Just as comments are useful in providing information for yourself and other developers in an HTML file, it can also be helpful to include comments in an external CSS file. CSS uses a different syntax than HTML for creating comments. In CSS, /* marks the start of a comment, and */ marks the end. Just like with HTML, CSS comments can be just a single like or can span multiple lines. Anything entered between the starting and ending comment characters is ignored by browsers. **CASE** ▸ *You add documentation to your external style sheet by adding a comment to the start of the file.*

STEPS

1. **Return to styles.css in your editor**

2. **Insert a blank line before the code** body {

QUICK TIP

Just as with HTML comments, you can enter the opening and closing characters for a CSS comment on the same line, with content between them.

3. **On the blank line you inserted, type** /*, **press [Enter] twice, then type** */

   Anything you enter between the opening and closing comment characters is ignored by browsers.

4. **Between the opening and closing comment characters, enter the following text, substituting your first and last name and today's date where indicated:**

   ```
   Lakeland Reeds Bed and Breakfast style sheet

   Filename: styles.css


   Author:    your first and last name

   Date:      today's date

   HTML5 and CSS3 Illustrated Unit C, Lessons
   ```
   FIGURE C-21 shows the completed style sheet, including the comment.

5. **Save your document, return to aboutus.html in your default browser, then click the Refresh or Reload button**

   As **FIGURE C-22** shows, the appearance of the page is unchanged, and the comment text you entered is not displayed in the browser window.

6. **Return to index.html in your browser, then click the Refresh or Reload button**

   Just like the About Us page, the appearance of the main web page is unaffected by the CSS comment.

Organizing CSS code

As a style sheet grows, it's important to keep it organized so you can quickly find style rules you want to edit. One of the most common methods of organization in CSS is to mirror the structure of the HTML document(s) to which the style sheet is applied. For instance, a style rule for the body element, which affects the entire document, would go at the start of a style sheet, followed by style rules for sections of the document in order, with style rules for specific elements occurring after the style rule for the section in which they're contained. Some developers also include a CSS comment at the start of each section in the style sheet to make it easier to figure out what part of the style sheet you're in while reading it. For instance, before styles for the footer element and elements nested within it, you might include a comment such as

```
/* footer section */
```
Sometimes it makes sense to style content in two different parts of the document with a single style rule—for instance, to apply similar styles to all p elements, or to both the header and footer sections. It generally makes sense to place a global style rule, such as a rule for all p elements, near the top of the style sheet. For style rules that apply to multiple separate parts of the document, you can use the same placement, or you may decide to break up the style rule so the styles for each part of the page are located in their own parts of the style sheet.

FIGURE C-21: Comment added to external style sheet

```
1    /*
2        Lakeland Reeds Bed and Breakfast style sheet         CSS start comment
3        Filename: styles.css                                 characters
4
5        Author:    your first and last name
6        Date:      today's date
7        HTML5 and CSS3 Illustrated Unit C, Lessons
8    */                                                       CSS end comment
9                                                             characters
10   body {
11       background-color: ivory;
12       text-align: left;
13   }
```

FIGURE C-22: Web page appearance unchanged by addition of CSS comment

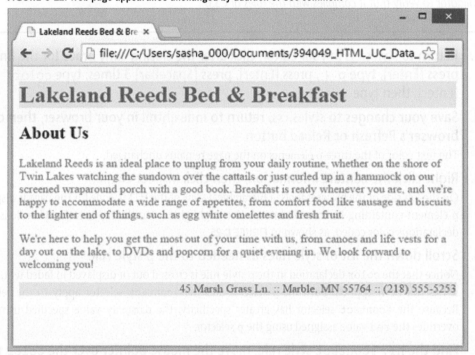

Viewing CSS comments in code editors

As with other parts of HTML and CSS code, many code editors automatically generate the closing comment characters for a CSS comment after you enter the opening characters, and they may automatically indent any lines between the opening and closing characters. In addition, some editors apply other informal standards to make CSS comments easier to view and read. One of these standards is to include an asterisk (*) at the start of every line between the opening and closing characters, aligned with the asterisk that starts the comment, as shown in **FIGURE C-23**. This creates the appearance of a vertical line in the code that indicates the size of the comment section at a glance. In addition, some code editors indent the closing comment characters

a single space, which aligns the * in the closing characters with the preceding line of asterisks. Because no characters within a CSS comment are parsed by browsers—including spaces and asterisks—these formatting choices have no effect on the website.

FIGURE C-23: CSS comment lines preceded by asterisks

```
1    /*
2     * Lakeland Reeds Bed and Breakfast style sheet
3     * Filename: styles.css
4     *
5     * Author:    Faduma Egal
6     * Date:      6/23/2018
7     * HTML5 and CSS3 Illustrated Unit C, Lessons
8     */
```

Debug and Validate CSS Code

Learning Outcomes
- Use browser developer tools to view CSS declarations and disable a CSS declaration
- Validate a CSS document

When multiple style rules select the same element and specify different values for the same property, CSS standards include rules for determining which declaration applies to the element. These rules calculate a selector's **specificity**, which is its priority relative to other selectors. The declaration whose selector has the highest specificity is applied to an element. **FIGURE C-24** illustrates the specificity rankings of basic selectors. If two selectors have the same specificity, the one that appears last in the style sheet is applied. If your CSS code does not affect the appearance of elements in browsers as you expect, you can use utilities known as **developer tools** that are built into all modern browsers to debug your code. These tools let you inspect the CSS properties and values for each element in a document and view which declarations are applied to an element. You can also validate your CSS code. **CASE** ➤ *You use browser tools to examine the style rules applied to the elements on the main Lakeland Reeds web page, and you upload your external style sheet to a CSS validator to verify that it complies with the rules of CSS.*

STEPS

1. **Return to** styles.css **in your editor, click after the closing curly brace for the final style rule, press [Enter], type** p { **, press [Enter], press [Spacebar] 3 times, type** color: red; **, press [Enter], then type** }

2. **Save your changes to** styles.css**, return to** index.html **in your browser, then click your browser's Refresh or Reload button**

   The text color of the three p elements on the page remains unchanged.

   QUICK TIP
   On a Mac, hold [command] and click the contact information, then click Inspect element.

3. **Right-click the contact information, then click Inspect element**

   On the left side of the browser tools, a hierarchical view of the HTML code for the page is displayed with the p element containing the contact information highlighted. On the right, each style rule is listed, with its declarations color coded, as shown in **FIGURE C-25**.

4. **Scroll down the list of style rules as needed to the** p **style rule**

   Notice that the color declaration in the p style rule is crossed out or displayed in faded text, indicating that it has not been applied. Both the p selector and the #contact selector apply to the selected element. Because the #contact selector has greater specificity, the dimgray value specified using that selector overrides the red value assigned using the p selector.

   QUICK TIP
   Tools in some browsers display a numerical code rather than a color name.

   QUICK TIP
   Edits to declarations in browser tools do not change your saved style sheet. To make the changes permanent, you must edit the style sheet in your editor and save the changes.

5. **Find the** h1, #contact **style rule, move the mouse pointer over the** color **property name until a check box is displayed to its left, then click the** check box **to uncheck it**

   Browser tools enable you to toggle or edit property values to see the effect in the browser. When you remove the color declaration associated with the #contact selector, the color declaration for the p selector is applied to the selected element because it has the highest specificity, and the contact information turns red. Note that the other p elements do not turn red because they are styled by the .accent style rule, which has higher specificity than the p style rule.

6. **Click the Refresh or Reload button, then scroll down to the** body **style rule**

   The browser reloads the saved style sheet, returning the contact information to its original gray color.

   QUICK TIP
   If the validator finds errors in your style sheet, use the validation result to edit your style sheet, save your changes, then repeat Steps 7–9 until no errors are found.

7. **In your browser, click the Close Developer Tools button** ☒ **in the top-right corner of the developer tools, click the Address Bar, type** jigsaw.w3.org/css-validator**, then press [Enter]**

   The web page for the CSS validation service provided by the W3C opens, as shown in **FIGURE C-26**.

8. **Click the By file upload tab, click Browse or Choose File, navigate to the Lessons folder where you store your Data Files for this unit, double-click** styles.css**, then click Check**

   The browser uploads your style sheet to the w3.org website and the result page opens.

9. **Scroll down to read the validation results, including any notes or warnings**

FIGURE C-24: Specificity rankings of basic CSS selectors

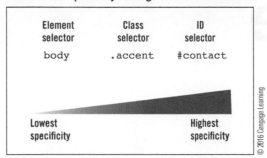

© 2016 Cengage Learning

FIGURE C-25: Developer tools in Chrome

FIGURE C-26: W3C CSS Validation Service page

Choosing between different possible selectors

Sometimes when creating a style rule, you'll find that you have a choice between two or more different selectors that could perform the same task. For instance, if you want to style all the elements within the footer element, you could use the footer type selector, or you could add a class attribute to each nested element and use a class selector for your style rule instead. In general, web developers aim to use the simplest selectors possible. In addition, using selectors, such as type selectors, that don't require additional HTML coding is generally preferred over using ID or class selectors when practical. Finally, it's important to consider the roles of inheritance and specificity when writing a style rule; in some cases, two selectors may appear as if they'll perform the same task, but due to interactions with other style rules, only one of the selectors is suited to the job. Writing CSS and checking the results of your style rules in browsers is one of the best ways to develop a feel for which selector is the best candidate in a given situation.

Practice

Concepts Review

Refer to FIGURE C-27.

FIGURE C-27

```
 1    /*
 2        Lakeland Reeds Bed and Breakfast style sheet
 3        Filename: styles.css
 4
 5        Author:    your first and last name
 6        Date:      today's date
 7        HTML5 and CSS3 Illustrated Unit C, Lessons
 8    */
 9
10    body {
11        background-color: ivory;
12        text-align: left;
13    }
14    #contact {
15        text-align: right;
16    }
17    .accent {
18        color: darkcyan;
19    }
20    h1, #contact {
21        background-color: palegoldenrod;
22        color: dimgray;
23    }
```

a →
b →
c →
d →
e →
f ↑
g ↑

1. Which style rule uses multiple selectors?
2. Which style rule uses an HTML id attribute value as the selector?
3. Which style rule uses an HTML class attribute value as the selector?
4. Which style rule uses the name of an HTML element as the selector?
5. Which item is a CSS property name?
6. Which item is ignored by a user agent?
7. Which item is the value assigned to a CSS property?

Match each term with the statement that best describes it.

8. **type selector**
9. **ID selector**
10. **class selector**
11. **style rule**
12. **declaration**
13. **embedded style sheet**
14. **external style sheet**

a. a line or block of CSS code that specifies the presentation of web page elements
b. a selector that applies the specified declarations only to the element with the specified ID
c. the most general kind of selector, which is the name of an HTML element
d. a selector that creates a style rule based on values assigned to elements using the HTML class attribute
e. CSS code that specifies a CSS property to apply to the selector(s) and the value to assign to the property
f. a separate file containing style information that multiple web pages can link to
g. CSS code entered in the head section of an HTML document

Select the best answer from the list of choices.

15. **Which part of a style rule identifies the HTML element or elements to which the style rule applies?**
    - **a.** property
    - **b.** selector
    - **c.** value
    - **d.** the code between the opening and closing curly braces

16. **A style rule ends with which of the following?**
    - **a.** */
    - **b.** }
    - **c.** ;
    - **d.** </style>

17. **A CSS comment ends with which of the following?**
    - **a.** */
    - **b.** :
    - **c.** ;
    - **d.** </style>

18. **A declaration ends with which of the following?**
    - **a.** :
    - **b.** }
    - **c.** ;
    - **d.** </style>

19. **An embedded style sheet ends with which of the following?**
    - **a.** */
    - **b.** :
    - **c.** ;
    - **d.** </style>

20. **Which is the most straightforward solution for affecting the presentation of a single web page?**
    - **a.** external style sheet
    - **b.** embedded style sheet
    - **c.** inline styles
    - **d.** multiple selectors

21. **Which of the following enables you to modify the presentation of multiple web pages with a single change?**
    - **a.** external style sheet
    - **b.** embedded style sheet
    - **c.** inline styles
    - **d.** multiple selectors

22. **Which of the following is a class selector?**
    - **a.** text-align: left
    - **b.** #logo
    - **c.** .pullquote
    - **d.** footer

Skills Review

1. **Create an embedded style sheet.**
   a. Open the file HTM_C-3.html in your editor from the SR folder where you store your Data Files for this unit, enter your name and today's date in the comment section where indicated, then save the file as **index.html** to the same SR folder.
   b. Preview index.html in your browser.
   c. Return to index.html in your editor, then within the head section and below the script element, add the opening and closing tags for a style element.
   d. Within the style element, add a style rule that uses a type selector to select the article element.
   e. Within the style rule you created, add a declaration that aligns text in the center.
   f. Save your document, refresh or reload it in your browser, then verify that the paragraphs beginning with "Eat in..." and "Voted..." are center-aligned.

2. **Implement an ID selector.**
   a. Return to index.html in your editor, then in the first p element, which contains the text "Authentic Chicago-style pies," add an id attribute with the value tagline.
   b. In the embedded style sheet in the head element, add a style rule that uses an ID selector to select the element with the id attribute value tagline.
   c. Within the style rule you created, add a declaration that aligns text on the right.
   d. Save your document, refresh or reload it in your browser, then verify that the paragraph below the heading is right-aligned.

Skills Review (continued)

3. Implement a class selector.

   a. Return to index.html in your editor, then in each of the three p elements within the footer element, add a class attribute with the value contact.

   b. In the embedded style sheet in the head element, add a style rule that uses a class selector to select the elements with the class attribute value contact.

   c. Within the style rule you created, add a declaration that aligns text on the right.

   d. Save your document, refresh or reload it in your browser, then verify that the contact information is right-aligned.

4. Use multiple selectors.

   a. Return to index.html in your editor, then, in the embedded style sheet in the head element, add a style rule that uses type selectors to select both the header and footer elements.

   b. Within the style rule you created, add a declaration that sets the background color to the value black, and a second declaration that sets the text color to the value red. (*Hint*: Use the color property to set the text color.)

   c. Save your document, refresh or reload it in your browser, then verify that the header and the footer contents are displayed in red on a black background. Your document should match **FIGURE C-28**.

5. Create an external style sheet.

   a. Return to your editor, save index.html as **index_embedded.html** to the SR folder where you store your Data Files for this unit, then close the file.

   b. Open index.html in your editor, then in the embedded style sheet, cut all the code between the opening and closing `<style>` tags to the clipboard.

   c. Create a new file, paste the contents of the clipboard, then save the new file as **styles.css** to the SR folder where you store your Data Files for this unit.

   d. Return to index.html in your editor, then delete the lines containing the opening and closing `<style>` tags along with any blank lines between them.

   e. Below the script element, insert a link element that points to styles.css.

FIGURE C-28

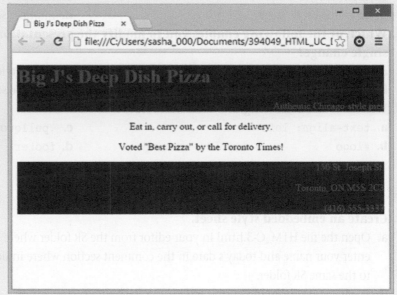

   f. Save your document, refresh or reload it in your browser, then verify that its appearance still matches **FIGURE C-28**.

6. Link to an external style sheet.

   a. Return to your editor, open the file HTM_C-4.html from the SR folder where you store your Data Files for this unit, enter your name and today's date in the comment section where indicated, then save the file as **history.html** to the same SR folder.

   b. Preview history.html in your browser.

   c. Return to your editor, then insert a link element below the script element that points to styles.css.

   d. Save the document, reload history.html in your default browser, then verify that the page is displayed using the styles in the external style sheet.

   e. Return to styles.css in your editor, change the value for text alignment in the style rule for the article element so the text is left-aligned, then save styles.css.

Skills Review (continued)

f. Refresh or reload history.html in your browser, then verify that its appearance matches **FIGURE C-29**.

g. Refresh or reload index.html in your browser, then verify that the main paragraphs are now left-aligned.

7. Add a comment to a style sheet.

a. Return to styles.css in your editor, then add opening and closing characters for a CSS comment on separate lines before the first style.

b. Between the comment tags, add the following comment text, substituting your name and today's date where indicated:

```
Big J's Deep Dish Pizza
style sheet
Filename: styles.css
Author:    your first and
           last name
Date:      today's date
HTML5 and CSS3 Illustrated
Unit C, Skills Review
```

c. Save your changes to styles.css, refresh or reload index.html and history.html in your browser, then verify that the appearance of both documents is unaffected.

8. Debug and validate CSS code.

a. Return to styles.css in your editor, add a declaration that aligns text in the center within the style rule for the `header` and `footer` elements.

b. Save your changes, refresh or reload index.html in your browser, then verify that only the main header is center-aligned.

c. Use your browser's developer tools to inspect the styles applied to the contact information at the bottom of the document.

d. In the style rule for the `contact` class in the browser developer tools, uncheck the declaration that sets the text alignment to right, then notice the effect on the footer text.

e. Refresh or reload the page in the browser, then notice the effect on the alignment of the contact information.

f. Close the developer tools, then open http://jigsaw.w3.org/css-validator/.

g. Upload styles.css, check it against the standards for CSS, review the validation results, then fix any errors that are identified.

FIGURE C-29

Independent Challenge 1

Sarah Nguyen, the owner and manager of the Spotted Wren Garden Center, is happy with your work so far on the company's website. She'd like you to add some presentation elements to the web page you created, so you incorporate some CSS style rules.

a. Open your editor, open the file HTM_C-5.html from the IC1 folder where you store your Data Files for this unit, enter your name and today's date where indicated in the comment section, then save the file as **index.html** to the same IC1 folder.

b. Add a `style` element in the head section, then create a style rule for the h1 element that sets the background color to `coral`.

c. Save your changes, open index.html in a browser, then verify that the heading is displayed with a background color.

d. Return to index.html in your editor, create a style rule for the h1 and p elements that aligns text in the center, save your changes, then refresh or reload the document in your browser and verify that all text content is centered.

e. Return to index.html in your editor, create a style rule for the `footer` element that sets the background color to `yellow`, save your changes, refresh or reload the document in your browser, then verify that the contact information has a yellow background and your document matches **FIGURE C-30**.

f. Validate your CSS code using the validator at http://jigsaw.w3.org/css-validator/. (*Note*: When you upload an HTML document containing an embedded style sheet to the CSS validator, it identifies and validates the CSS code in the document.)

FIGURE C-30

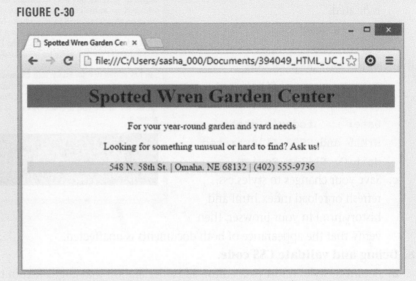

Independent Challenge 2

As you continue developing the website for the Murfreesboro Regional Soccer League, you decide to add presentation features to the web pages. You've created two web pages for the site, so you create an external style sheet.

a. Open your editor, open the file HTM_C-6.html from the IC2 folder where you store your Data Files for this unit, enter your name and today's date where indicated in the comment section, then save the file as **index.html** to the same IC2 folder.

b. Add a `style` element in the head section, then create a style rule for the h1 element that sets the background color to `orangered`.

c. Save your changes, open index.html in a browser, then verify that the heading is displayed with a background color.

d. Return to index.html in your editor, create a style rule for the h1 and `article` elements that aligns text in the center, save your changes, then refresh or reload the document in your browser and verify that all content except the contact information is centered. (*Note*: The contact information is not centered because those p elements are part of the `footer` element and not the body text.)

e. Return to index.html in your editor, create a style rule for the `footer` element that sets the background color to `green` and the text color to `white`, save your changes, then refresh or reload the document in your browser and verify that the contact information is displayed as white text on a green background.

Independent Challenge 2 (continued)

f. Return to index.html in your editor, add class attributes with the value contact to the two p elements in the footer section, create a style rule that right-aligns the text in these paragraphs, save your changes, refresh or reload the document in your browser, then verify that your document matches **FIGURE C-31**.

g. Save index.html as index_embedded.html, close the file, then reopen index.html.

h. Cut the CSS code from your embedded style sheet to the Clipboard, create a new file, paste the CSS code into it, then save the new file as **styles.css** to the IC2 folder where you store your Data Files for this unit.

i. In index.html, delete the style element, add an element that links to the styles.css file you created, save your changes, refresh or reload index.html in your browser, then verify that the document still matches **FIGURE C-31**.

j. Return to styles.css in your editor, add a comment at the start of the document that includes the text **Murfreesboro Regional Soccer League style sheet**, the filename, your first and last name, today's date, and the text **HTML5 and CSS3 Illustrated Unit C, Independent Challenge 2**, then save your changes.

k. Open the file HTM_C-7.html in your editor from the IC2 folder, enter your name and today's date where indicated in the comment section, then save the file as **started.html** to the same folder.

l. Add an element that links to the styles.css file, save your changes, open started.html in a browser, then verify that the document matches **FIGURE C-32**.

m. Validate your CSS code using the validator at http://jigsaw.w3.org/css-validator/.

FIGURE C-31

FIGURE C-32

Independent Challenge 3

As you continue your work on the website for Hotel Natoma, you incorporate a color scheme and basic text alignment using CSS.

a. Open your text editor, open the file HTM_C-8.html from the IC3 folder where you store your Data Files for this unit, enter your name and today's date where indicated in the comment section, then save the file as **index.html** to the same IC3 folder. Repeat for HTM_C-9.html, saving it as **nearby.html**.

b. Preview both files in a browser.

c. Return to your editor, create a new document, enter a CSS comment containing the text **Hotel Natoma style sheet**, the filename **styles. css**, your first and last names, today's date, and the text **HTML5 and CSS3 Illustrated Unit C, Independent Challenge 3**, then save the document with the name **styles.css** to the IC3 folder.

FIGURE C-33

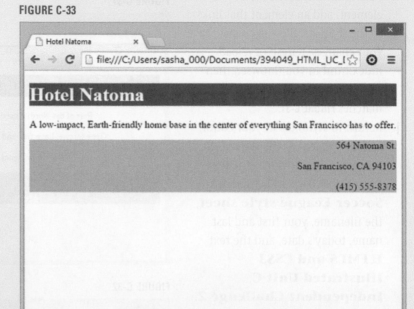

d. Create style rules to apply the following presentation details, adding HTML attributes to both web documents when necessary:

- set the background color of h1 elements to darkgreen and the text color to white

- set the text color of h2 elements to darkgreen

- center-align h2 elements and all p elements except the contact information, which should be right-aligned (*Hint*: Use a general selector for all p elements, then create a more specific selector for just the elements containing the contact information.)

- set the background color of the footer element to darkseagreen

FIGURE C-34

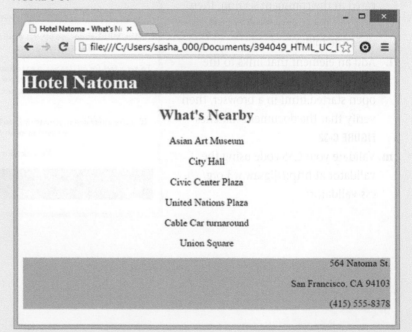

e. Save your work, add a link to your external style sheet to both index.html and nearby.html, then save your changes.

f. Preview index.html and nearby.html in a web browser. Compare index.html to **FIGURE C-33** and nearby.html to **FIGURE C-34**, making corrections to your code as needed.

g. Validate your CSS code using the validator at http://jigsaw.w3.org/css-validator/.

Independent Challenge 4—Explore

You've been hired to create a website for Eating Well in Season (EWIS), a business in Glover, Vermont, that delivers produce from local farms to its customers. Another team member has created a style sheet for the site but has been unable to resolve some errors in the code. You continue your work on the site by linking to and debugging the style sheet, incorporating a color scheme, and aligning the page content.

a. Open your text editor, open the file HTM_C-10.html from the IC4 folder where you store your Data Files for this unit, enter your name and today's date where indicated in the comment section, then save the file as **index. html** to the same IC4 folder. Repeat for HTM_C-11.css, saving it as **styles.css**. Preview index.html in a browser.

b. Return to styles.css in your browser, enter a CSS comment containing the text **Eating Well in Season style sheet**, the filename **styles.css**, your first and last names, today's date, and the text **HTML5 and CSS3 Illustrated Unit C, Independent Challenge 4**, then save your changes.

c. Create style rules to apply the following presentation details, adding HTML attributes to the web document when necessary:

- set the background color of the `header` and `footer` elements to `olive` and the text color to `floralwhite`
- set the text color of the `h1` element and of the `p` element in the `footer` element containing the text Eating Well in Season to `khaki` (*Hint*: You will need to add a `class` or `id` attribute to this `p` element.)
- set the background color of the `h2` elements to `khaki`

d. Save your changes to styles.css, link index.html to the external style sheet, save your changes to index.html, then preview the document in a browser.

e. Using the debugging methods you learned in this unit, edit your CSS as necessary until your document matches **FIGURE C-35**. (*Hint*: Debugging may include making changes to both the CSS and HTML code.)

f. Validate your CSS code using the validator at http://jigsaw.w3.org/css-validator/.

FIGURE C-35

Visual Workshop

Open your text editor, then open the file HTM_C-12.html from the VW folder where you store your Data Files for this unit. Add your first and last names and today's date to the comment section, save the file as **index.html**, then preview it in a browser. Use your text editor to add the necessary CSS code to make your web page match the one shown in FIGURE C-36. Use the color navy for the main heading text and for the first two lines of the address. Use the color lightblue for the background at the top and bottom of the document. Use the color maroon as the text color for the phone number. Validate your CSS using the online validator at http://jigsaw.w3.org/css-validator/.

FIGURE C-36

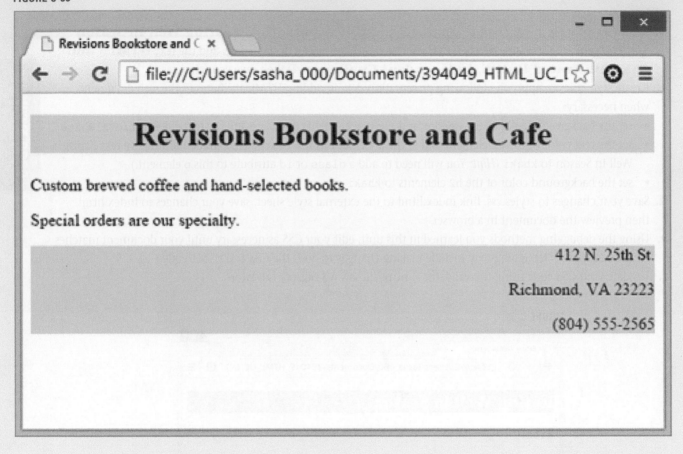

Laying Out Elements With CSS

As you continue building a website for Lakeland Reeds Bed & Breakfast, you want to more precisely influence where elements are positioned in a browser window and in relation to each other. In this unit, you practice using CSS properties that give you control over web page layout.

Unit Objectives

After completing this unit, you will be able to:

- Assess the CSS box model
- Set element width and borders
- Set margins and padding
- Align elements with `float`
- Control page flow with `clear`

- Implement fixed positioning
- Implement relative positioning
- Control stacking order
- Implement absolute positioning

Files You Will Need

 L   4 files   IC3   3 files

 SR   3 files   IC4   3 files

 IC1   3 files   VW   3 files

 IC2   3 files

For specific filenames, see Filenames_D.pdf in the Unit D Data Files folder.

Assess the CSS Box Model

Learning
Outcomes
• Describe the
components of the
CSS box model

CSS represents the characteristics of every web page element using the **box model**, which treats each element as a rectangular box having several global properties. The properties most significant to the box model are described in **TABLE D-1**. **CASE** ▶ *Before you enhance the layout of the Lakeland Reeds About Us page, you familiarize yourself with the CSS box model.*

DETAILS

A few concepts are important for using box model properties effectively:

- **Distinguishing between padding, border, and margin**

  The `padding`, `border`, and `margin` properties all create space around the contents of a web page element; it's important to understand the relationship of these components to each other in order to create the results you want. Of these three aspects of the box model, **border**, which represents a line around an element formatted with the width, style, and color that you specify, is the only one that can be seen in a web browser. A border serves as a reference point for the other two properties, as illustrated in **FIGURE D-1**. **Padding** is the space inside a border between the border and the element content, while **margin** is the space outside the border between the border and adjacent or parent elements.

- **Understanding CSS units of measure**

  You specify a number as the value of the `padding`, `margin`, and `width` properties. In addition, the `border` property takes a number as one of the three components of its value. All of these numbers must be accompanied by the abbreviation for a unit of measure. CSS supports many units of measure, but the four most commonly used are ems (`em`), percent (`%`), pixels (`px`), and rems (`rem`), which are described in **TABLE D-2**. Ems, percent, and rems are **relative units**, meaning that they are calculated based on the sizes of other elements on a web page. Pixels are **absolute units**, meaning that they represent a specific length or height that doesn't change.

- **Calculating box size**

  Positive values for `padding`, `border`, and `margin` all increase the amount of space on a web page that an element occupies. However, an element's `width` and `height` values (and their `min-` and `max-` variants) do not include these properties. When you specify an element's `width` value or `height` value, it applies only to the element content. Any values you specify for `padding`, `border`, or `margin` are added to the `width` value or `height` value when a browser calculates the space occupied by an element. To determine how much horizontal room an element will occupy, you add the `width` value to the `padding`, `border`, and `margin` values, as **FIGURE D-2** illustrates. There is one exception to this rule: when the bottom margin of one element is adjacent to the top margin of another element, the margins combine, or **collapse**, into a single margin equal to the greater of the two values.

TABLE D-1: Box model properties

property	description	example*
border	a visible border around an element specified with a thickness value, a style keyword, and a color name or value	border: 1px solid black;
padding	the space inside a border between the border and the element content	padding: 5%;
margin	the space outside a border between the border and adjacent or parent elements	margin: 10px;
width	the horizontal size of an element's content, excluding border, padding, and margin	width: 25%;
min-width	the minimum horizontal size of an element's content, excluding border, padding, and margin	min-width: 320px;
max-width	the maximum horizontal size of an element's content, excluding border, padding, and margin	max-width: 1000px;
height	the vertical size of an element's content, excluding border, padding, and margin	height: 5rem;
min-height	the minimum vertical size of an element's content, excluding border, padding, and margin	min-height: 2em;
max-height	the maximum vertical size of an element's content, excluding border, padding, and margin	max-height: 5em;

* Values in CSS units, with a % value based on width of parent element

© 2016 Cengage Learning

FIGURE D-1: The CSS box model

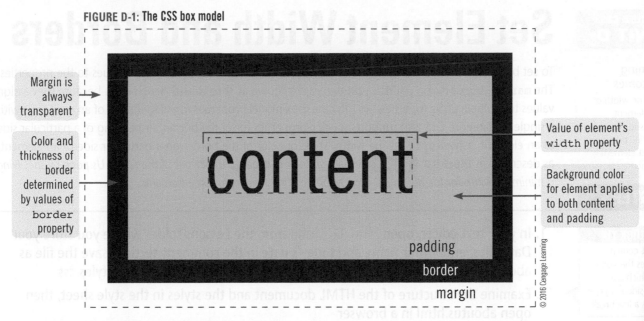

Margin is always transparent

Color and thickness of border determined by values of `border` property

Value of element's `width` property

Background color for element applies to both content and padding

content

padding

border

margin

© 2016 Cengage Learning

FIGURE D-2: Calculating web page space occupied by an element

```
p {
    width: 10em;
    padding: 0.5em;
    border: 0.25em solid black;
    margin: 1em;
}
```

left and right margin

left and right padding

1em + 0.25em + 0.5em + 10em + 0.5em + 0.25em + 1em = 13.5em

width

left and right border

Total horizontal space occupied

© 2016 Cengage Learning

TABLE D-2: Commonly used CSS units of measure

abbreviation	unit	description	example
em	em	A multiple of the computed font size for the current element, where 1em represents 100% of this size	`padding: 1.4em;`
%	percent	A percentage of another value for the current element or an ancestor element; each CSS property that takes a value in % specifies what value the % calculation is based on	`margin: 10%;`
px	pixel	A unit equal to approximately 1/96 inch or 0.26 millimeter	`padding: 10px;`
rem	rem	A multiple of the computed font size for the `html` element, where 1rem represents 100% of this size	`margin: 0.25rem;`

© 2016 Cengage Learning

Set Element Width and Borders

Learning Outcomes
- Set the width of an element
- Use shorthand and specific properties to set element borders

To set box properties for web page elements, you create declarations that assign values to the properties. The margin, border, and padding properties are known as **shorthand properties** because they assign values to multiple CSS properties—in this case, box model properties for all four sides of an element—with a single declaration. CSS also supports specific properties to set the border, or padding of a particular side of an element, as well as to set the width, style, or color of the border on a particular side of an element, as described in **TABLE D-3**. **CASE** ▶ *You start your changes to the layout of the About Us page by specifying a minimum width for the document content and adding borders to some elements.*

STEPS

1. **In your text editor, open HTM_D-1.html from the Lessons folder where you store your Data Files, enter your name and today's date in the comment section, save the file as aboutus.html, then repeat for the file HTM_D-2.css, saving the file as styles.css**

2. **Examine the structure of the HTML document and the styles in the style sheet, then open aboutus.html in a browser**

   The content is grouped within header, article, aside, and footer elements. All the content sections are enclosed in a div element with the class attribute value container. The style sheet contains comments identifying the section of the page that each rule or rules apply to.

3. **In styles.css, add the declaration** max-width: 640px; **in the** .container **rule before the existing declaration**

   This declaration limits the width of the document content, making it easier to read on larger screens.

4. **Below the first comment in the document, add a new line containing the comment** /* reset styles */, **type** article, body, div, footer, header, h1, h2, p { **below the comment, press [Enter] twice, then type** }

   This style rule uses multiple type selectors to select all the elements containing text in aboutus.html.

5. **Within the style rule you created in Step 4, type** border: 0;

   This removes the border from all elements displayed in the browser window. This type of style rule is known as a **reset rule** because it resets one or more common properties (the border, in this example) of multiple elements to a common baseline, ensuring that default values that may be different between browsers do not cause a web page to be displayed inconsistently. When you set the value of a CSS property to 0, there's no need to specify units.

6. **Below the** aside **style rule in the** /* sidebar */ **section of the style sheet, type** aside p { **on a new line, press [Enter] twice, then type** }

7. **Within the style rule you created in Step 6, type** border-bottom: 1px solid black; **on a new line, press [Enter], then type** border-top: 1px solid black;

   FIGURE D-3 shows the changes to the style sheet.

8. **Save your work, then reload aboutus.html in your browser**

   The document content is now exactly 640px wide and surrounded by a border. In addition, each paragraph in the aside element has a horizontal border above and below it.

9. **Right-click the text What a weekend!, click Inspect Element, then in the developer tools, click Computed (Chrome), Box Model (Firefox), or Layout (IE)**

   The developer tools illustrate the box model values for the selected p element, as shown in **FIGURE D-4**.

10. **Open aboutus.html on a handheld device such as a smartphone**

    The page is displayed at a narrower width to fit the device. This is because you set the width using max-width, allowing browsers to display the page at a narrower width when appropriate.

FIGURE D-3: width and border declarations added to style sheet

```
10    /* reset styles */
11    article, body, div, footer, header, h1, h2, p {
12        border: 0;
13    }
14
15    /* body and page container */
16    .container {
17        max-width: 640px;
18        background-color: beige;
19    }
```

Using max-width allows content to be displayed at a narrower width on smaller screens; note that declarations for box model properties are listed first within a style rule by convention

```
30    /* sidebar */
31    aside {
32        background-color: goldenrod;
33    }
34    aside p {
35        border-bottom: 1px solid black;
36        border-top: 1px solid black;
37    }
```

Declarations add top and bottom borders to aside p element without adding left or right borders

FIGURE D-4: Width and border properties applied to About Us page

Maximum width of element with container class value set to 640px

br element adds a line break within the h1 element, splitting the content into two lines

1px black border added to top and bottom of p element within aside element

Illustration of box model values in Chrome developer tools

Browser default value for margin; your browser may also add a default value for padding

p element within aside element selected in browser tools

TABLE D-3: Specific properties for components of box model

component	properties	description	values
border	border-*side*-width	thickness of a visible border	a border thickness, such as 1px
	border-*side*-style	style of a visible border	dashed, solid, or another keyword
	border-*side*-color	color of a visible border	a color name or value, such as black
padding	padding-*side*	space between border and content	a value in a CSS unit, such as 5%
margin	margin-*side*	space between border and adjacent elements	a value in a CSS unit, such as 1.2em

Set Margins and Padding

You can assign different margin and padding values to different sides of an element by providing multiple values for the `margin` and `padding` shorthand properties, with a space separating each value, as described in **TABLE D-4**. In addition to numbers, the `margin` property supports the value `auto`. If you assign the value `auto` to the left and right margins of an element, the element is centered horizontally within its parent element. **CASE** ▸ *You continue your changes to the layout of the About Us page by specifying margins and padding.*

STEPS

1. **Return to** styles.css **in your editor, within the style rule below the** `/* reset styles */` **comment, add the declarations** `padding: 0;` **and** `margin: 0;` **on separate lines**

   These declarations expand your reset style rule to set the margin and padding to 0 on all sides of all elements.

2. **In the** `.container` **style rule, add the declaration** `margin: 0 auto;` **below the** `max-width` **declaration**

   The declaration sets the left and right margins to `auto`, centering the element horizontally within the browser window.

3. **In the** `h1` **style rule, add the declaration** `padding: 0.4em;` **before the existing declarations**

4. **Below the** `h1` **style rule, type** `h2 {`**, press [Enter], insert 3 spaces, type** `padding: 0.4em 0.6em;`**, press [Enter], then type** `}`

   The declaration sets the top and bottom padding to 0.4em and the left and right padding to 0.6em.

5. **Below the** `h2` **style rule, add a new line containing the comment** `/* main content */`**, type** `article p {` **below the comment, press [Enter], insert 3 spaces, type** `padding: 0 1em 1em;`**, press [Enter], then type** `}`

   This style rule uses 3 values to set padding for all p elements within the `article` element. The first value applies to the top, the second value applies to the right and left, and the third value applies to the bottom.

6. **In the** `aside` **style rule, add the declaration** `padding: 1em 0;` **before the existing declaration, then in the** `aside p` **style rule, add the declarations** `padding: 0.4em 0;` **and** `margin: 0 0.6em;` **on separate lines**

7. **In the** `footer` **style rule, add the declaration** `padding: 0.6em;` **below the selector**

8. **Below the** `footer` **style rule, add a new line containing** `footer p {`**, press [Enter], insert 3 spaces, type** `margin: 0.4em;`**, press [Enter], then type** `}`

   Your updated style sheet should match **FIGURE D-5**.

9. **Save your work, then reload** aboutus.html **in your browser**

   The document layout is updated to include the margins and padding you specified as shown in **FIGURE D-6**.

10. **Right-click the text** What a weekend!**, click** Inspect Element**, then in the developer tools, click** Computed (Chrome), Box Model (Firefox), **or** Layout (IE)

    The box model illustration in the developer tools is updated to include the margin and padding you specified for p elements within the `aside` element.

FIGURE D-5: padding and margin declarations added to style sheet

```
10    /* reset styles */
11    article, body, div, footer, header, h1, h2, p {
12        border: 0;
13        padding: 0;
14        margin: 0;
15    }
16
17    /* body and page container */
18    .container {
19        max-width: 640px;
20        margin: 0 auto;
21        background-color: beige;
22    }
23
24    /* headings */
25    header {
26        background-color: darkgreen;
27    }
28    h1 {
29        padding: 0.4em;
30        color: white;
31        text-align: center;
32    }
33    h2 {
34        padding: 0.4em 0.6em;
35    }
36
37    /* main content */
38    article p {
39        padding: 0 1em 1em;
40    }
41
```

Code continued with line 42 in figure to the right

```
42    /* sidebar */
43    aside {
44        padding: 1em 0;
45        background-color: goldenrod;
46    }
47    aside p {
48        border-bottom: 1px solid black;
49        border-top: 1px solid black;
50        padding: 0.4em 0;
51        margin: 0 0.6em;
52    }
53
54    /* footer section */
55    footer {
56        padding: 0.6em;
57        color: white;
58        background-color: darkgreen;
59        text-align: center;
60    }
61    footer p {
62        margin: 0.4em;
63    }
64    footer p.accent {
65        color: goldenrod;
66    }
```

Code continued from figure on the left

FIGURE D-6: padding and margin properties applied to About Us page

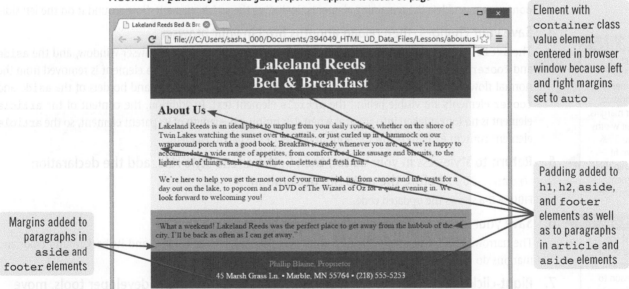

Element with container class value element centered in browser window because left and right margins set to auto

Padding added to h1, h2, aside, and footer elements as well as to paragraphs in article and aside elements

Margins added to paragraphs in aside and footer elements

TABLE D-4: Interpretation of different numbers of values for the margin and padding shorthand properties

# of values	values apply to	example
four	top, right, bottom, left	margin: 0 5% 5% 0;
three	top, left/right, bottom	padding: 0 2em 1em;
two	top/bottom, left/right	margin: 0 10px;
one (shorthand property)	top/left/bottom/right	padding: 5%;

Align Elements with `float`

By default, a browser renders elements in a web document in the order they appear, with most elements displayed below the element that precedes them. This default arrangement of elements is known as **normal flow**. In some cases, though, you want the elements that follow an element to wrap around it, rather than being stacked below it. To do so, you use the CSS `float` property. The `left` and `right` values of the `float` property align the element horizontally with the left or right edge of the parent element, respectively, and allow elements that follow to fill in the remaining horizontal space. **FIGURE D-7** illustrates the effect of the `float` property on web page elements. **CASE** ▶ The design of the About Us page calls for the aside element to be displayed as a sidebar along the right edge of the page, and the main content to be displayed to its left. You resize the aside and article elements so they fit side-by-side within the container element, and you use the `float` property to display them next to each other.

STEPS

1. **Return to** styles.css **in your editor, enter** `article {` **on a new line below the** `/* main content */` **comment, press [Enter] twice, then type** `}`

2. **In the** `article` **style rule, add the declaration** `width: 70%;`
   A percentage value for `width` is calculated based on the width of the parent element, which in this case is the element with the `class` value `container`. Using a percentage value for the `article` width allows it to scale if the document is displayed at a narrower width on a small screen. Setting the width to 70% leaves the remaining 30% of the parent width for the content of the `aside` element.

3. **In the** `article` **style rule, add the declaration** `float: right;`
   The `article` element comes before the `aside` element in the HTML document. Assigning it a `float` value of `right` aligns it with the right edge of the parent element, which is the element with the `class` value `container`, and lets the remaining elements, including the `aside` element, flow around it on the left side.

4. **Save your changes, then reload** aboutus.html **in your browser**
   The `article` element is narrower and displayed on the right side of the browser window, and the `aside` and `footer` elements are displayed to its left. However, because the `article` element is removed from the normal flow and has no background color specified, the background colors and borders of the `aside` and `footer` elements are visible behind the `article` element text. In addition, the content of the `article` element is no longer taken into account when determining the length of its parent element, so the `article` element content extends below the bottom border of the parent element.

5. **Return to** styles.css **in your editor, then in the** `aside` **style rule, add the declaration** `width: 30%;` **before the** `padding` **declaration**
   FIGURE D-8 shows the updated code.

6. **Save your changes, then reload** aboutus.html **in your browser**
   The narrower `aside` element fits next to the `article` element content and its background color and margins do not extend across the page.

7. **Right-click the text** About Us, **click** Inspect Element, **then in the developer tools, move the mouse pointer over the opening** `<article>` **tag**
   The element is highlighted. Notice that it is only as wide as the area it occupies in the browser window, which is 70% of the width of its parent element, as shown in **FIGURE D-9**.

8. **Move the mouse pointer over the tags for the** `aside`, `footer`, **and** `header` **elements in the developer tools**
   Each element is highlighted in the browser window. The dimensions of the `aside` element reflect the `width` value you specified, while the `header` and `footer` elements extend the full width available within the parent element.

FIGURE D-7: Using the `float` property

float: left;

Elements that follow the floated element in HTML document now fill in the space next to it

Layout in normal flow

Layout using `float`

© 2016 Cengage Learning

FIGURE D-8: Updated code for floating main content

```
37      /* main content */
38      article {
39          width: 70%;
40          float: right;
41      }
42      article p {
43          padding: 0 1em 1em;
44      }
45
46      /* sidebar */
47      aside {
48          width: 30%;
49          padding: 1em 0;
50          background-color: goldenrod;
51      }
```

FIGURE D-9: About Us page with floated `article` element

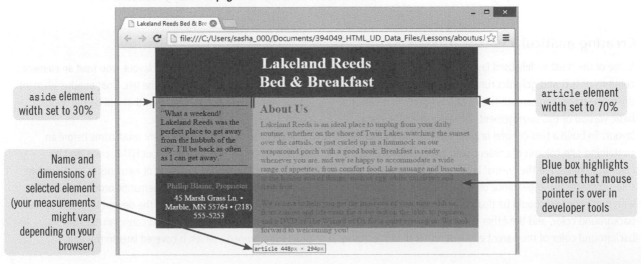

aside element width set to 30%

Name and dimensions of selected element (your measurements might vary depending on your browser)

article element width set to 70%

Blue box highlights element that mouse pointer is over in developer tools

Control Page Flow with `clear`

Learning
Outcomes
• Clear a float on a
  web page

The CSS `float` property gives you basic control over how web page elements are rendered in relation to each other. However, in some situations, using `float` is not enough to create the layout you want. For instance, sometimes you want to ensure that text or another object follows a floated element, rather than running alongside it. You can control the flow of web page elements more precisely with the CSS `clear` property, which prevents floated elements from being displayed to the left, right, or on either side of another element. **TABLE D-5** describes the effects of common `clear` values, and **FIGURE D-10** illustrates the effect of specifying a `clear` value for an element. **CASE** ▸ *You use the* `clear` *property to ensure that the* footer *element is displayed below the* aside *element.*

STEPS

1. **Return to** styles.css **in your editor**

2. **In the** `footer` **style rule, add the declaration** `clear: right;` **below the existing declarations**

   Specifying the value `right` for the `clear` property prevents a floated element from being displayed to the right of the current element. **FIGURE D-11** shows the `clear` property inserted in the style sheet.

3. **Save your work**

4. **Reload aboutus.html in your browser**

   As **FIGURE D-12** shows, the `footer` element is now displayed below the `aside` element.

TABLE D-5: Values of the clear property

value	description
left	element is displayed at next location in the document where no element is floated to the left
right	element is displayed at next location in the document where no element is floated to the right
both	element is displayed at next location in the document where no element is floated either to the left or to the right
none	element is displayed at next available location in the document, regardless of surrounding floated elements

Creating multicolumn layouts with `float`

Some of the most widely used layouts in print media involve columns of text and graphics running parallel to each other down the page. You can use the `float` property to create a basic version of this arrangement, known as a multicolumn layout. To build a two-column layout, you float an element containing one column of content, and either allow the other column to remain in the normal flow, or float it on the other side. To create the appearance of even columns, the column with more content should be floated and assigned a distinct background color, and the other column should use the background color of the parent element rather than specifying its own. To create a three-column layout, you float an element that will serve as one column on the left, float another element on the right, and allow the element that will be the middle column to remain the normal flow.

Remember that a floated element must come before an element that runs alongside it in your HTML code, and it's important not to change the order of elements in HTML simply for presentational purposes. If the semantic order of your HTML code doesn't lend itself to creating the desired layout using the `float` property, you should instead consider using the `position` property, which is covered later in this unit.

FIGURE D-10: Using the `clear` property

float: left; →

float: left; →

clear: left; →

Layout using `float`

clear: left; declaration prevents floated element (green box) from being displayed to the left of this element (yellow box), moving this element down the page past the floated element

Layout using `float` and `clear`

© 2016 Cengage Learning

FIGURE D-11: Updated code including `clear` property

```
59    /* footer section */
60    footer {
61        padding: 0.6em;
62        color: white;
63        background-color: darkgreen;
64        text-align: center;
65        clear: right;
66    }
```

FIGURE D-12: About Us page with footer using `clear` property

Footer element displayed in normal flow after right margin is clear of floated elements

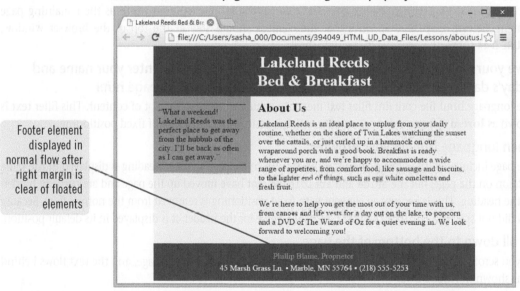

Dealing with floated content that's longer than its parent element

An element's content can extend below the bottom of its container element, especially when the content of a floated element is longer than other elements on a page. When a floated element is followed by another element in the normal flow, the `clear` property can be useful in extending the formatting of the parent element to all the content within it. However, in some cases the order of elements in HTML code does not lend itself to this layout. In these cases, you can add the declaration `overflow: auto;` to the parent element

to extend it horizontally to give the appearance of the floated element still being in the normal flow.

In some browsers, this declaration results in a scroll bar being displayed on the right side of the parent element, which some designers find unsightly. Other approaches to solving this same problem that use more advanced CSS tools are in wide use. One popular method, known as a clearfix, is detailed at http://css-tricks.com/snippets/css/clear-fix/.

Laying Out Elements With CSS

Implement Fixed Positioning

So far, your layouts have been limited to web page elements being displayed in the order they appear in your HTML documents, or by moving elements outside the normal flow using the `float` property. CSS also lets you specify more precisely where an element should be positioned on a web page using the `position` property. **TABLE D-6** describes commonly used values for the `position` property. One popular effect that developers create with the `position` property, known as **fixed positioning**, involves an element remaining in the same position in the browser window while a user scrolls the remaining page content. To implement fixed positioning, you use the `position` property with a value of `fixed`. You then specify either a horizontal position using the `left` or `right` property, or a vertical position using the `top` or `bottom` property, or both a horizontal and vertical position. **TABLE D-7** describes the properties used in fixed positioning and their values. **FIGURE D-13** illustrates how fixed positioning affects the flow of elements in a web page. **CASE ▶** *You anticipate other pages in the Lakeland Reeds website will include so much information that users will need to scroll; you'd like the main heading to stay on the page as they do so. You use fixed positioning to do this.*

STEPS

1. **Return to styles.css in your text editor**

2. **Below the /* headings */ comment and in the header style rule, add the declarations** `width: 100%;`, `max-width: 640px;`, **and** `position: fixed;`

   Fixed positioning removes the element from the normal flow, and it is sized relative to the browser window. Setting the `width` to 100% ensures that the `header` width is not limited to the width of its content, and setting the `max-width` to 640px gives the element the same maximum width as the remaining page content. Setting `top` to 0 specifies that the element should stay at the top of the browser window. **FIGURE D-14** shows the new rule in the style sheet.

3. **Save your work, open HTM_D-3.html from the Lessons folder, enter your name and today's date in the comment section, then save the file as longpage.html**

   The longpage.html file contains filler text meant to simulate a page with a lot of content. This filler text is known as **lorem ipsum**. A long document makes it easier to see the effect of fixed positioning.

4. **Open longpage.html in your browser**

   The page includes all the same elements as the aboutus.html file. The main heading is displayed in the same location on the page, but the `aside` and `article` content have moved up the page and are partially hidden by the heading. This is because an element with fixed positioning is removed from the normal flow. Because you did not specify a `top`, `bottom`, `left`, or `right` value for the header, it is displayed in its default position.

5. **Scroll down to the bottom of the page**

   As you scroll, the main header remains in the same place at the top of the page, and the text flows behind it, as shown in **FIGURE D-15**.

TABLE D-6: Commonly used values of the `position` property

value	description
`absolute`	element is removed from the normal flow and positioned relative to the nearest ancestor element that has a position value other than `static`
`fixed`	element is removed from the normal flow and positioned relative to the browser window, and remains in this position even as a user scrolls through the document
`relative`	element remains in the normal flow and is positioned relative to its default position
`static` (default)	element is displayed in its default position in the normal flow

FIGURE D-13: Implementing fixed positioning

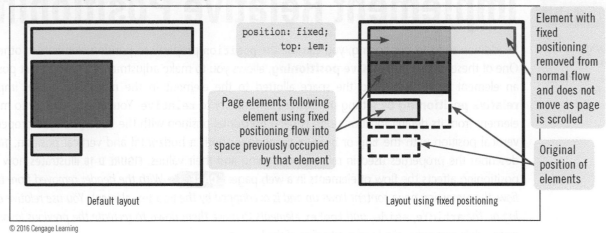

© 2016 Cengage Learning

FIGURE D-14: header style rule added to style sheet

```
24    /* headings */
25    header {
26        width: 100%;
27        max-width: 640px;
28        position: fixed;
29        background-color: darkgreen;
30    }
```

FIGURE D-15: Test page showing header element using fixed positioning

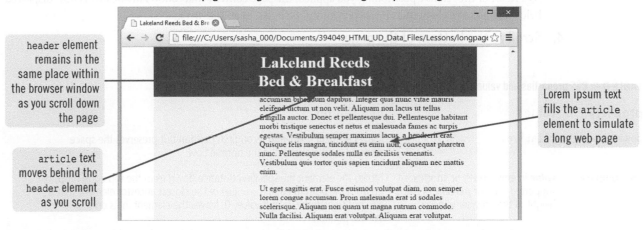

TABLE D-7: CSS properties and values used in fixed positioning

property	value	description
position	fixed	Removes element from normal flow, positions it relative to the browser window, and keeps it in this position even as a user scrolls through the document
top, bottom	*value* in ems, pixels, or another supported unit, or *percent* of the height of the browser window	Moves the element the specified distance down from the top edge (top) or up from the bottom edge (bottom) of the browser window; the default value, 0, leaves the element in its original vertical position
left, right	*value* in ems, pixels, or another supported unit, or *percent* of the width of the browser window	Moves the element the specified distance right from the left edge (left) or left from the right edge (right) of the browser window; the default value, 0, leaves the element in its original horizontal position

© 2016 Cengage Learning

Implement Relative Positioning

In addition to fixed positioning, you can use the position property to position elements in other ways. One of these, known as **relative positioning**, allows you to make adjustments to the default position of an element while preserving the space allotted to the element in the normal flow. You implement **relative positioning** by setting the position property to relative. You specify how far to move the element from its default location using either a horizontal position with the left or right property, or a vertical position with the top or bottom property, or both a horizontal and vertical position. **TABLE D-8** describes the properties used in relative positioning and their values. **FIGURE D-16** illustrates how relative positioning affects the flow of elements in a web page. **CASE** *With the header removed from the page flow, the remaining page content flows up and is overlapped by the* header *element. You use relative positioning on the* article, aside, *and* footer *elements to move them down to recreate the previous layout of the page, while preserving the fixed positioning of the header.*

STEPS

1. **Return to styles.css in your editor**

QUICK TIP
While horizontal and
vertical positions can
sometimes be
calculated, it's often
a process of trial and
error to arrive at the
correct values.

2. **In the .container rule, add the declarations** position: relative; **and** top: 6.2em; **after the existing declarations**

   The value of 6.2em for the element's top value moves it down from the top of the parent element exactly the height of the header element. **FIGURE D-17** shows the updated code.

3. **Save your work, refresh longpage.html in your browser, then scroll to the top of the page if necessary**

   As a result of the relative positioning you applied, the page content that follows the header is now displayed below the header element as it was previously, as shown in **FIGURE D-18**.

4. **Scroll to the bottom of the page.**

TABLE D-8: CSS properties and values used in relative positioning

property	value	description
position	relative	Moves element relative to its original position but preserves the space reserved for the element in the normal flow
top, bottom	**value** in ems, pixels, or another supported unit, or **percent** of the height of the browser window	Moves the element the specified distance down from the top edge (top) or up from the bottom edge (bottom) of the closest ancestor element that is also positioned; the default value, 0, leaves the element in its original vertical position
left, right	**value** in ems, pixels, or another supported unit, or **percent** of the width of the browser window	Moves the element the specified distance from the left edge (left) or from the right edge (right) of the closest ancestor element that is also positioned; the default value, 0, leaves the element in its original horizontal position

© 2016 Cengage Learning

Maintaining accessibility with positioning

When you alter the layout of your web pages using positioning, it's important to plan for non-visual user agents, as well as devices with smaller screens, to make sure your page content still flows logically. User agents that don't process positioning continue to render all content from top to bottom in the document. Thus, your HTML code should contain elements in the order users will encounter them. In addition, you can help all user agents understand the content of your pages and present it appropriately by using semantic elements to indicate the content of different columns; for instance, aside for a sidebar, article for main page content, and footer for the page footer.

FIGURE D-16: Implementing relative positioning

position: relative;
left: 20em;

Other page elements do not reflow into space originally occupied by another element to which relative positioning has been applied

Element position changed relative to original position in normal flow

Default layout

Layout using relative positioning

© 2016 Cengage Learning

FIGURE D-17: Styles for relative positioning added to style sheet

```
17    /* body and page container */
18    .container {
19        max-width: 640px;
20        margin: 0 auto;
21        background-color: beige;
22        position: relative;
23        top: 6.2em;
24    }
```

FIGURE D-18: Test page with relatively positioned element

Top of container element is below header element as a result of relative positioning

Control Stacking Order

One of the side effects of using positioning in your layouts is the possibility of two elements occupying the same space on a web page. Elements with either a fixed or relative position can be moved to positions occupied by other elements, or two positioned elements can be moved to the same place. While it requires careful planning to ensure that a positioned element doesn't unintentionally obscure the view of another element, the ability to overlap, or **stack**, elements introduces additional possibilities for creative layouts. A positioned element is placed in a new **layer**, which is a new level displayed on top of the normal flow. As **FIGURE D-19** illustrates, the arrangement of layers is similar to placing clear sheets of plastic over a sheet of paper. By default, positioned elements are stacked based on their order in the HTML code, with the first element at the bottom and subsequent elements stacked on top. You can change the stacking order of positioned elements by assigning values for the z-index property of one or more elements. Values can be positive or negative, and an element with a larger z-index value is displayed on top of an element with a smaller value. **CASE** ▶ *You explore the effect of stacking order on the* header *element and the container using the* z-index *property.*

STEPS

1. **Return to** styles.css **in your editor**

QUICK TIP
Values for the
z-index property
can be any number,
including a negative
number. Stacking
order is based solely
on which element
has a larger
z-index value.

2. **In the** header **style rule, add the declaration** z-index: -1; **below the existing declarations**
   FIGURE D-20 shows the declaration inserted in the style sheet.

3. **Save your changes to** styles.css

4. **Reload** longpage.html **in your browser, scroll to the top of the page if necessary, then scroll down the page**
   The header element, which includes the main heading text, is now covered by the aside and article content in the stacking order, as shown in **FIGURE D-21**.

5. **Return to** styles.css **in your editor**

6. **In the** header **style rule, add** /* **before the declaration** z-index: -1; **, then add** */ **after the declaration**
   You do not want the container element to be displayed above the header element, so you remove the z-index declaration. Formatting the declaration as a comment preserves it in your code while ensuring that user agents ignore it when rendering documents.

7. **Save your changes to** styles.css

8. **Reload** longpage.html **in your browser, scroll to the top of the page if necessary, then scroll down the page**
   The header element once again remains above the aside and article content in the stacking order.

Understanding stacking context

Controlling stacking order with the z-index property is straightforward in many cases. However, in some situations, it's important to understand some of the finer details of the property in order to achieve the results you want. The z-index property determines stacking order based on a **stacking context**, which is the element containing elements to be stacked. When stacking sections of a page, stacking order works pretty predictably, as all elements share a stacking context—the html element. However, when both a parent and child element are positioned, you cannot use the z-index property to stack the child element above another element on the page. This is because the stacking context for this child element is its parent element, rather than the html element containing all page contents. You can learn more about the details of stacking context and strategies for working with it at developer.mozilla.org/en-US/docs/Web/Guide/CSS/Understanding_z_index.

FIGURE D-19: Stacking elements

Element with the lowest z-index value is stacked below other positioned elements

z-index: 1;

z-index: 3;

z-index: 2;

Element with the highest z-index value is stacked on top of other positioned elements

© 2016 Cengage Learning

FIGURE D-20: `z-index` declaration added to `header` style rule

```
26    /* headings */
27    header {
28        width: 100%;
29        max-width: 640px;
30        position: fixed;
31        background-color: darkgreen;
32        z-index: -1;
33    }
```

FIGURE D-21: Test page with `z-index` value added to `header` element

container element displayed on top of `header` element because `header` has lower `z-index` value

Evaluating website layout types

By default, web page content occupies the entire width of a user's browser window. When most users accessed the web with a desktop computer, designers often used a **static layout**, which specifies a fixed width for the web page content. However, a static layout that's sized appropriately for a desktop computer often doesn't fit on the screen of a smaller device such as a smartphone. Designers for some websites find that setting a fixed width and expecting users to scroll and/or zoom to view the entire page is still their best option. However, many other sites have replaced static layouts with **fluid layouts**—also known as **liquid layouts**—in which the content size is constrained with the `min-width` and `max-width` properties and the columns are sized using percentages. A liquid layout fills the width of whatever window it's displayed in, up to the maximum width limit. This allows designers to take advantage of larger screens on desktop computers while still making the entire width of the site viewable on a handheld device.

Implement Absolute Positioning

Another type of CSS positioning is **absolute positioning**, which takes an element out of the normal flow and positions it in a location you specify. The `top`, `right`, `bottom`, and `left` properties specify the new location of an absolutely positioned element relative to the closest ancestor element that is also positioned. **TABLE D-9** describes the properties used in absolute positioning and their values. **FIGURE D-22** illustrates how absolute positioning affects the flow of elements in a web page. **CASE** ▶ *The owners of Lakeland Reeds would like you to add and position a text placeholder for a logo. You add a new* `p` *element for the logo text and use absolute positioning to position it next to the existing main heading text.*

STEPS

1. **Return to longpage.html in your text editor, then below the `h1` element and before the closing `</header>` tag, enter the following code on a new line:**
   `<p class="logo">&#8466;&#8475;</p>`
   This code creates a new p element with the class `attribute` value `logo`, as shown in **FIGURE D-23**.

2. **Save your changes to longpage.html, then reload longpage.html in your browser**
   The cursive characters L and R are displayed in the bottom left corner of the `header` element, increasing the height of the `header` element so it overlaps some of the content below it.

3. **Return to styles.css in your editor, then enter the following style rule below the `/* headings */` comment and below the `h2` style rule:**
   ```
   p.logo {
       padding: 0.2em;
       border: 2px solid beige;
       color: goldenrod;
   }
   ```
   This style rule sets the padding, border, and color for the element with the `logo` class.

4. **Within the `p.logo` style rule, insert the declarations** `position: absolute;`, `top: 2em;`, **and** `left: 2em;` **below the existing declarations, as shown in FIGURE D-24**
   These declarations set the position of the element to `absolute`, and position it 2em from the top and left of the nearest positioned ancestor element. Because the parent element, which is the `header` element, has a `position` value of `fixed`, the `top` and `left` values are calculated in relation to the `header` element.

5. **Save your changes to styles.css, reload longpage.html in your browser, then scroll up to the top of the page if necessary**
   The logo placeholder text is displayed next to the main heading and the space reserved for it in the normal flow is removed, as shown in **FIGURE D-25**.

6. **Load longpage.html on a smartphone, then scroll the page and verify that the layout is displayed as expected.**

7. **Validate your HTML and CSS code**

Creating a Cohesive Website

All the pages on a website should be visually similar enough that users can tell that they're on the same site. Visual design, including a color scheme and logo, plays an important role. In addition, page elements, such as headings and sidebars, should appear in a consistent place on every page. Your website designs should also make use of elements that are standard on most other websites, making your website instantly familiar to even first-time visitors. Thus, an important part of creating a new web design is exploring other websites sharing similar audiences or topics to get a clear understanding of the standard elements that users may expect to see.

FIGURE D-22: Implementing absolute positioning

Default layout

Element following absolutely positioned element reflows into space originally occupied by absolutely positioned element

position: absolute; right: 0;

Element position changed relative to original position in normal flow

Layout using absolute positioning

© 2016 Cengage Learning

FIGURE D-23: Logo placeholder element added to longpage.html

```
20          <header>
21              <h1>Lakeland Reeds<br>Bed &amp; Breakfast</h1>
22              <p class="logo">&#8466;&#8475;</p>
23          </header>
```

code for cursive capital L

code for cursive capital R

FIGURE D-24: Style rule to absolutely position element with `logo` class value

```
39   h2 {
40       padding: 0.4em 0.6em;
41   }
42   p.logo {
43       padding: 0.2em;
44       border: 2px solid beige;
45       color: goldenrod;
46       position: absolute;
47       top: 2em;
48       left: 2em;
49   }
```

FIGURE D-25: Logo placeholder absolutely positioned

Logo placeholder text placed next to main heading using absolute positioning

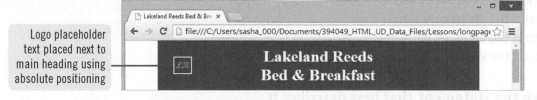

TABLE D-9: CSS properties and values used in absolute positioning

property	value	description
position	absolute	Removes element from normal flow and positions it relative to the closest ancestor element that is also positioned
top, bottom	**value** in ems, pixels, or another supported unit, or **percent** of the height of the browser window	Moves the element the specified distance down from the top edge (top) or up from the bottom edge (bottom) of the closest ancestor element that is also positioned; the default value, 0, leaves the element in its original vertical position
left, right	**value** in ems, pixels, or another supported unit, or **percent** of the width of the browser window	Moves the element the specified distance right from the left edge (left) or left from the right edge (right) of the closest ancestor element that is also positioned; the default value, 0, leaves the element in its original horizontal position

© 2016 Cengage Learning

Practice

Concepts Review

Refer to FIGURE D-26 **to answer the questions that follow.**

FIGURE D-26

© 2016 Cengage Learning

1. **Which item represents the element border?**
2. **Which item represents the element content?**
3. **Which item represents the element width?**
4. **Which item represents the element padding?**
5. **Which item represents the element margin?**

Match each term with the statement that best describes it.

6. **relative positioning**
7. **absolute positioning**
8. **fixed positioning**
9. **lorem ipsum**
10. **layer**

a. a new level of content displayed on top of the normal flow

b. effect in which an element remains in the same position in the browser window while a user scrolls the remaining page content

c. standard filler text used for print layouts

d. lets you make adjustments to the default position of an element while preserving the space allotted to the element in the normal flow

e. takes an element out of the normal flow and allows other elements to flow into the space it would have occupied

Select the best answer from the list of choices.

11. **Which property do you use to align an element horizontally with the left or right edge of its parent element?**
    a. `position`
    b. `z-index`
    c. `float`
    d. `clear`

12. **Which property do you use to precisely specify the location of an element on a web page?**
    a. `position`
    b. `z-index`
    c. `float`
    d. `clear`

13. **Which property do you use to control the stacking order of positioned elements?**
    a. `position`
    b. `z-index`
    c. `float`
    d. `clear`

14. **Which property creates space that is unaffected by an element's background color?**
    a. `width`
    b. `padding`
    c. `margin`
    d. `border`

15. **Which declaration sets an element's padding to 0 on top, 1em on the right and left, and 2.5em on the bottom?**
    a. `padding: 0 1em 1em 2.5em;`
    b. `padding: 1em 2.5em;`
    c. `padding: 0 2.5em 1em;`
    d. `padding: 0 1em 2.5em;`

Skills Review

1. **Set element width and borders.**
    a. In your editor, open HTM_D-4.html from the SR folder where you store your Data Files for this unit, enter your first and last name and today's date in the comment section, save the file as **index.html**, then repeat for HTM_D-5.css, saving it as **styles.css**.
    b. Below the first comment section in styles.css, add a comment containing the text **reset styles**, then create a style rule that applies to the `article`, `body`, `div`, `footer`, `header`, `h1`, `h2`, `h3`, and `p` elements and sets all border widths to 0.
    c. Set the maximum width of the element with the `class` value `container` to 640px.
    d. Set the width of the `div` element within the `header` element to 70% and set 3px solid red borders on all sides.
    e. Add 3px solid black borders to all sides of `p` elements within the `header` element.
    f. Create a style rule that selects the `p` element nested in the `header` element with the `class` value `established`, set its width to 25%, then repeat for the `p` element nested in the `header` element with the class value `award` and for the `p` element nested in the `header` element with the class value `options`.
    g. Set the width of the `p` element nested in the `header` element with the `class` value `phone` to 50%, then set 3px solid red borders on all sides.
    h. Set the width of the `article` element to 65%.
    i. Add 3px solid black borders on all sides of the `footer` element.
    j. Save your changes, preview index.html in a browser, then verify that all the properties you set were applied successfully.

2. **Set margins and padding.**
    a. Return to styles.css in your editor, then in the style rule below the `reset styles` comment, add declarations that set padding and margins to 0.
    b. Set the top and bottom margins of the element with the `class` value `container` to 0 and the left and right margins to auto, then repeat for the `p` element within the `header` element with the `class` value `options` and for the `article` element. (*Hint*: You can set all four values with a single declaration.)
    c. For the `div` element within the `header` element, set the top margin to 0, the bottom margin to 0.6em, and the left and right margins to auto.
    d. Set padding for all `p` elements nested in the `header` element to 6px on all sides.

e. For the p element within the header element with the class value phone, set the top and bottom margins to 0.4em and the left and right margins to auto.

f. Set the padding for the article element to 5em on top and 1em on all other sides, and for the footer element to 0.5em on all sides.

g. Set margins for the h3 element to 1em on top, 0 on the right and left sides, and 0.4em on the bottom.

h. Create a style rule for p elements nested in the article element, then set the bottom margin of these elements to 0.5em.

i. Create a style rule for p elements with the class value myo nested within the article element, then set the left margin of these elements to 1em.

j. Create a style rule for p elements with the class value list nested within the article element, then set the left margin of these elements to 2em.

k. Save your changes, refresh or reload index.html in your browser, then verify that all the properties you set were applied successfully. Refer to **FIGURE D-27** as needed to compare your results to the completed document.

FIGURE D-27

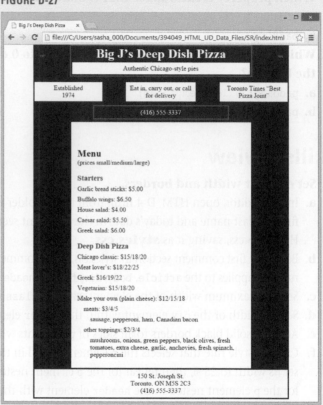

3. Align elements with float and control page flow with clear.

a. Return to styles.css in your editor, float the p element with the class value established nested within the header element to the left, then float the p element with the class value award nested within the header element to the right.

b. Set the p element with the class value phone nested within the header element to clear floats on both margins.

c. Save your changes, refresh or reload index.html in your browser, then verify that all the properties you set were applied successfully.

4. Implement fixed positioning.

a. Return to styles.css in your editor, set the width of the header element to 100% and set its maximum width to 640px.

b. Give the header element a fixed position at the top of the browser window. (*Hint*: Set the top property to 0.)

c. Save your changes, refresh or reload index.html in your browser, scroll down the page, then verify that the properties you set were applied successfully. (*Hint*: Reduce the height of your browser window if necessary to check the scrolling behavior of the document.)

5. Implement relative positioning.

a. Return to styles.css in your editor, then relatively position the element with the class value container, setting its position to be 11em lower than its starting position.

b. Save your changes, refresh or reload index.html in your browser, then verify that all the properties you set were applied successfully.

6. Control stacking order.

a. Return to styles.css in your editor, then stack the header element below the container element. (*Hint*: Use -1 as the stacking value.)

b. Save your changes, refresh or reload index.html in your browser, scroll down to the bottom of the page, then verify that the header is displayed behind the scrolling content.

Skills Review (continued)

 c. Return to styles.css in your editor, then mark the declaration you added in Step a as a comment.

 d. Save your changes, refresh or reload index.html in your browser, scroll down to the bottom of the page, then verify that the header content remains on top of the scrolling content.

7. Implement absolute positioning.

 a. Return to index.html in your editor, add a p element with the class value pointright containing the character code ☛ just before the closing </header> tag, then add another p element below it with the class value pointleft and containing the character code ☚.

 b. Save your changes to index.html, then in styles.css, create style rules for the two elements you created in the previous step, setting the character color to red and the background color to black.

 c. Absolutely position the two elements you created in Step a, setting the element with the class value pointright 0.4em from the top of the parent element and 0.4em from its left side, and setting the element with the class value pointleft 0.4em from the top of the parent element and 0.4em from its right side.

 d. Save your changes, reload index.html in your browser, then verify that pointing finger icons are shown in the top left and right corners of the header. Your completed document should match **FIGURE D-27**.

 e. Open index.html on a smartphone and verify that the layout is displayed as expected.

 f. Validate your HTML and CSS code.

Independent Challenge 1

Sarah Nguyen, the owner of the Spotted Wren Garden Center, has asked you to enhance the layout of the website you created for the store. You start by implementing the new layout on the main page.

 a. In your editor, open HTM_D-6.html from the IC1 folder where you store your Data Files for this unit, enter your first and last name and today's date in the comment section, save the file as **index.html**, then repeat for HTM_D-7.css, saving it as **styles.css**.

 b. In styles.css, create a reset styles comment, then add a style rule under the comment that sets border, margin, and padding to 0 for the article, body, div, footer, header, h1, h2, h3, and p elements.

 c. Below the reset styles style rule, create a global styles section, set the bottom margin of h2 and h3 elements to 0.4em, then set the top and bottom margins of p elements to 0.4em.

 d. Set a bottom border on the header element of 3px solid red, then use the same settings for the top border of the footer element and the left border of the article element.

 e. Set the maximum width of the element with the class value container to 640px, then set the width of the article element to 52% and create a style rule to set the aside element to 38%.

 f. Float the aside element to the left and the article element to the right, then set the footer element to be displayed only when the left and right margins are clear of floated elements.

 g. Set the left and right margins of the element with the class value container to auto.

 h. Add 0.5em padding to the header and footer elements, and 2% padding to the article and aside elements.

 i. Create a style rule for p elements within the article element, then set the left margin of these elements to 1em.

 j. Save your changes to styles.css, open index.html in a browser, then compare your document to **FIGURE D-28**.

 k. Open index.html on a smartphone and verify that the layout is displayed as expected.

 l. Validate your HTML and CSS code.

FIGURE D-28

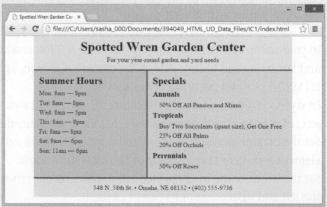

Independent Challenge 2

As you continue your volunteer work creating a website for the Murfreesboro Regional Soccer League, you incorporate some of the layout properties and techniques you've learned to enhance the appearance of the organization's main web page.

a. In your editor, open HTM_D-8.html from the IC2 folder where you store your Data Files for this unit, enter your first and last name and today's date in the comment section, save the file as **index.html**, then repeat for HTM_D-9.css, saving it as **styles.css**.

b. In styles.css, create a reset styles comment, then add a style rule that sets border, margin, and padding to 0 for the article, aside, body, div, footer, header, h1, h2, and p elements.

c. Create a body and page container comment, add a style rule for the element with the class value container below the comment, then set the maximum width of the element to 640px.

d. Create a main content comment, create a style rule for the article element, then set the width of the element to 55%

e. Set the width of the aside element to 35%.

f. Float the aside element to the left and the article element to the right, then set the footer element to be displayed only when the left and right margins are clear of floated elements.

g. Set the margins of the element with the class value container so the element is centered horizontally in the browser window.

h. Add 0.5em padding to the header and footer elements, 2% padding to the aside element, and 3% padding to the article element.

i. Create a style rule for the h2 element within the aside element, then set the bottom margin to 0.4em.

j. Create a style rule for p elements within the aside element, then set the top and bottom margins to 0.4em.

k. Create a style rule for p elements with the class value description within the aside element, then set the left margin to 1em.

l. Add a 3px solid black border around the element with the class value container.

m. Save your changes to styles.css, open index.html in a browser, then compare your document to **FIGURE D-29**.

n. Open index.html on a smartphone and verify that the layout is displayed as expected.

o. Validate your HTML and CSS code.

FIGURE D-29

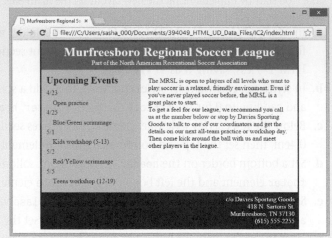

Independent Challenge 3

You've been working with Diego Merckx, the manager of Hotel Natoma, to develop a new layout for the website. You style a page of museum listings with the new layout.

a. In your editor, open HTM_D-10.html from the IC3 folder where you store your Data Files for this unit, enter your first and last name and today's date in the comment section, save the file as **museums.html**, then repeat for HTM_D-11.css, saving it as **styles.css**.

b. In styles.css, create a reset styles comment, then add a style rule that sets border, margin, and padding to 0 for the article, body, div, footer, header, h1, h2, and p elements.

c. Set the maximum width of the element with the class value container to 800px, then set its margins so the element is centered horizontally in the browser window.

d. Set the width of the article element to 60%, then set its margins so its content is horizontally centered between the left and right edges of its parent element.

Independent Challenge 3 (continued)

e. Add 3px solid black borders to the left and right sides of the element with the `class` value `container`, and to the top and bottom of the `header` and `footer` elements.

f. Add 10px padding to the header and footer elements and 15px padding to the article element.

g. Apply fixed positioning to the `header` element 0 px from the top of the browser window, then specify a maximum width of 780px and a width of 100%.

h. Apply 4em of padding to the top of the element with the `class` value `container`, then save styles.css.

i. In museums.html, add 2 p elements as children of the `header` element, each containing the character code `&#9728;`, one with the `class` value `logoleft`, and the other with the `class` value `logoright`, then save museums.html.

j. In styles.css, create a style rule for the p elements nested in the `header` element, then set the text color for the elements to `linen`.

k. Create a style rule for the p element with the `class` value `logoleft` nested in the `header` element, absolutely position the element, then set the element 1em from the top and 3em from the left of the positioned ancestor element.

l. Create a style rule for the p element with the `class` value `logoright` nested in the `header` element, absolutely position the element, then set the element 1em from the top and 3em from the right of the positioned ancestor element.

m. Save your changes to styles.css, open museums.html in a browser, then compare your document to **FIGURE D-30**.

FIGURE D-30

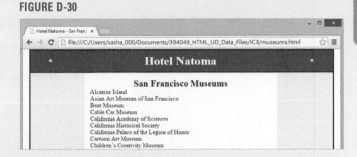

n. Reduce the height of your browser window if necessary so not all page contents are visible, scroll down the page, then verify that the `header` element remains fixed at the top of the window and the remaining text scrolls under it.

o. Open museums.html on a smartphone and verify that the layout is displayed as expected.

p. Validate your HTML and CSS code.

Independent Challenge 4—Explore

As you continue your work building the website for your client Eating Well in Season, you've developed a new visual layout for the site. You'll use positioning to apply the new layout to the main page of the site.

a. In your editor, open HTM_D-12.html from the IC4 folder where you store your Data Files for this unit, enter your first and last name and today's date in the comment section, save the file as **index.html**, then repeat for HTM_D-13.css, saving it as **styles.css**.

b. Add reset styles that set margins, padding, and border to 0 for all elements in use on the page.

c. Create a style rule for the element with the `class` value `container`, set the maximum width of the element to 800px, then center it in the browser window.

d. Set the width of the `article` element to 62.5%, create a style rule for the `aside` element, set its width to 37.5%, then use absolute positioning to display it against the top and right of the element with the `class` value `positioncontainer`. (*Hint*: You can use a `position` value of `relative` to make the parent element the positioning context without changing its location in the layout.)

FIGURE D-31

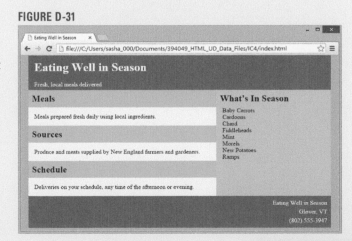

e. Set margins and padding for page elements until your document matches **FIGURE D-31** in a browser.

f. Open index.html on a smartphone and verify that the layout is displayed as expected.

g. Validate your HTML and CSS code.

Visual Workshop

In your editor, open the file HTM_D-14.html from the VW folder where you store your Data Files for this unit, enter your first and last name and today's date in the comment section, save the file as **index.html**, then repeat for HTM_D-15.css, saving it as **styles.css**. Edit styles.css to create the layout shown in FIGURE D-32. When you are finished, open index.html in a browser and on a smartphone and verify that the layout is displayed as expected, then validate your HTML and CSS code.

FIGURE D-32

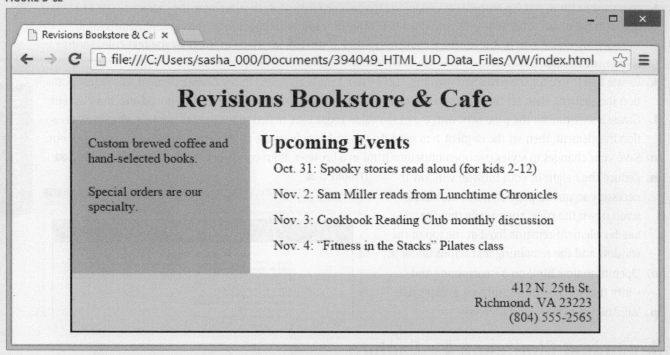

Laying Out Elements With CSS

Formatting Text with CSS

CASE You can use CSS to change the font, size, and color of text, and you can style text with bold, italic, and other variations. As you continue your work on the Lakeland Reeds Bed & Breakfast website, you customize the appearance of text in the web pages.

Unit Objectives

After completing this unit, you will be able to:

- Assess web fonts
- Declare a font family
- Use a custom font
- Declare font size and line height
- Implement bold and italics

- Style pseudo-elements
- Specify hex and RGB colors
- Add shadows
- Create a media query

Files You Will Need

 L   3 files   IC3   3 files

 SR   3 files   IC4   3 files

 IC1   3 files   VW   3 files

 IC2   3 files

For specific filenames, see Filenames_E.pdf in the
Unit E Data Files folder.

Assess Web Fonts

Learning Outcomes
- Describe how to customize web fonts
- Identify the components of a font stack

When you create a document in a word processing program such as Microsoft Word, you can format text with any font installed on your computer. When you create a web document in an editor, you can likewise use CSS to format web page text with different fonts. However, when you style web page text with CSS, you are limited by the fonts available on your *users'* machines. This limitation makes it a challenge to ensure that your web pages appear consistently on different devices. **CASE** *One of your colleagues has created a mock-up of the Lakeland Reeds Bed & Breakfast About Us web page with text formatting. As you prepare to incorporate the fonts and other text characteristics into the web page, you review strategies for working with fonts in web pages.*

DETAILS

Strategies for implementing fonts consistently on the web include the following:

QUICK TIP

Values specified for the font-family property are not case sensitive, but it's common practice to capitalize the first letter of each font family.

- **Specifying multiple font families**

  You specify the font family for the text of an element using the CSS font-family property. The value consists of names of one or more **font families**, which are collections of single typefaces and their variants. For example, the Arial font family contains characters in the standard Arial typeface, including italic and bold versions of those characters. Every operating system has some font families installed by default, but different operating systems often have different fonts installed, meaning that not every browser or user agent has a given font available for rendering. To bridge this discrepancy, CSS enables you to use a font stack as the value of the font-family property. A **font stack** is a list of font families in order of preference, separated by commas. For example,

  ```
  font-family: Tahoma, Arial;
  ```

  specifies that a user agent should display the text of associated elements in the Tahoma font, but if that's not available, the user agent should use Arial instead, as shown in **FIGURE E-1**. **TABLE E-1** lists some font stacks. Note that you surround any font family name containing a space with quotes (for instance, "Times New Roman").

QUICK TIP

When used as one of the values for the font-family property, the name of a default font family is generally all lower case, as sans-serif is in this example.

- **Specifying a generic font family**

  CSS also defines five **generic font families**, which are groupings of font families according to shared characteristics. Two generic font families are based on whether a font incorporates **serifs**, which are small finishing strokes at the ends of lines making up each character. A font that uses these strokes is known as a **serif font**, while a font without these strokes is called a **sans-serif font**. Serif and sans-serif fonts are the most commonly used fonts both online and in print. **TABLE E-2** shows examples of all five generic font families.

  You add the name of a generic font family to the end of a font stack to provide guidance to user agents when your other font family choices are not available. For example,

  ```
  font-family: Tahoma, Arial, sans-serif;
  ```

  instructs user agents without access to either Tahoma or Arial to use the default sans-serif font on the user's system instead. In general, all font stacks should end with a generic font family.

QUICK TIP

Some fonts for creating printed materials are not licensed for use on websites as custom fonts. Always verify that you have permission to use a particular font on your website before doing so.

- **Implementing custom fonts**

  User agents can also download and apply **custom fonts** or **downloadable fonts** that are not installed on a user's computer. Many companies that create and license fonts also enable you to link to fonts on their web servers. To do so, you add a link element to your HTML file using a URL provided by the font host as the value for the href attribute. The URL links to a font-specific style sheet on a web server run by the font provider, which provides the necessary CSS code to make the font available to style elements on your site. Because web server issues can prevent a font from downloading correctly, you should always use a font stack when you use a custom font.

FIGURE E-1: Fonts applied from a font stack

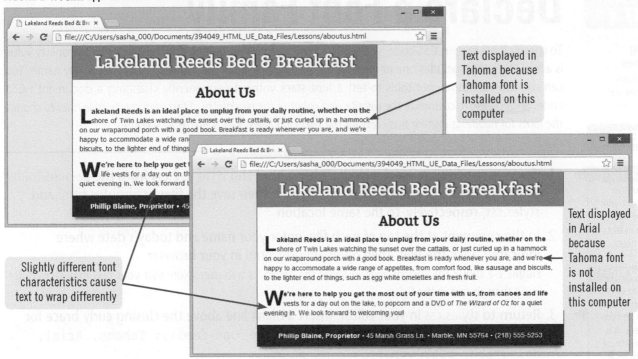

Text displayed in Tahoma because Tahoma font is installed on this computer

Text displayed in Arial because Tahoma font is not installed on this computer

Slightly different font characteristics cause text to wrap differently

TABLE E-1: Commonly used font stacks

font type	font stack
wide sans-serif	Verdana, Geneva, sans-serif
narrow sans-serif	Tahoma, Arial, Helvetica, sans-serif
wide serif	Georgia, Palatino, "Palatino Linotype", serif
narrow serif	"Times New Roman", Times, serif
monospace	"Courier New", Courier, monospace

© 2016 Cengage Learning

TABLE E-2: Generic font families

generic font family	examples	characteristics	best for
Serif	Times New Roman Georgia	Finishing strokes at the end of each line making up a character	Headings on computer screens and other backlit displays
Sans-serif	Arial Tahoma	Lack of serifs	Paragraphs of text on computer screens and other backlit displays
Monospace	Courier New Lucida Console	Each character uses the same amount of horizontal space	Code samples
Cursive	Monotype Corsiva Comic Sans	Flowing strokes that simulate handwritten text	Decorative purposes only, not main web page text, as font families in these groups can be difficult to read
Fantasy	Papyrus Impact	Exaggerated style	

© 2016 Cengage Learning

Declare a Font Family

To specify fonts in your CSS code, you use the `font-family` property. The `font-family` property value is a font stack that includes one or more font family names and ends with a generic font family name. You can use browser developer tools to test a font stack without permanently changing a document's CSS code. **CASE** ▸ *To customize the website and enhance the readability of text, you create style rules to change the fonts for headings and for body text for the Lakeland Reeds Bed & Breakfast website.*

STEPS

1. **Open your editor, open the files HTM_E-1.html and HTM_E-2.css from the Lessons folder where you store your Data Files for this unit, then save the files as aboutus.html and styles.css, respectively, to the same location**

2. **In the comment at the top of each file, enter your name and today's date where indicated, save the files, then open aboutus.html in your browser**
   FIGURE E-2 shows the current appearance of the About Us web page. Note that your text may wrap differently than shown in the figure.

3. **Return to styles.css in your editor, insert a blank line above the closing curly brace for the body style rule, indent as needed, then type** `font-family: Tahoma, Arial, Helvetica, sans-serif;`
   This declaration specifies the default font for all text within the body element. User agents without access to the first choice, Tahoma, should look next for Arial, then, if necessary, for Helvetica. If none of these are available, the text should be displayed in the user agent's default sans-serif font.

4. **Insert a blank line above the closing curly brace for the h1, h2 style rule, indent as needed, then type** `font-family: "Times New Roman", Times, serif;`
   This declaration overrides the default font family you set for the body element. The font name Times New Roman is enclosed in quotes because the name is more than one word. **FIGURE E-3** shows the completed code.

5. **Save your changes to styles.css, then refresh or reload aboutus.html in your browser**
   As **FIGURE E-4** shows, the headings are displayed in Times New Roman or another serif font, and the remaining body text is displayed in Tahoma or another sans-serif font. If the Tahoma font is not installed on your computer, the appearance of body text of your web page may differ from **FIGURE E-4**.

6. **Right-click (Win) or press [control] and click (Mac) the paragraph that begins "We're here," then click Inspect Element**
   The developer tools are displayed.

7. **On the right side of the developer tools pane, click Styles (IE and Chrome) or Rules (Firefox), then scroll down the list of style rules in the right pane to the body rule**

8. **Click the value of the `font-family` property as many times as necessary until it is highlighted in blue, click after the comma following Tahoma to position the insertion point, press [Backspace] (Win) or [delete] (Mac) until the word Tahoma is deleted, then press [Enter]**
   The font Tahoma is removed from the font stack, and the browser displays the body text in Arial instead.

9. **Repeat Step 8 for each of the remaining font families until only `sans-serif` is left**
   Testing all the fonts in your font stack ensures that your layout appears as expected no matter which of the fonts a system uses. Remember that any changes you make to a document's code in browser developer tools are only temporary, and are discarded the next time you refresh or reload the page.

10. **Click the h2 element on the left side of the developer tools pane, scroll as needed on the right side to view the h1, h2 rule, then repeat Steps 8 and 9 to test all fonts in the font stack for the headings**

FIGURE E-2: The About Us web page

Lakeland Reeds Bed & Breakfast

About Us

Lakeland Reeds is an ideal place to unplug from your daily routine, whether on the shore of Twin Lakes watching the sunset over the cattails, or just curled up in a hammock on our wraparound porch with a good book. Breakfast is ready whenever you are, and we're happy to accommodate a wide range of appetites, from comfort food, like sausage and biscuits, to the lighter end of things, such as egg white omelettes and fresh fruit.

We're here to help you get the most out of your time with us, from canoes and life vests for a day out on the lake, to popcorn and a DVD of The Wizard of Oz for a quiet evening in. We look forward to welcoming you!

Phillip Blaine, Proprietor • 45 Marsh Grass Ln. • Marble, MN 55764 • (218) 555-5253

FIGURE E-3: Style sheet containing `font-family` declarations

```
17    /* body */
18    body {
19        max-width: 640px;
20        margin: 0 auto;
21        border-left: 1px solid black;
22        border-right: 1px solid black;
23        background-color: aliceblue;
24        font-family: Tahoma, Arial, Helvetica, sans-serif;
25    }
26
27    /* headings */
28    h1, h2 {
29        padding: 0.4em;
30        text-align: center;
31        font-family: "Times New Roman", Times, serif;
32    }
```

FIGURE E-4: About Us page with updated fonts

h1 and h2 text displayed in Times New Roman

Remaining body text displayed in Tahoma

Lakeland Reeds Bed & Breakfast

About Us

Lakeland Reeds is an ideal place to unplug from your daily routine, whether on the shore of Twin Lakes watching the sunset over the cattails, or just curled up in a hammock on our wraparound porch with a good book. Breakfast is ready whenever you are, and we're happy to accommodate a wide range of appetites, from comfort food, like sausage and biscuits, to the lighter end of things, such as egg white omelettes and fresh fruit.

We're here to help you get the most out of your time with us, from canoes and life vests for a day out on the lake, to popcorn and a DVD of The Wizard of Oz for a quiet evening in. We look forward to welcoming you!

Phillip Blaine, Proprietor • 45 Marsh Grass Ln. • Marble, MN 55764 • (218) 555-5253

Choosing fonts

When deciding which fonts to use for a website, it's important not to use too many fonts, which can make a page chaotic and make it hard for users to understand the relationships among the page contents. A common practice for a basic web page is to start with just two fonts: one serif font and one sans-serif font. The rule of thumb for web design is serif fonts for headings and sans-serif fonts for paragraphs. You can use your browser's developer tools to identify the fonts used by sites you visit.

Use a Custom font

Limiting the fonts in your web pages to those installed on users' devices can result in layouts that don't display uniformly and can greatly reduce your font options. To create a more uniform appearance and open a wider set of font possibilities in your layouts, you can incorporate custom fonts. **CASE** ▶ *You've identified a more modern serif font, which is hosted by Google, to use for the headings on the Lakeland Reeds website. You download the code to link to the font definition from the Google Fonts website and add the new font to your font stack for headings.*

STEPS

1. **In your browser, open** google.com/fonts
   Google makes a collection of custom fonts available for free use. This web page allows you to browse fonts, as shown in **FIGURE E-5**, and generates the appropriate link element for any font you decide to use.

2. **In the search box, type** Bitter
   A preview of the Bitter font is displayed.

3. **Click** Add to Collection, **then at the bottom of the window click** Use
   The Almost done! page opens. To minimize the amount of font data your users have to download, Google defaults to providing only the normal version of a font. You can use the check boxes on this page to make other versions of the font available as well, such as the italic and bold versions.

4. **Scroll down the page to the text** 3. *Add this code to your website,* **click the** link element **below the text to select it, then press [Ctrl][C] (Win) or [command][C] (Mac) to copy the code**
   This element links to a stylesheet containing all the CSS code you need to use the selected font on your website.

5. **Return to** aboutus.html **in your editor, insert a new line below the** script **element in the head section, indent as needed, then press [Ctrl][V] (Win) or [command][V] (Mac) to paste the code**
   The link element is added to the head section, as shown in **FIGURE E-6**.

6. **Save your changes, then return to** styles.css **in your editor**

7. **In the** h1, h2 **style rule, click after the colon for the** font-family **declaration, press [Spacebar], then type** Bitter,
   Adding the link element to the HTML file makes the font available to your website, but you must reference it in a font-family declaration to implement it in your layout. **FIGURE E-7** shows the updated style sheet code.

8. **Save your changes, then open** aboutus.html **in your browser**
   As **FIGURE E-8** shows, the h1 and h2 headings are now displayed using the downloaded Bitter font.

9. **In the developer tools, open the downloaded style sheet using the steps for your browser:**
   • **Chrome: Click** Sources, **on the left side double-click** fonts.googleapis.com, **then click** css?family=Bitter
   • **Firefox: Click** Style Editor (Firefox), **then on the left side click** css 1 rule

   The downloaded style sheet containing an @font-face rule is displayed on the right side of the browser tools.

FIGURE E-5: Google Fonts web page

Search box

Options for viewing only fonts with certain characteristics

Preview text displayed for each font

Click to select font

Click to continue the process of using selected fonts

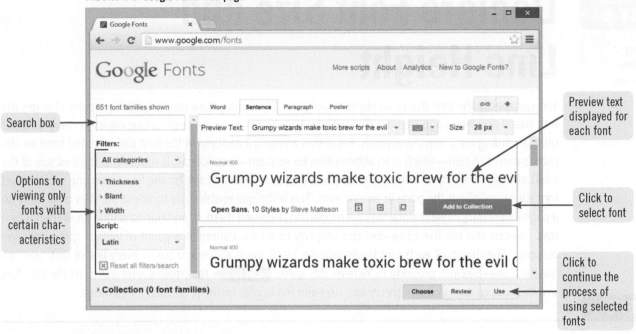

FIGURE E-6: `link` element added to aboutus.html

```
15        <script src="modernizr.custom.62074.js"></script>
16        <link href='http://fonts.googleapis.com/css?family=Bitter' rel='stylesheet'
17        type='text/css'>
18        <link rel="stylesheet" href="styles.css">
```

link element copied from Google Fonts website

href value references an address on a web server

link element for font placed before link element for website style sheet

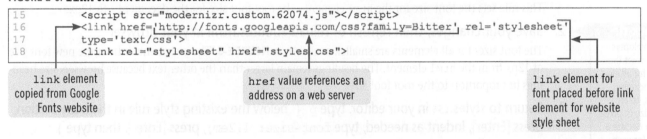

FIGURE E-7: Bitter font added to start of font stack

```
28    h1, h2 {
29        padding: 0.4em;
30        text-align: center;
31        font-family: Bitter, "Times New Roman", Times, serif;
32    }
```

FIGURE E-8: Headings displayed with downloaded font

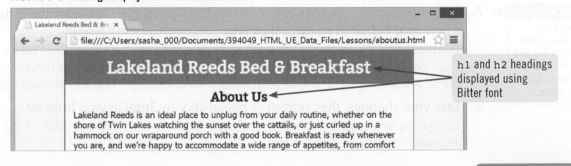

h1 and h2 headings displayed using Bitter font

Learning
Outcomes
• Set font size
• Set line height

Declare Font Size and Line Height

You can specify the font size of an element using the CSS `font-size` property. This property changes the font size of any web page element that includes text. You can specify `font-size` values in many different units, including ems, rems, and pixels. Recall that an em is a multiple of the font size inherited from an element's parent. A rem—which is an abbreviation for root em—is specifically a multiple of the font size of the `html` element. Developers commonly use pixels (px) to set a default size for the `html` element, and then set font sizes throughout the page in ems or rems. This technique enables you to adjust the sizes of all fonts on a page if necessary while maintaining the proportions between them. In addition to setting an element's font size, you can also use the `line-height` property to set the minimum amount of vertical space each line occupies. The design of each font family includes blank space above and below every line of text; you can use the `line-height` property to increase this space. **CASE** ▸ *You create a reset rule to set the base font size for the document. You also specify font sizes and line heights for the* p, h1, *and* h2 *elements.*

STEPS

1. **Return to** styles.css **in your editor, in the reset styles section and above the existing style rule, type** html {, **press [Enter], indent as needed, type** font-size: 12px;, **press [Enter], then type** }

   This rule sets the font size for the `html` element—the root font size for the document—to 12px.

Some developers prefer to reset the font size for all elements, including headings, to an explicit size in pixels, and then declare a font size for each heading.

2. **Save your changes, then refresh or reload aboutus.html in your browser**

   The font sizes for all elements are smaller, as shown in **FIGURE E-9**. The p elements inherit the new font size of 12px from the `html` element. The headings remain larger than the other text because browsers size headings in proportion to the root font size.

3. **Return to** styles.css **in your editor, type** p { **below the existing style rule in the body section, press [Enter], indent as needed, type** font-size: 1.2em;, **press [Enter], then type** }

   This rule sets the font size for all p elements to 1.2 times the inherited font size ($12px \times 1.2 = 14.4px$).

4. **Before the closing curly brace for the** h1 **style rule, add a new line, indent as needed, then type** font-size: 3em;

   This sets the font size for the h1 element to 3 times the inherited font size, or 36px.

5. **Below the** h1 **style rule, type** h2 {, **press [Enter], indent as needed, type** font-size: 2.4em;, **press [Enter], then type** }

   This sets the font size for the h2 element to 2.4 times the inherited font size, or 28.8px.

6. **Save your changes, then refresh or reload aboutus.html in your browser**

   The font size of all elements increases, with the headings slightly larger than their default sizes, and the body text slightly smaller.

Choosing a line height value is often a process of trial and error to find the value that works best for your layout.

7. **Return to** styles.css **in your editor, before the closing curly brace for the** p **style rule, add a new line, indent as needed, then type** line-height: 1.4em;

   This declaration sets the line height for all p elements to 1.4 times the font size of the element itself. For many font families, the default line height is 1.2em, so this rule slightly increases the vertical space for lines of text, which results in more space between lines of text. Your style sheet should match **FIGURE E-10**.

8. **Save your changes, then refresh or reload aboutus.html in your browser**

   The spacing between lines of text in the article section is increased as a result of the line-height declaration, as shown in **FIGURE E-11**.

FIGURE E-9: About Us page after setting root font size

Font sizes of all elements reduced based on smaller inherited font size

FIGURE E-10: Style sheet including `font-size` and `line-height` declarations

```
10    /* reset styles */
11    html {
12        font-size: 12px;
13    }
14    article, body, div, footer, header, h1, h2, p {
29    p {
30        font-size: 1.2em;
31        line-height: 1.4em;
32    }
```

```
40    h1 {
41        color: ivory;
42        background-color: darkgoldenrod;
43        font-size: 3em;
44    }
45    h2 {
46        font-size: 2.4em;
47    }
```

FIGURE E-11: About Us page with new font sizes and line heights

Font sizes of all elements increased based on `font-size` declarations

Space between lines of text in p elements increased as a result of `line-height` declaration

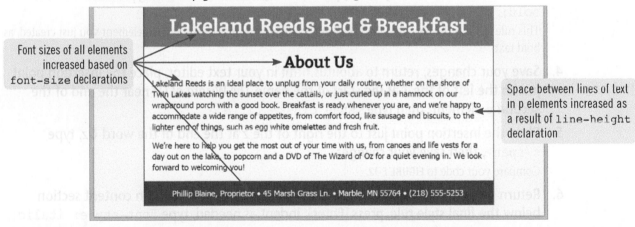

Using white space

Graphic designers refer to empty space in a layout as **white space**. In general, every visual design needs some white space. Empty space in a design helps make it clear where one element ends and another begins. In addition, you can create specific visual effects by varying the amount of white space in a design. You can use the padding property to create white space around an element that shares that element's background color, and you can use the margin property to create white space that uses the background color of the parent element.

Implement Bold and Italics

Learning
Outcomes
• Create a span
  element
• Format text in
  bold
• Format text in
  italics

CSS enables you to modify web page text in a number of ways. Two of the most common are making text bold and italic. You can make text bold using the `font-weight` property, and you can make text italic using the `font-style` property. **TABLE E-3** summarizes the CSS properties related to fonts that you've learned so far in this unit and describes the syntax for the `font` shorthand property. Bold and italic styles are often applied to words or phrases, rather than to entire paragraphs or pages, so you often need a way to indicate the section of a paragraph to format. You can use the `span` element for this purpose. The `span` element is a generic element, like `div`; however, it allows you to isolate a specific section of a larger element. All of the elements you have worked with so far are **block-level elements**, which are boxes occupying the full length of their parent elements and rendered with a line break before and after. The `span` element is an **inline element**, meaning that it does not expand to fill the space of its parent and is not rendered with line breaks before or after. **CASE** *You use the `font-weight` property to apply bold to the name of the owner in the contact information. You also use the `font-style` property to italicize the title of the DVD in the second paragraph.*

STEPS

1. **Return to aboutus.html in your editor, place the insertion point just to the left of the *P* in the name *Phillip Blaine* at the start of the text in the `footer` element, then type** `<span class="accent">`

2. **Place the insertion point just to the right of the *r* at the end of the word *Proprietor*, then type** `</span>`

   The phrase Phillip Blaine, Proprietor is enclosed within the `<span>` tags. This creates an inline element that you can style separately from the surrounding content.

3. **Save your changes, return to styles.css in your editor, type** `.accent {` **in the footer section below the final style rule, press [Enter], indent as needed, type** `font-weight: bold;`, **press** `[Enter]`, **then type** `}`

   This rule formats the element with the `class` value accent, which is the span element you just created, as bold text.

4. **Save your changes, return to aboutus.html in your text editor, place the insertion point just to the left of the *T* at the start of the name *The Wizard of Oz* near the end of the second p element, then type** `<span class="title">`

5. **Place the insertion point just to the right of the *z* at the end of the word *Oz*, type** `</span>`, **then save your changes**

   Compare your code to **FIGURE E-12**.

6. **Return to styles.css in your text editor, type** `.title {` **in the main content section below the final style rule, press [Enter], indent as needed, type** `font-style: italic;`, **press** `[Enter]`, **then type** `}`

   This rule formats the element with the `class` value title as italic text. Your completed style sheet should match **FIGURE E-13**.

7. **Save your changes, then refresh aboutus.html in your browser**

   The movie title *The Wizard of Oz* is displayed in italics, and the text Phillip Blaine, Proprietor in the footer appears in bold, as shown in **FIGURE E-14**.

FIGURE E-12: span elements added to text

Owner's name enclosed within `<span>` tags with class value accent

Movie title enclosed within `<span>` tags with class value title

```
        <p>We&rsquo;re here to help you get the most out of your time w
        canoes and life vests for a day out on the lake, to popcorn and
        <span class="title">The Wizard of Oz</span> for a quiet evening
        forward to welcoming you!</p>
        </article>
        <footer>
          <p><span class="accent">Phillip Blaine, Proprietor</span> &bull; 45 Marsh Grass
          Ln. &bull; Marble, MN 55764 &bull; (218) 555-5253</p>
40      </footer>
```

FIGURE E-13: .title and .accent rules added to style sheet

```
53    article p {
54        padding: 0 1em 1em;
55    }
56    .title {
57        font-style: italic;
58    }
59
60    /* footer section */
                                        //
67    footer p {
68        margin: 0.4em;
69    }
70    .accent {
71        font-weight: bold;
72    }
```

FIGURE E-14: Text formatted in bold and italics

Text styled with the `font-weight` property appears in bold

We're here to help you get the most out of your time with us, from canoes and life vests for a day out on the lake, to popcorn and a DVD of *The Wizard of Oz* for a quiet evening in. We look forward to welcoming you!

Phillip Blaine, Proprietor • 45 Marsh Grass Ln. • Marble, MN 55764 • (218) 555-5253

Text styled with the `font-style` property appears in italics

TABLE E-3: Font properties

property	description	example
font-style	Provides access to a font family's italic or oblique style	`font-style: italic;`
font-variant	Provides access to a font family's small caps style	`font-variant: small-caps;`
font-weight	Sets the weight of text using keywords or values including normal, bold, or a multiple of 100 up to 900, where 100 is lightest and 900 is heaviest	`font-weight: bold;`
font-size	Changes an element's font size to a value specified in an applicable unit, including px, %, rem, or em	`font-size: 2em;`
line-height	Specifies the height of each line containing text in an applicable unit, including px, %, rem, or em	`line-height: 1.4em;`
font-family	Specifies one or more font families and/or a generic font, separated by commas; font family names composed of multiple words must be surrounded by quotes	`font-family: "Times New Roman", Times, serif;`
font	Shorthand property that can set all 6 preceding properties in a single declaration, using the syntax [font-style] [font-variant] [font-weight] font-size [/line-height] font-family; at minimum, both font-size and font-family values must be specified, and all values within square brackets are optional	`font: italic small-caps bold 2em/1.4em "Times New Roman", Times, serif`

Style Pseudo-Elements

As an alternative to the span element, CSS supports another means of selecting specific parts of a block element. A **pseudo-element** is a selector that identifies a specific part of an element and lets you style the selection as if it were its own element. To use a pseudo-element, you begin your selector with a standard selector that identifies the element you wish to style a portion of. You then add a colon (:) followed by the name of the pseudo-element. TABLE E-4 describes five commonly used pseudo-elements. **CASE** *You implement the :first-letter and :first-line pseudo-elements to enhance the appearance of the paragraphs in the article element.*

STEPS

1. **Return to** styles.css **in your editor**

2. **In the main content section and below the closing curly brace for the** article p **style rule, insert a new line, then type** article p:first-line {
   The selector starts with the descendant selector article p. The :first-line pseudo-element is added to the end, resulting in a style rule that modifies the first line of each p element within the article element.

3. **Press [Enter], indent as needed, type** font-weight: bold;, **press [Enter], then type** }

4. **Save your changes, then refresh or reload aboutus.html in your browser**
   As **FIGURE E-15** shows, the entire first line of each paragraph within the article element is displayed in bold.

5. **Return to** styles.css **in your editor, in the main content section and below the closing curly brace for the** article p:first-line **style rule, insert a new line, then type** article p:first-letter {

6. **Press [Enter], indent as needed, type** font-size: 3em;, **press [Enter], indent as needed, type** float: left;, **press [Enter], indent as needed, type** line-height: 0.9em;, **press [Enter], then type** }
   The :first-letter selector allows you to create a **drop cap**, a common visual effect in print media in which the first letter of a paragraph or section is enlarged and drops below the first line of text. You use the float property to make the text that follows the enlarged letter flow around it. Setting the line height for a drop cap is commonly necessary to integrate the letter optimally with the remaining paragraph text. Your code should match **FIGURE E-16**.

7. **Save your changes, then refresh or reload aboutus.html in your browser**
   As **FIGURE E-17** shows, the first letter of each paragraph within the article element is enlarged, and multiple lines of text run to its right.

TABLE E-4: CSS pseudo-elements

pseudo-element	effect	properties commonly used with
:first-line	styles the first line of text in the current element	font-family, font-size, font-weight
:first-letter	styles the first letter of text in the current element	font-family, font-size, line-height
:before	inserts specified content before the content of the current element	content
:after	inserts specified content after the content of the current element	content
:selection	styles web page content selected by user	background-color, color

FIGURE E-15: `:first-line` pseudo-elements styled in paragraphs

Font weight for
entire first line of
each paragraph
set to bold

FIGURE E-16: Style rules using pseudo-elements added to style sheet

```
49    /* main content */
50    article {
51        background-color: ivory;
52    }
53    article p {
54        padding: 0 1em 1em;
55    }
56    article p:first-line {
57        font-weight: bold;
58    }
59    article p:first-letter {
60        font-size: 3em;
61        float: left;
62        line-height: 0.9em;
63    }
64    .title {
65        font-style: italic;
66    }
```

FIGURE E-17: `:first-letter` pseudo-elements styled in paragraphs

First letter
of each
line is
styled as a
drop cap

Specify Hex and RGB Colors

Learning Outcomes
- Specify a color using the hexadecimal system
- Specify a color using the RGB system

You've already practiced setting the color and background color of text using color names. CSS also allows you to specify a color using several other common systems, as described in TABLE E-5. In the **hexadecimal system**—also known as the **hex system**—the value starts with a pound sign (#), followed by six characters, which may include the numbers 0–9 and the letters a–f. The first two characters specify the red value, the middle two characters indicate the green value, and the final pair of characters represents the blue value. The **RGB system** uses a set of comma-separated values known as an **RGB triplet**. Each value ranges from 0–255 or 0–100%, which represent the amounts of red, green, and blue in the color. **CASE** > *You'll specify new colors using hexadecimal and RGB color codes.*

STEPS

1. **Return to** styles.css **in your text editor**

2. **In the** body **style rule, delete the value** aliceblue **in the** background-color **declaration, then replace it with the value** #dee9f9

   This hexadecimal value specifies a light blue color that's slightly different than the aliceblue shade.

3. **In the** h1 **style rule, delete the value** darkgoldenrod **in the** background-color **declaration, then replace it with the value** rgb(184,148,77)

   This RGB value specifies a different medium brown color than the previous one.

4. **In the** footer **style rule, delete the value** saddlebrown **in the** background-color **declaration, then replace it with the value** rgb(52,24,15)

   Compare your updated style sheet to **FIGURE E-18**.

5. **Save your work, then refresh or reload aboutus.html in your browser**

   The background color surrounding the content changes as well as the background colors for the h1 and footer elements, as shown in **FIGURE E-19**.

TABLE E-5: CSS color systems

system	format	support
name	*name* where *name* is a name from the CSS3 list of 147 colors	all browsers
hexadecimal	#*rrggbb* or #*rgb* where *rr* (or *r*) is the red value, *gg* (or *g*) is the green value, and *bb* (or *b*) is the blue value in hexadecimal absolute value (00–FF or 0–F)	all browsers
RGB	rgb(*rrr*,*ggg*,*bbb*) where *rrr* is the red value, *ggg* is the green value, and *bbb* is the blue value in absolute value (0–255) or percent (0%–100%)	all browsers
RGBa	rgba(*rrr*,*ggg*,*bbb*,*a*) same as RGB but where *a* is a decimal value representing the alpha (transparency); 0 is fully transparent and 1 is fully opaque	modern browsers (not IE8)
HSL	hsl(*hhh*,*sss*%,*lll*%) where *hhh* is the hue value in degrees (0–360), *sss* is the saturation value in percent (0%–100%), and *lll* is the light value in percent (0%–100%)	modern browsers (not IE8)
HSLa	hsla(*hhh*,*sss*,*lll*,*a*) same as HSL but where *a* is a decimal value representing the alpha (transparency); 0 is fully transparent and 1 is fully opaque	modern browsers (not IE8)

FIGURE E-18: Color names replaced with hex and RGB colors

```
20    /* body */
21    body {
22        max-width: 640px;
23        margin: 0 auto;
24        border-left: 1px solid black;
25        border-right: 1px solid black;
26        background-color: #dee9f9;
27        font-family: Tahoma, Arial, Helvetica, sans-serif;
28    }
```

Hex value where first two characters specify the red value, next two the green value, and last two the blue value

```
34    /* headings */
35    h1, h2 {
36        padding: 0.4em;
37        text-align: center;
38        font-family: Bitter, "Times New Roman", Times, serif;
39    }
40    h1 {
41        color: ivory;
42        background-color: rgb(184,148,77);
43        font-size: 3em;
44    }
```

RGB value where the first number specifies the red value, the next one the green value, and the last one the blue value

```
68    /* footer section */
69    footer {
70        padding: 0.6em;
71        color: ivory;
72        background-color: rgb(52,24,15);
73        text-align: center;
74    }
```

OK to use different color schemes in the same style sheet

FIGURE E-19: About Us page with updated colors

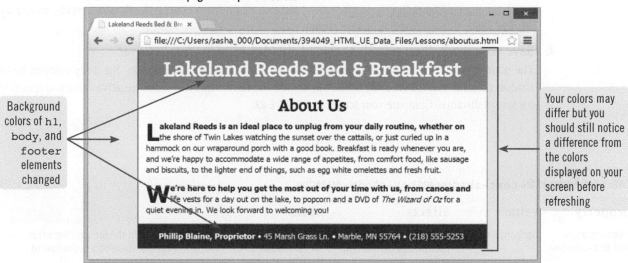

Background colors of h1, body, and footer elements changed

Your colors may differ but you should still notice a difference from the colors displayed on your screen before refreshing

Understanding hexadecimal values

The two RGB color systems—using a triplet of RGB values or using hexadecimal values—allow you to specify the same 16.7 million colors. Each value in an RGB triplet can range from 0 to 255, giving you 256 possible values (1–255, plus the value 0). Hexadecimal values provide the same range using only two characters. The standard decimal numbering system allows 10 possibilities for each digit: the numbers 0–9. Hexadecimal (from roots meaning "six" and "ten") offers 16 possibilities for each character: the numbers 0–9 plus the letters A–F.

Many common colors are represented in hexadecimal notation with repeating pairs of characters (such as #00DDFF). CSS supports shortening these values to three characters, with the assumption that any three-character hexadecimal value represents the color created by doubling each character. For example, a user agent would interpret the hexadecimal value #0DF as #00DDFF.

Add Shadows

Learning
Outcomes
- Add a shadow to text
- Add a shadow to a box element

CSS includes the `text-shadow` and `box-shadow` properties, which automate the creation of shadows for text and box elements, respectively. Each property can take the same basic values for horizontal offset, vertical offset, blur, and shadow color. In addition, box-shadow supports a couple of additional options. **TABLE E-6** and **FIGURE E-20** detail how each value affects the appearance of a shadow for each property. You can add multiple shadows to an element to create more complex effects by separating the values for each shadow with a comma. **CASE** ▸ *You enhance the main heading by adding a text shadow, using the background color of the* `footer` *element for contrast. You also add a box shadow to the body to give the page the appearance of being raised above its background.*

STEPS

QUICK TIP

Many websites such as css3gen.com allow you to create text and box shadows visually using a set of controls, which then generates the code you need based on your selections.

1. **Return to** styles.css **in your editor**

2. **Just above the closing curly brace for the** h1 **style rule, add a new line, indent as needed, then type** `text-shadow: 2px -1px 2px rgb(52,24,15);`

   This code creates a text shadow with a positive horizontal offset (placing the shadow to the right of the text), a negative vertical offset (placing the shadow above the text), a blur radius, and a shadow color that matches the dark brown color used as the background for the `footer` element.

3. **Just above the closing curly brace for the** body **style rule, add a new line, indent as needed, then type** `box-shadow: 0 10px 6px -6px #777;`

   This code creates a box shadow with no horizontal offset, a positive vertical offset (placing the shadow below the box), a blur radius, a negative spread distance that reduces how far the shadow spreads, and a gray shadow color. Your code should match **FIGURE E-21**.

4. **Save your work, then refresh or reload aboutus.html in your browser**

   The main heading text has a dark shadow above it and to its right. In addition, the `body` element has a shadow below it that moves away from both the left and right edges due to the negative value you specified for spread distance. Compare your screen to **FIGURE E-22**.

TABLE E-6: Syntax of the `text-shadow` **and** `box-shadow` **properties**

property	value	affects	notes
`text-shadow` and `box-shadow`	horizontal offset	location of shadow horizontally behind text or box	Required value; must be the first number in the list; positive value offsets shadow to the right, and negative value offsets shadow to the left
	vertical offset	location of shadow vertically behind text or box	Required value; must be the second number in the list; positive value offsets the shadow down, and negative value offsets the shadow up
	blur radius	blurriness of shadow	Optional value; must be positive; must be third number in list; value of 0 creates a shadow with a sharp edge
	color	color of shadow behind text or box	Optional value; may appear before or after numerical settings
`box-shadow` only	spread distance	expansion or contraction of shadow	Optional value; must be the fourth number in the list; positive value expands shadow by the specified value, and negative value contracts the shadow
	inset	whether shadow is displayed outside or inside of border	Optional `inset` keyword makes the shadow display inside the element border; may appear before or after other settings

FIGURE E-20: text-shadow and box-shadow examples

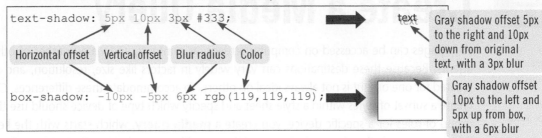

```
text-shadow: 5px 10px 3px #333;                        text
```

Horizontal offset   Vertical offset   Blur radius   Color

Gray shadow offset 5px to the right and 10px down from original text, with a 3px blur

```
box-shadow: -10px -5px 6px rgb(119,119,119);
```

Gray shadow offset 10px to the left and 5px up from box, with a 6px blur

FIGURE E-21: Code for text shadow and box shadow

```
20   /* body */
21   body {
22       max-width: 640px;
23       margin: 0 auto;
24       border-left: 1px solid black;
25       border-right: 1px solid black;
26       background-color: #dee9f9;
27       font-family: Tahoma, Arial, Helvetica, sans-serif;
28       box-shadow: 0 10px 6px -6px #777;
29   }
30   p {
```

```
41   h1 {
42       color: ivory;
43       background-color: rgb(184,148,77);
44       font-size: 3em;
45       text-shadow: 2px -1px 2px rgb(52,24,15);
46   }
```

FIGURE E-22: About Us page with text shadow and box shadow

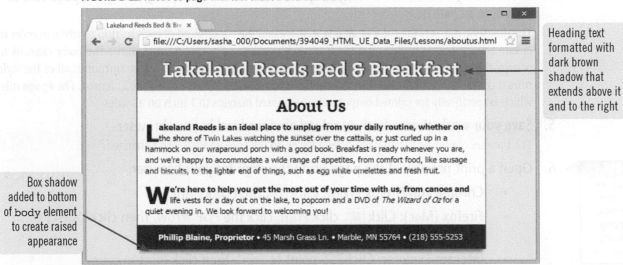

Heading text formatted with dark brown shadow that extends above it and to the right

Box shadow added to bottom of body element to create raised appearance

Picking a color scheme

Although hex and RGB values make over 16 million colors available for use on your web pages, it's best not to try to use all of them at once. In fact, visual designs often use only two or three colors that complement each other.

In any color scheme, the colors are not used equally—generally, one or two of the colors are reserved as accent colors. Many free tools are available to help you create color schemes. You can use a website such as paletton.com to identify complementary colors and create a color scheme. You can also install the free Adobe Color app on a mobile device to automatically generate a color scheme using your camera.

Create a Media Query

Learning Outcomes
• Create a media query
• View a print preview of a web page

Web pages can be accessed on computer screens, as printouts, and via a number of other types of user agents. Because these destinations can vary widely in factors like size, resolution, and contrast, styling created for one output is not always ideal on others. To accommodate these differences, CSS allows you to create a subset of styles within a style sheet and specify which type of device should use them. To create a group of rules for a specific device, you create a **media query**, which starts with the keyword @media, lists one or more values for media type, and then specifies style rules specific to this media, enclosed within curly braces. **TABLE E-7** describes the available media type values. For printed output, CSS also supports the @page **rule**, which is used in a way that is similar to a selector and which enables you to set properties that apply to a printed page. The @page rule is commonly used to specify margins for printed output. Recall that if a style sheet contains two declarations with the same specificity that apply to the same element, the last one is applied. For this reason, you should place media queries after the general style rules in your style sheets. **CASE** ▶ *You create a media query for printed output.*

STEPS

1. **Return to** styles.css **in your editor**

2. **Below the closing curly brace for the final style rule, add two blank lines, then add the comment** /* print styles */

3. **Below the comment you added, add a new line, type** @media print {, **press** [Enter], **then indent as needed**

   The print value specifies that the associated style rules are for rendering the output on a printer.

4. **Enter the style rules, the closing curly brace for the media query, and the** @page **rule as shown in FIGURE E-23.**

   The first style rule sets the color of all text to black and the background of each section to white in order to ensure the content is legible on a black and white printer. The second rule allows the body element to occupy the entire width of the page and removes the borders. The media query surrounds all of the style rules it contains in a set of curly braces, and the style rules in the media query are indented. The @page rule, which is specifically for printed output, sets the printed margins to 1 inch on all sides.

5. **Save your work, then refresh or reload aboutus.html in your browser**

   The browser continues to apply the default styles, so the appearance doesn't change.

6. **Open a print preview of the page using the steps for your browser:**

   • **Chrome and Firefox (Win): Click** ≡, **then click** Print

   • **Firefox (Mac): Click** ≡, **click** Print, **click the** PDF arrow, **then click** Open PDF in Preview

   • **Internet Explorer: Click** ⚙, **point to** Print, **then click** Print preview

   A preview of the printed page is displayed, showing the text in black with a white background and no border. **FIGURE E-24** shows the preview in Chrome.

TABLE E-7: Media type values for media queries

media type	intended use
all	All devices
print	Printed output and print preview on a screen
screen	Computer screen
speech	Screen reader

FIGURE E-23: Media query for printed output added to style sheet

```
84    /* print styles */
85    @media print {
86        body, h1, article, footer {
87            color: #000;
88            background-color: #fff;
89        }
90        body {
91            max-width: 100%;
92            border: 0;
93        }
94    }
95    @page {
96        margin: 1in;
97    }
```

Style rules indented within curly braces for media query

FIGURE E-24: Print preview of About Us web page in Chrome

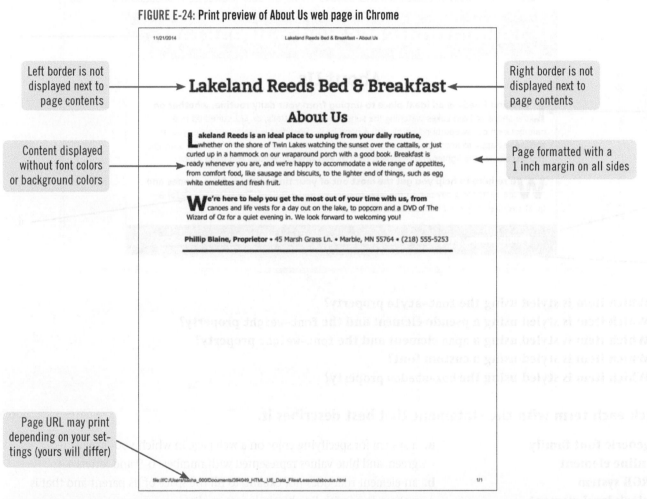

Left border is not displayed next to page contents

Right border is not displayed next to page contents

Content displayed without font colors or background colors

Page formatted with a 1 inch margin on all sides

Page URL may print depending on your settings (yours will differ)

Creating media-specific styles using other methods

In addition to creating a media query within a style sheet, you can incorporate styles targeted at specific media in your web documents in different ways. One option is to place the media-specific styles in their own style sheet document, link that style sheet to the HTML file using a separate link element, and then use the media attribute to specify the appropriate media type(s). Especially on a larger website where the style sheets consist of hundreds or thousands of lines of code, dividing up style sheets in this manner can help keep the styles organized, and can allow different team members to work on different documents simultaneously without interfering with each other's work. Note that if you use multiple link elements, the general style sheet should come first in the HTML code, followed by the media-specific styles so that the general styles do not override the media-specific styles when rendered by a user agent.

Practice

Concepts Review

Refer to FIGURE E-25 **to answer the questions that follow.**

FIGURE E-25

1. **Which item is styled using the** font-style **property?**
2. **Which item is styled using a pseudo-element and the** font-weight **property?**
3. **Which item is styled using a** span **element and the** font-weight **property?**
4. **Which item is styled using a custom font?**
5. **Which item is styled using the** box-shadow **property?**

Match each term with the statement that best describes it.

6. **generic font family**
7. **inline element**
8. **RGB system**
9. **block-level element**
10. **font stack**
11. **hexadecimal system**
12. **media query**

a. a system for specifying color on a web page in which you provide red, green, and blue values represented with numbers 0–9 and letters a–f

b. an element that does not expand to fill the space of its parent and that is not rendered with line breaks before or after

c. a system for specifying color on a web page in which you provide red, green, and blue values represented as one-, two-, or three-digit numbers

d. a grouping of font families according to shared characteristics

e. a variation of a style rule that you use to create a group of rules for a specific device

f. a list of font families in order of preference, separated by commas

g. an element rendered as a box occupying the full length of its parent element, with a line break before and after

Select the best answer from the list of choices.

13. You set the amount of vertical space a line of text occupies using the CSS _____ property.
    a. `font-weight`
    b. `font-style`
    c. `line-height`
    d. `font-family`

14. You format web page text as bold using the CSS _____ property.
    a. `font-family`
    b. `font-weight`
    c. `font-style`
    d. `font-size`

15. You specify the size of web page text using the CSS _____ property.
    a. `font-size`
    b. `line-height`
    c. `font-family`
    d. `font-weight`

16. You format web page text as italic using the CSS _____ property.
    a. `font-size`
    b. `line-height`
    c. `font-family`
    d. `font-style`

17. The _____ element is a generic element that allows you to isolate a specific section of a larger element.
    a. `div`
    b. `span`
    c. `p`
    d. `h1`

18. `sans-serif` is an example of a(n) _____.
    a. font stack
    b. inline element
    c. font family
    d. generic font family

19. `:first-line` is an example of a(n) _____.
    a. font family
    b. media query
    c. pseudo-element
    d. `@page` rule

Skills Review

1. **Declare a font family.**
   a. In your editor, open the file HTM_E-3.html from the SR folder where you store your Data Files for this unit, save it as **history.html**, then repeat to save the file HTM_E-4.css as **styles.css**.
   b. Within the comment section at the top of each file, enter your first and last names and today's date, then save your changes.
   c. Preview history.html in your browser.
   d. Return to styles.css in your editor, in the body and container section (the code following the body and container comment), create a rule for the `p` element, then add a declaration to style the text with the font stack Arial, Helvetica, sans-serif.
   e. Save your changes, then refresh or reload history.html in your browser and verify that all `p` elements are styled with the appropriate font.
   f. Use the developer tools in your browser to test the layout with each font family in the font stack.

2. **Use a custom font.**
   a. In your browser, open google.com/fonts.
   b. Search on the font name Playfair, then add the font Playfair Display to your collection. (*Hint*: Do not select Playfair Display SC.)
   c. Click Use, select the Normal 400 and Ultra-Bold 900 styles, then copy the generated `link` element.
   d. Return to history.html in your editor, paste the `link` element into the head section before the `link` element for styles.css, then save your changes.

Skills Review (continued)

e. Return to styles.css in your editor, then in the h1, h2 style rule, add a declaration to style the text with the font stack Playfair Display, Times New Roman, Times, serif. (*Hint*: Remember to use quotation marks around a font name that consists of multiple words, and be sure that the commas separating font names are outside of the quotes.)

f. Save your changes, then refresh or reload history.html in your browser and verify that the h1 and h2 elements are styled with the appropriate font.

g. Use the developer tools in your browser to test the layout with each font family in the font stack for the h1 and h2 elements.

3. Declare font size and line height.

a. Return to styles.css in your editor, then, at the top of the reset styles section, create a style rule for the html element that sets the font size to 12px.

b. Set the font size for p elements to 1.6em and line height to 1.4em.

c. Set the font size for h1 elements to 4em and the font size for h2 elements to 2.8em

d. Save your changes, then refresh or reload history.html in your browser and verify that the p, h1, and h2 elements are styled with the appropriate font size and line height.

4. Implement bold and italics.

a. Return to history.html in your text editor, then create a span element with the class value title containing the text Toronto Times in the second paragraph in the article element.

b. Create a span element with the class value accent containing the text (416) 555-3337 in the footer element, then save your changes.

c. Return to styles.css in your text editor, add a declaration to set the font weight for the h1 element to 900.

d. Add a declaration to set the font weight for the element with the class value contrastbox to bold, then add a declaration to set the font weight for the element with the class value accent to bold.

e. Add a declaration to set the font style for the element with the class value title to italic, then save your changes.

f. Save your changes, then refresh or reload history.html in your browser and verify that the appropriate elements are styled with bold and with italics.

5. Style pseudo-elements.

a. Return to styles.css in your editor, then, in the main content section, create a style rule to select the first letter of the paragraph element with the class value firstparagraph within the article element.

b. Add declarations to the new style rule that set its font size to 3em, its line height to 0.9em, and float it to the left.

c. Save your changes, then refresh or reload history.html in your browser and verify that the first letter of the first paragraph after the h2 heading is displayed as a drop cap.

6. Specify hex and RGB colors.

a. Return to styles.css in your editor.

b. Set the background color of the body element to #ddd, the background color of the element with the class value container to rgb(255,204,102), and the background color of the article element to #fff.

c. Set the background color of the element with the class value contrastbox to #ddd, and add a 1px solid border using the color #777.

d. Save your changes, then refresh or reload history.html in your browser and verify that the page is styled with the appropriate background and border colors.

Skills Review (continued)

7. Add shadows.

  a. Return to styles.css in your editor.

  b. Add a text shadow to the h2 element with 2px horizontal offset, -1px vertical offset, 2px blur radius, and a color of rgb(255,204,102).

  c. Add a box shadow to the element with the `class` value `contrastbox` with 3px horizontal and vertical offset, 0 blur radius, and a color of #777.

  d. Save your changes, then refresh or reload history.html in your browser and verify that the appropriate elements have been styled with the text shadow and box shadow you specified. Your document should match **FIGURE E-26**.

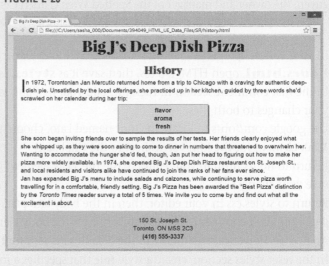

8. Create a media query.

  a. Return to styles.css in your editor.

  b. At the bottom of the document, add a comment containing the text **print styles** and then create a media query for print devices.

  c. Within the media query, add the following style rules:

    • a style rule for the body, h2, and `article` elements that sets text color to #000 and background-color to #fff.

    • a style rule for the body element that sets its maximum width to 100%.

  d. Below the media query, create a style rule for printed pages that sets all margins to 1in. (*Hint*: Use the @page selector.)

  e. Save your changes, refresh or reload history.html, open a print preview of your document, then verify it matches the one shown in **FIGURE E-27**.

FIGURE E-27

Independent Challenge 1

Sarah Nguyen, the owner and manager of the Spotted Wren Garden Center, is happy with your work so far on the company's website. She'd like you to begin to personalize the site by using a new font, styling the text, and incorporating a new set of colors.

a. In your editor, open HTM_E-5.html from the IC1 folder where you store your Data Files for this unit, save it as **hours.html**, open HTM_E-6.css, then save it as **styles.css**.

b. In the first comment section in each file, add your first and last names and today's date where indicated, then save your changes to both files.

c. Use google.com/fonts to locate the font named Lato, choose the Normal 400 and Bold 700 styles, then copy the `link` element for the font's stylesheet to the Clipboard

d. Return to hours.html in your editor, paste the `link` element just before the `link` element for your stylesheet, then save your changes.

e. Return to styles.css in your editor, then in the body and page container section (the code following the body and page container comment), create a style rule for the `body` element that uses Lato as the font family and falls back to Arial, then Helvetica, and finally to the default sans-serif font, and sets a background color of `#fff`.

f. In the reset styles section, create a style rule that specifies a font size of 12px for the `html` element.

g. In the global styles section, set the font size for the p element to 1.2em.

h. In the header section, create a style rule for the h1 element that sets the font size to 3em and the font weight to `bold`.

i. In the main content section, set the font size for the h2 element to 2.4em and the font weight to `bold`.

j. Return to hours.html in your editor, in the `article` element enclose each day of the week and the colon that follows it in a `span` element, then save your changes.

k. Return to styles.css in your editor, then in the main content section, set the font weight for `span` elements nested in p elements within the `article` element to `bold` and set their text color to `green`.

l. In the header section, specify a text color of #f15a24 for the p element nested within the `header` element.

m. In the body and page container section, set the background color of the element with the `class` value `container` using the following RGB values: red: 106, green: 194, blue: 56.

n. In the main content section, set the background color of the `article` element to `#fff`.

o. In the page and body container section, add a box shadow to the element with the `class` value `container` that has 0 horizontal and vertical offsets, 10px of blur, and uses the color `#000`.

FIGURE E-28

p. Preview your web page in a browser and compare your screen to **FIGURE E-28**.

q. Validate both your HTML and CSS documents.

r. Use the developer tools in your browser to test the layout with each font family in the font stack for the `body` element.

Independent Challenge 2

As you continue developing the website for the Murfreesboro Regional Soccer League, you incorporate font styling and colors into the site.

a. In your editor, open HTM_E-7.html from the IC2 folder where you store your Data Files for this unit, save it as **index.html**, open HTM_E-8.css, then save it as **styles.css**.

b. In the first comment section in each file, add your first and last names and today's date where indicated, then save your changes to both files.

c. In the reset styles section (the code following the reset styles comment), create a style rule that specifies a font size of 14px for the `html` element.

d. In the body and page container section, set the font family for the `body` element to Arial, specifying Helvetica as a fallback and sans-serif as the generic font.

e. In the body and page container section, create a style rule that sets the font size for p elements to 1.2em.

f. In the header section, set the background color of the `header` element to the color with the following RGB values: red: 140, green: 198, blue: 63.

g. In the header section, create a style rule for the `h1` element that sets the font size to 2em, the line height to 1.4em, the font family to Georgia with Times New Roman and Times as fallbacks and serif as the generic font, and creates a text shadow with 0 horizontal and vertical offsets, 10px of blur, and a color of ivory.

h. In the header section, create a style rule for p elements nested in the `header` element that sets the font style to italic.

i. In the main content section, create a style rule for the first line of the p element with the `class` value `firstparagraph` nested within the `article` element that sets the font weight to bold.

j. In the sidebar section, set the background color of the `aside` element to the value #c8f098.

k. In the sidebar section, set the font family for the `h2` element nested in the `aside` element to Georgia, with Times New Roman and Times as fallbacks and a generic font of serif, and set the font size to 1.6em.

l. In the sidebar section, set the font weight of p elements with the `class` value `accent` nested in the `aside` element to bold.

m. In the footer section, create a style rule for p elements with the `class` value `accent` nested in the `footer` element that sets the font weight to bold.

n. Save your changes, open index.html in a browser, then compare your document to **FIGURE E-29**.

o. Use the developer tools in your browser to test the layout with each font family in the font stack for the `body` and `h1` elements.

FIGURE E-29

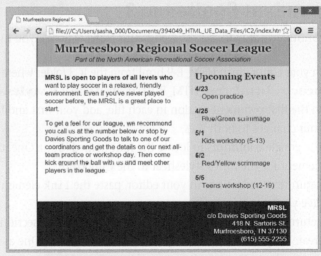

Independent Challenge 2 (continued)

p. Return to styles.css in your editor, add a comment at the bottom of the style sheet containing the text **print styles**, then use a media query to specify the following styles for printed output:

- For the aside, body, footer, and header elements and the element with the class value container, set the text color to #000, the background color to #fff, and the border to 0.
- For the body element, set the maximum width to 100%.
- For the header element, add a 2px solid black bottom border.
- For the aside element, add a 2px solid black left border.
- For the footer element, add a 2px solid black top border.

q. Below the media query, create a style rule that specifies 1in margins on all sides of a printed page.

r. Save your changes, refresh or reload index.html in your browser, display a print preview of the document, then compare your preview to **FIGURE E-30**.

FIGURE E-30

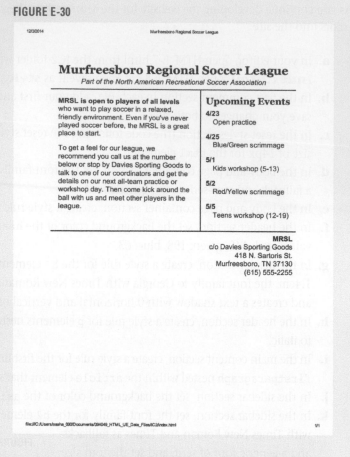

Independent Challenge 3

As you continue your work on the website for Hotel Natoma, you incorporate fonts and colors using CSS.

a. In your editor, open HTM_E-9.html from the IC3 folder where you store your Data Files for this unit, save it as **nearby.html**, open HTM_E-10.css, then save it as **styles.css**.

b. In the first comment section in each file, add your first and last names and today's date where indicated, then save your changes to both files.

c. Use google.com/fonts to locate the font named Krona One, choose the Normal 400 style, then copy the link element for the font's stylesheet to the Clipboard

d. Return to nearby.html in your editor, paste the link element just before the link element for your stylesheet, then save your changes.

e. Return to styles.css in your editor, then in the header section (the code following the header section comment), create a style rule for the h1 element that uses Krona One as the font family and falls back to Arial, then Helvetica, and finally to the default sans-serif font. Repeat in the aside section for the h2 element nested within the aside element.

f. In the style rule for the h1 element, set the font size to 2.4em, the line height to 1.6em, and the font weight to 400.

g. In the style rule for the h2 element nested within the aside element, set the font size to 1.6em, the line height to 2em, and the font weight to 400.

Independent Challenge 3 (continued)

h. In the reset styles section, create a style rule that specifies a font size of 14px for the `html` element.

i. In the body and page container section, create a style rule that sets the font family for the `body` element to Arial, with a fallback of Helvetica and a generic font of sans-serif. Also create a style rule for the `p` element that sets the font size to 1.4em.

j. In the main content section, set the font size for the `p` element within the `article` element to 2.1em and the line height to 1.4em.

k. In the header section, set the background color of the `header` element using the following RGB values: red: 8, green: 32, blue: 8, repeat in the footer section for the `footer` element, then in the sidebar section set the background color for the `aside` element using the following RGB values: red: 147, green: 173, blue: 120.

l. In the header section, create a style rule for the first letter of the h1 element that sets the text color using the following RGB values: red: 8, green: 32, blue: 8, and sets the background color using the following RGB values: red: 147, green: 173, blue: 120.

FIGURE E-31

m. In the sidebar section, create a style rule for the first letter of each p element nested within the `aside` element that creates a text shadow with 1px horizontal offset, -1px vertical offset, 2px blur, and a color of `linen`.

n. In the body and page container section, add a box shadow to the element with the `class` value `container` with 0 horizontal offset, 10px vertical offset, 6px blur, -6px spread, and a color of #777.

o. Save your changes, open nearby.html in a browser, then compare your document with **FIGURE E-31**.

p. Use the developer tools in your browser to test the layout with each font family in the font stack for the `body`, h1 and h2 elements.

q. Return to styles.css in your editor, add a comment at the bottom of the style sheet containing the text **print styles**, then use a media query to specify the following styles for printed output:

- For the `article`, `aside`, `body`, `footer`, and `header` elements, set the text color to #000 and the background color to #fff.
- For the `body` element, set the maximum width to 100%.

r. Below the media query, create a style rule that specifies 1in margins on all sides of a printed page.

s. Save your changes, refresh or reload nearby.html in your browser, display a print preview of the document, then compare your preview to **FIGURE E-32**.

FIGURE E-32

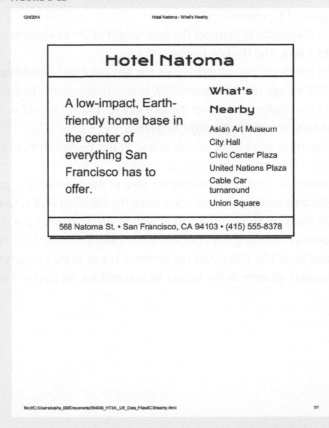

Independent Challenge 4 – Explore

As you continue your work creating the website for Eating Well in Season, a local food delivery company, you customize the design's fonts and colors.

a. In your editor, open HTM_E-11.html from the IC4 folder where you store your Data Files for this unit, save it as **index.html**, open HTM_E-12.css, then save it as **styles.css**.

b. In the first comment section in each file, add your first and last names and today's date where indicated, then save your changes to both files.

c. Use google.com/fonts to locate the font named Alegreya Sans, choose the Normal 400 style, then copy the `link` element for the font's stylesheet to the Clipboard

d. Return to index.html in your editor, paste the `link` element just before the `link` element for your stylesheet, then save your changes.

e. Return to styles.css in your editor, then in the body and page container section (the code following the body and page container comment), create a style rule that sets the font family for the `body` element to Alegreya Sans with a fallback to Arial, then Helvetica, and finally to the default sans-serif font. Also set the background color for the `body` element using the following RGB values: red: 170, green: 189, blue: 126.

f. In the body and page container section, create a style rule for the `p` element that uses the `font` shortcut property to set the font size to 1.6em and the font family to Verdana with a fallback to Geneva and a generic font of sans-serif.

g. In the reset styles section, create a style rule that specifies a font size of 12px for the `html` element.

h. In the body and page container section, specify a background color for the element with the `class` value `container` using the following HSL values: hue: 53 degrees, saturation: 91%, light: 61%. (*Hint*: Use the syntax for the HSL color system rather than the RGB color system, and be sure to include the % symbol after the second and third values.) In the header section, use the same color as the text color for the `h1` element nested in the `header` element.

i. In the header section, set the background color for the `header` element using the following RGB values: red: 161, green: 127, blue: 67.

j. In the header section, set the font weight of the `h1` element nested in the `header` element to normal, the font size to 4.6em, and the line height to 0.8em.

k. In the main content section, set the text color for `h2` elements nested in the `article` element using the following RGB values: red: 152, green: 192, blue: 61. Also set the font size to 2.8em and the font weight to `normal`.

l. In the sidebar section, set the font size for the `h2` element nested in the `aside` element to 2.8em, the line height to 0.8em, and the font weight to `normal`.

m. Return to index.html in your editor, in the `footer` element enclose each instance of the `&bull;` character code in a `span` element, then save your changes.

n. Return to styles.css in your editor, then in the footer section, add a style rule for `span` elements nested in the `footer` element that sets the font color using the following RGB values: red: 161, green: 127, blue: 67.

o. In the body and page container section, create an inset box shadow for the element with the `class` value `container` using 0 horizontal offset, 0 vertical offset, 3px blur, 5px spread, and the RGB values red: 170, green: 189, and blue: 126. (*Hint*: Add the keyword `inset` to the property value to create an inset shadow.) Repeat for the `header` element in the header section and for the `footer` element in the footer section.

Independent Challenge 4 – Explore (continued)

p. In the main content section, create an inset box shadow for the article element using 5px horizontal offset, 0 vertical offset, 3px blur, and the RGB values red: 170, green: 189, and blue: 126. (*Hint*: Add the keyword `inset` to the property value to create an inset shadow.)

q. Save your changes, open index.html in a browser, then compare your document with **FIGURE E-33**.

r. Use the developer tools in your browser to test the layout with each font family in the font stack for the `body` and `p` elements.

s. Return to styles.css in your editor, add a comment at the bottom of the style sheet containing the text **print styles**, then use a media query to specify the following styles for printed output:

- For the `article`, `article h2`, `aside`, `body`, `.container`, `footer`, `header`, `header h1`, and `header p` selectors, set the text color to #000, the background color to #fff, and the box shadow to `none`.
- For the `body` element, set the maximum width to 100%.

t. Below the media query, create a style rule that specifies 1in margins on all sides of a printed page.

u. Save your changes, refresh or reload index.html in your browser, display a print preview of the document, then compare your preview to **FIGURE E-34**.

FIGURE E-33

FIGURE E-34

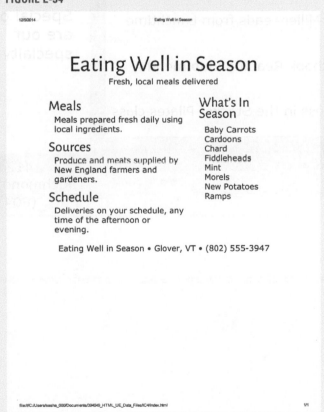

Visual Workshop

In your text editor, open the file HTM E-13.html from the VW folder where you store your Data Files for this unit, save the file as **events.html**, then repeat to save HTM_E-14.css as **styles.css**. Preview events.html in a browser. Use your text editor to style the web page to match the one shown in **FIGURE E-35**. Specify a font stack starting with Verdana as the default font family for the body element. Use the ultra-bold style of the downloadable Google wide serif font Playfair Display for the h1 and h2 headings. Use the RGB triplet 189,204,212 for the background color of the header and footer sections, and the RGB triplet 198,156,109 for the background color of the article element containing the Upcoming Events list. Be sure to format the dates in bold. Add text shadows to the first letters of the h1 and h2 headings, as well as to the first letter of each p element in the sidebar using the RGB triplet 198,156,109. Add a box shadow around the upcoming events list and another one around the parent element of the page contents.

FIGURE E-35

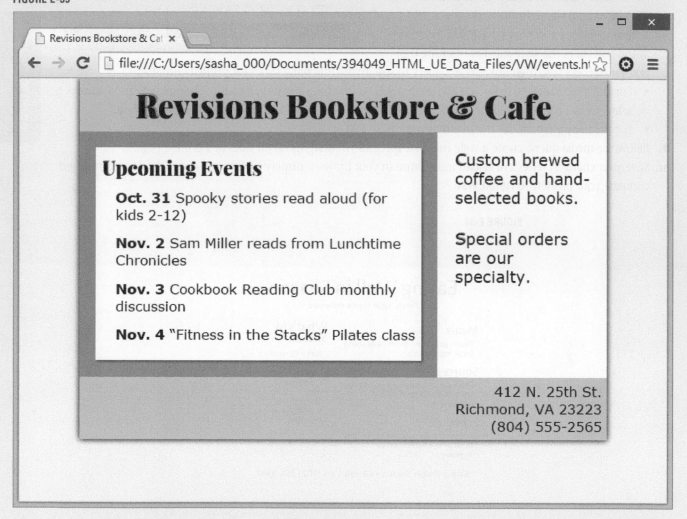

Formatting Text with CSS

Inserting and Working with Links

CASE ▶ Now that you have created a basic set of web pages for Lakeland Reeds Bed & Breakfast, you integrate them together as a website by creating links between the pages. You also link to relevant information available on another website.

Unit Objectives

After completing this unit, you will be able to:

- Understand links
- Create relative links
- Create absolute links
- Change CSS display type
- Style links with a pseudo-class

- Style multiple link states
- Open links in new tabs
- Link within a document
- Aid navigational accessibility

Files You Will Need

 L   7 files   IC3   4 files

 SR   6 files   IC4   5 files

 IC1   5 files   VW   5 files

 IC2   5 files

For specific filenames, see Filenames_F.pdf in the
Unit F Data Files folder.

Understand Links

Learning
Outcomes
• Describe how
  to link web
  documents
• Identify the
  components of
  a URL

While a website is made up of a collection of web pages, another important element sets a website apart from a simple group of pages: linking. A **hyperlink**, more commonly known as a **link**, is text or another web page element that users can select to move to related content in the same page or in another document. Links let you widen the scope of a web page from a stand-alone source of information to an integral part of a set of options available on a website. In turn, links enable you to integrate the contents of a website with anything available on the web. **CASE** *As you prepare to incorporate links into the Lakeland Reeds B&B website, you review how to create and organize web page links.*

DETAILS

Use the following techniques to implement links effectively:

• **Creating links**

To create a link, you enclose the text or other element you want to serve as a link within an a element using the <a></a> tag pair. You use the href attribute to specify the filename of the location, web page, or other document to link to, which is known as the **target document**. TABLE F-1 explains the most common values for the href attribute. When a user agent encounters an a element, it enables users to interact with the element to open the linked document; for example, in a browser, users most commonly click linked text or images to follow links.

Visual browsers apply colors to linked text to indicate that it is a link and to convey a user's interactions with the link at a glance. By convention, an unclicked link is blue, a link that is in the process of being clicked by a user is red, and a link to a web page or document that has already been viewed by a user is purple. However, because CSS allows you to customize these colors, it's uncommon to see this color combination on the web today.

• **Organizing links**

Virtually every website includes a set of links for moving between web pages on the site. This design element is known as a **navigation bar** or **nav bar**, and usually occurs near the top of a web page, as shown in FIGURE F-1, or along one of the sides. A navigation bar should maintain the same location and appearance on every page on a website in order to give users a reliable way to move between pages. Some larger websites include a second set of links at the bottom of each page for information that most users may need only occasionally, such as the site's privacy policy or contact information.

When a web page is longer than an average user's screen, it can be useful to create an additional page-specific navigation bar that scrolls the user's screen to a section of the current page.

QUICK TIP
While several other
protocols are in use
on the Internet, the
web uses only http
and https.

• **Referencing web resources**

Every web page and other document available on the web can be referred to using a **uniform resource locator (URL)**, also known as a **web address**, which is a standard format for specifying how and where to access a resource on the Internet. As shown in FIGURE F-2, a URL consists of three parts: the scheme, the server name, and the path. The **scheme** is the way that computers ask for and communicate about the requested document. Web servers make documents available using the **Hypertext Transfer Protocol (http)** or **Hypertext Transfer Protocol Secure (https)** schemes. The **server name**, such as course.com or mail.google.com, identifies the general location of the target document on the web. The **path** is the sequence of folders in which the target document is stored on the server. A path may end with a filename such as compatibility.html, like the first URL in FIGURE F-2. The filename at the end of the URL is the name of the document a user agent should open in response to a user selecting the link. However, some URLs, such as the second one shown in FIGURE F-2, terminate instead with a series of variable names and values that a program on the web server uses to generate content dynamically. For instance, a link to a specific location on a map website includes information in the URL that enables the website to show the desired spot.

FIGURE F-1: A navigation bar

Navigation bar provides a consistent set of links for moving around within the site

Source: mozilla.org

FIGURE F-2: Two uniform resource locators (URLs)

© 2016 Cengage Learning

TABLE F-1: Possible values for the `href` attribute

value	description	example
filename	the filename of a web page or other document located in the same directory as the current page	`history.html`
path and filename	the path and filename of a web page in a different location on the same server	`/docs/register.pdf`
URL	scheme, server name, and, optionally, path for a resource located on another server	`https://mail.google.com/mail/?shva=1#inbox`
id **value**	named location within the current web document, preceded by a pound sign (#); can also be appended to a filename or URL	`#section3`

© 2016 Cengage Learning

Creating links to documents other than web pages

Most web page links are to other web pages. However, sometimes it's useful to create a link to another type of document, such as a PDF file or a CSV file. You can specify any type of computer-readable document as the value for an `href` attribute. Although you can link to documents in almost any format from your web pages, it's important to keep in mind that HTML documents are the only ones that your users are guaranteed to be able to access. To be able to access documents in other formats, users' computers must have programs installed that interpret these files. The PDF format has become an unofficial web standard for documents that require a specific printed format, such as forms that must be filled out by hand and/or signed, and you can rely on most of your users

having the capability to view and print PDFs. You should make documents in other formats available based on the likely computer configurations of your target audience. For instance, on a website by and for users of a highly specialized type of software, you'd be safe in making files in that software format available; however, on a site for the general public, it's unlikely that most users would be able to access such files.

Keep in mind that web-focused formats such as HTML and PDF minimize file sizes as much as possible, meaning that documents usually download quickly. If you are making a document available in another format, pay attention to the file size and take any steps available to reduce the size.

Create Relative Links

Learning Outcomes
- Create a relative link to a web page
- Create a relative link to a non-HTML document

You can use an a element to link to other documents in two basic ways. When you enter a URL as the href value, you create an **absolute link**, which is the full and complete address for the target document on the web. In some situations, however, it makes more sense to create a **relative link**, which gives only the path and filename information necessary to locate the target document based on the location of the current web page. Because web pages on a small website almost always share the same folder on a web server, it's most efficient to create relative links when creating a nav bar. **CASE** ▸ *You create a nav bar for the Lakeland Reeds B&B website and use relative links to reference the other pages on the site.*

STEPS

1. **In your text editor, open HTM_F-1.html from the Lessons folder where you store your Data Files for this unit, save it as index.html, then repeat to save HTM_F-2.html as aboutus.html, HTM_F-3.html as rooms.html, HTM_F-4.html as reserve.html, and HTM_F-5.css as styles.css**

2. **In the comment at the top of each file, enter your name and today's date where indicated, then save the files**

QUICK TIP
Because a web page can contain multiple nav elements, you should include a class value for each nav element that indicates its role.

3. **In reserve.html, add a new line beneath the header element, indent the same number of spaces, type `<nav class="sitenavigation">`, press [Enter] twice, then type `</nav>`**
   You use the nav element to create a nav bar.

4. **On the blank line between the opening and closing `<nav>` tags, indent three additional spaces, type `<p>Home<p>`, then press [Enter]**

5. **Repeat Step 4 to add the following p elements on separate lines: `<p>About Us</p>`, `<p>Rooms</p>`, `<p>Reservations</p>`, `<p>Local Weather</p>`, `<p>Directions</p>`**
   FIGURE F-3 shows the nav and p elements added to your code.

6. **Place the insertion point just to the left of the word *Home*, type `<a href="index.html">`, move the insertion point just after the word *Home*, then type `</a>`**
   The href value index.html is a relative link to the main page of the website.

QUICK TIP
If a user selects a link to the current page, the user agent simply reloads the page. It's important to include this link on the nav bar for use on other pages on the website.

7. **Repeat Step 6 to add a elements to the text for the following three links:**
   `<a href="aboutus.html">`**About Us**`</a>`
   `<a href="rooms.html">`**Rooms**`</a>`
   `<a href="reserve.html">`**Reservations**`</a>`

8. **In the last p element within the article element, place the insertion point to the left of the word *Read*, type `<a href="weddings.pdf">`, move the insertion point just after *event.*, then type `</a>`**
   You make files in other formats available as well by using links. **FIGURE F-4** shows the completed code.

9. **Save your changes, then open reserve.html in a browser**
   FIGURE F-5 shows the main Reservations web page containing the nav bar and the linked body text. The width and float are set by a rule in styles.css using the nav.sitenavigation selector.

10. **Click About Us on the nav bar**
    The About Us web page opens.

11. **Click your browser's Back button to return to reserve.html, then click the link that begins Read about reserving...**

FIGURE F-3: `nav` element and link text added to index.html

```
23          <header>
24              <h1>Lakeland Reeds Bed &amp; Breakfast</h1>
25          </header>
26          <nav class="sitenavigation">
27              <p>Home</p>
28              <p>About Us</p>
29              <p>Rooms</p>
30              <p>Reservations</p>
31              <p>Local Weather</p>
32              <p>Directions</p>
33          </nav>
34          <article>
```

Each p element within the nav element contains the text for a link

FIGURE F-4: Navigation bar code with relative links

```
27          <nav class="sitenavigation">
28              <p><a href="index.html">Home</a></p>
29              <p><a href="aboutus.html">About Us</a></p>
30              <p><a href="rooms.html">Rooms</a></p>
31              <p><a href="reserve.html">Reservations</a></p>
32              <p>Local Weather</p>
33              <p>Directions</p>
34          /nav>
35          article>
36              <h2 id="main">Reserva
37              <p>We're happy to take reservations up to a year in advance by phone, fax, or
38              email.</p>
39              <p>Feel free to contact us with any queries about Lakeland Reeds, or about
40              planning your trip.</p>
41              <p><a href="weddings.pdf">Read about reserving Lakeland Reeds for a wedding
42              or other special event.</a> (PDF)</p>
43          </article>
```

href attribute value specifies target document of link

Opening and closing <a> tags added around text for each link

Link target can be a document in a format other than HTML

FIGURE F-5: Web page displaying links

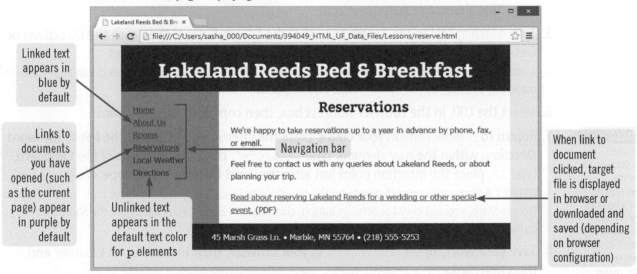

Linked text appears in blue by default

Links to documents you have opened (such as the current page) appear in purple by default

Unlinked text appears in the default text color for p elements

Navigation bar

When link to document clicked, target file is displayed in browser or downloaded and saved (depending on browser configuration)

Creating effective link text

You can create a link on any text on a web page. However, keeping a few rules in mind can enhance your site's accessibility and usability. Above all, link text should describe the target document. In a nav bar, a word or two that summarizes the content is usually sufficient. When you're inserting a link within a paragraph, a few words or a phrase may make more sense. For instance, instead of linking a phrase such as *click here*, creating a link on text such as *read more about your local watershed* helps users verify they're accessing the information they want. Users of screen readers may also check the link text on a web page as a means of scanning the page; using descriptive text increases accessibility in this instance.

Create Absolute Links

Learning Outcomes
• Add an absolute link to a web document

Providing entire URLs in a elements isn't necessary for links to other pages on the same web server. However, when you want to link to information on another website, you must use absolute links, which include the full and complete address for the target document on the web. **CASE** ▶ *Phillip Blaine, the owner of Lakeland Reeds B&B, wants to include a link to an online weather forecast for the town where Lakeland Reeds is located. He'd also like the page to incorporate a link that enables users to easily generate customized driving directions to the establishment. You add absolute links targeting external websites to the last two items on the nav bar.*

STEPS

1. **In your browser, open a site that provides current weather conditions, such as wunderground.com or weather.com, type Marble, MN in the location search box, then press [Enter]**

   The website displays current weather conditions in Marble, MN, along with a forecast.

2. **Select the URL in the browser Address box, then copy it to the Clipboard**

   On wunderground.com, you can click the Share button, then click the Short Link box to display a shortened URL.

QUICK TIP
If a URL you paste contains the & symbol, replace each occurrence with & to ensure your code validates.

3. **Return to reserve.html in your editor, place the insertion point just to the left of the phrase *Local Weather* within the nav element, type `<a href="`, paste the contents of the Clipboard, type `">`, place the insertion point just after the phrase *Local Weather*, type `</a>`, then save your changes**

   The `href` value is an absolute link consisting of the entire URL for the target web page.

4. **Return to your web browser, open a site that provides driving directions, such as maps.google.com or mapquest.com**

5. **Type Marble, MN in the Search box, click the Search button, then click the Directions or Get Directions button when the map showing Marble, MN is displayed**

   A web page opens with a destination of Marble, MN, selected. If your home address doesn't appear automatically, you may be prompted to enter a starting point.

6. **Select the URL in the browser Address box, then copy it to the Clipboard**

TROUBLE
If the URL in the address bar contains no text after the server name, explore the page for a way to create a link containing the information you've entered, such as the "Share or embed map" option under Settings on maps.google.com or the Link/Embed link on mapquest.com, and verify that the link text begins with http.

7. **Return to reserve.html in your editor, place the insertion point just to the left of the word *Directions* within the nav element, type `<a href="`, paste the contents of the Clipboard, type `">`, place the insertion point just after the word *Directions*, then type `</a>`**

   FIGURE F-6 shows the completed code for the two absolute links, using short links for both `href` values. In Google Maps, you can click the Settings button, click Share or Embed Map, then click the Short URL box to display a shortened URL like the one shown in the figure.

8. **Save your work, open reserve.html in your browser, then test the Local Weather and Directions links**

   FIGURE F-7 shows the completed nav bar.

9. **Return to reserve.html in your text editor, select the entire code for the nav bar, including the opening and closing `<nav>` tags, copy the code to the Clipboard, paste it below the header element in index.html, aboutus.html, and rooms.html, then save each document**

10. **In your web browser, use the links on the reserve.html nav bar to open the other pages in the website, then verify that all the links work on each page**

    Notice that the nav bar is longer than the `article` element on index.html. You'll adjust the layout in the next lesson to address this issue.

```
26      <nav class="sitenavigation">
            <p><a href="index.html">Home</a></p>
            <p><a href="aboutus.html">About Us</a></p>
            <p><a href="rooms.html">Rooms</a></p>
            <p><a href="reserve.html">Reservations</a></p>
            <p><a href="http://wxug.us/1hn14">Local Weather</a></p>
32          <p><a href="https://goo.gl/maps/bwf5R">Directions</a></p>
33      </nav>
```

Absolute link contains the entire URL for the target document

Short links used in place of full URLs (your URLs may differ)

FIGURE F-7: Nav bar with absolute links

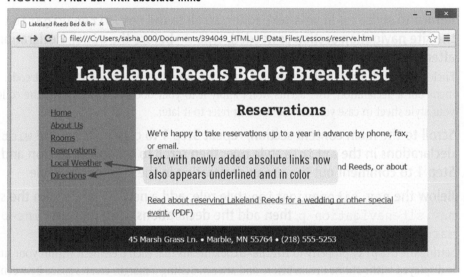

Text with newly added absolute links now also appears underlined and in color

Understanding mailto links

In addition to creating links that target web pages and other documents, you can construct a link that creates a new email to a specified recipient. Instead of beginning with `http://`, these links start with `mailto:` and are often referred to as **mailto links**. Despite their usefulness, mailto links present both usability and security issues and are not widely used by themselves. When a mailto link is activated, it's up to the user agent to identify which program should complete the request. This program is known as the default mail client. On some systems, the default mail client is a program; on other systems, a web-based email system is the default. This situation, especially on a shared computer, can mean that accessing the link creates unpredictable results, including failure to create the email, accompanied by an error message. In addition, because a mailto link includes a real email address and is publicly available on the Internet, these links are prime targets for

programs known as **email harvesters**, which continually explore web pages looking for email addresses that can then be targeted for spam emails.

If communication from your users is important, a few alternatives have replaced mailto links. Using more advanced HTML elements, you can create a form where users can enter comments and contact information, and then submit it to you without your email address or the sender's being exposed on the web. You can also create a personal or organizational social network feed and make it available on your website, inviting users to direct feedback or questions to you through that network instead of via email. If including a mailto link is a priority for a client, you can incorporate JavaScript code into your page that makes it harder for email harvesters to access the email address.

Change CSS display Type

The main nav bar for a website is usually displayed in one of two places: vertically along the left side of the page, or horizontally at or near the top of the page. It's easiest to work with and style link text when each link is a separate block-level element, allowing you to style it with padding, border, and/or margins. However, by default a block-level element is rendered with a line break before and after. You can change how an element is rendered by changing its display type using the CSS display property. **TABLE F-2** describes commonly used display property values. **CASE** ▶ *Your contacts at Lakeland Reeds like the nav bar you've created, but they would prefer the links to be displayed horizontally below the header. You set the* display *property to* inline-block *and change other properties to implement this new layout.*

STEPS

1. **Return to** styles.css **in your text editor, scroll to the** nav.sitenavigation **style rule in the site navigation section as needed, type** /* **before the** width **declaration and** */ **after it, then repeat for the** float **and** padding **declarations**

   Enclosing a declaration within comment characters is known as **commenting out** code. When you comment out a declaration, user agents won't apply it to your documents. However, the code is preserved in your style sheet in case you want to use it or refer to it later.

2. **Scroll to the main content section, repeat Step 1 to comment out the** width **and** float **declarations in the** article **style rule, then scroll to the footer section and repeat Step 1 to comment out the** clear **declaration in the** footer **style rule**

3. **Below the** nav.sitenavigation **style rule, add a new style rule with the selector** nav.sitenavigation p, **then add the declarations** display: inline-block; **and** margin: 0.5em;

   Setting the display property to inline-block means that each p element within your site navigation bar is displayed without line breaks before and after it. Setting a margin creates space between the p elements, which are now displayed next to each other in a row.

4. **In the** nav.sitenavigation **rule, add the declaration** text-align: center;

   Because inline-block elements do not occupy 100% of the width of their parent elements, the text-align value of the parent element determines how they are aligned, just like it determines how words are aligned within a parent element. Your code should match **FIGURE F-8**.

5. **Save your changes, then refresh or reload reserve.html in your browser**

   As **FIGURE F-9** shows, the nav bar is now displayed horizontally below the header element, and the article element occupies the full width of the container.

6. **Use the nav bar links to view all the pages on the site and verify that the layout changes have been applied to all documents**

7. **Return to** styles.css **in your editor, then in the media query at the end of the document, create a new style rule below the** h2 **rule with the selector** nav **and the declaration** display: none;

   Because nav elements are not functional in a printout, you set the display value to none to hide them in printed output. **FIGURE F-10** shows the code added to the media query.

8. **Save your changes, refresh or reload reserve.html in your browser, then open a print preview**

   The page is formatted for printing without the site nav bar, and the page is laid out as if the nav bar was not part of the document.

FIGURE F-8: Style sheet with changes for new layout

```
47    /* site navigation bar */
48    nav.sitenavigation {
49    /*    width: 19%; */
50    /*    padding: 3%; */
51    /*    float: left; */
52        color: #34180f;
53        text-align: center;
54    }
55    nav.sitenavigation p {
56        display: inline-block;
57        margin: 0.5em;
58    }
59
60    /* main content */
61    article {
62    /*    width: 69%; */
63        padding: 0 3% 1em;
64        background-color: ivory;
65    /*    float: right; */
66    }
```

text-align property affects the alignment of child inline-block elements as well as text

display value for p elements within the site nav bar set to inline-block

Unneeded declarations commented out

```
87    /* footer section */
88    footer {
89        padding: 0.6em;
90        background-color: #34180f;
91        color: ivory;
92        text-align: center
93    /*    clear: both; */
94    }
```

FIGURE F-9: Nav bar orientation changed to horizontal

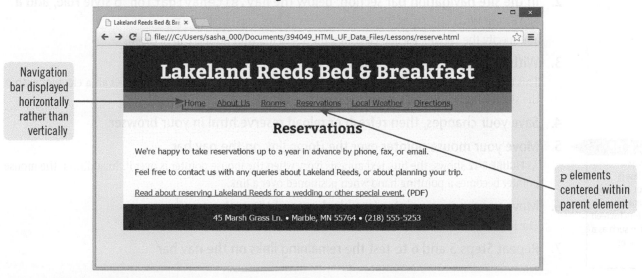

Navigation bar displayed horizontally rather than vertically

Lakeland Reeds Bed & Breakfast

Home   About Us   Rooms   Reservations   Local Weather   Directions

Reservations

We're happy to take reservations up to a year in advance by phone, fax, or email.

Feel free to contact us with any queries about Lakeland Reeds, or about planning your trip.

Read about reserving Lakeland Reeds for a wedding or other special event. (PDF)

45 Marsh Grass Ln. • Marble, MN 55764 • (218) 555-5253

p elements centered within parent element

FIGURE F-10: Code added to style sheet to exclude `nav` elements from printed output

```
175        h2 {
176            font-size: 2.2em;
177        }
178        nav {
179            display: none;
180        }
181    }
182    @page {
```

TABLE F-2: Commonly used values of the `display` property

value	rendered as	line breaks before and after?	box model support
block	box occupying the full width of its parent element	yes	all properties
inline	content that does not expand to the full width of its parent	no	margin-left, margin-right
inline-block	box that does not expand to the full width of its parent	yes	all properties
none	document rendered as if element does not exist		

Style Links with a Pseudo-Class

Learning Outcomes
• Style the :hover pseudo-class

In addition to creating basic styles for a elements, you can create CSS styles to change the format of a link in response to a user's interaction with the link. To do so, you use a **pseudo-class**, which is a categorization of a web page element based on a relationship or condition of the element at a given moment, rather than on a static attribute value. The word *pseudo* means *like* or *similar to*, so the term *pseudo-class* means *like a class*, referencing its similarity to the class attribute. A pseudo-class is analogous to a class value being assigned temporarily to an element only when the element meets certain criteria. One of the most useful pseudo-classes is the :hover pseudo-class, which applies to an element when a user moves the mouse pointer over the element. The a element is the only HTML element that supports the :hover pseudo-class. Often used to change the appearance of a link before a user clicks it, :hover provides visual confirmation that the user is about to click the desired link. **CASE** *You use the :hover pseudo-class for the links in the site navigation bar to change the color of link text when a user moves the mouse pointer over a link.*

STEPS

1. **Return to styles.css in your text editor**

2. **In the site navigation bar section, below the nav.sitenavigation p style rule, add a style rule with the selector nav.sitenavigation a:hover**
   You specify the :hover pseudo-class after the a selector, with no space in between.

3. **Within the new style rule, add the declaration color: ivory;**
   This declaration changes the font color to ivory when a user's mouse pointer is over an a element within the site nav bar. **FIGURE F-11** shows the new style rule.

4. **Save your changes, then refresh or reload reserve.html in your browser**

5. **Move your mouse pointer over the Home link on the nav bar**
   As **FIGURE F-12** shows, the link text appears ivory when the mouse pointer is over it. In addition, the mouse pointer becomes a pointing hand when positioned over a link.

6. **Move your mouse pointer to a blank area of the web page**
   The link text returns to its default color.

7. **Repeat Steps 5 and 6 to test the remaining links on the nav bar**

QUICK TIP
The :hover pseudo-class is usually not applied when interacting with the touchscreen on a device such as a smartphone or tablet.

Styling the :hover pseudo-class

You can style the :hover pseudo-class using any property that is valid for an a element. However, it's best to avoid changing the values of properties for the :hover pseudo-class that affect the line height of text, such as line-height, font-size, or font-weight. Changing any of these properties can affect the page layout—for instance, it can cause the elements below a nav bar to move down temporarily because the height of the nav bar increases to accommodate the new value while the mouse pointer is over a link. Instead, properties such as color, background-color, and text-shadow are commonly used to affect the appearance of links while the mouse pointer is over them but without affecting the overall layout.

Note that because the a element is an inline element, you cannot set box model properties including width, padding, border, or margin unless you first change its display type. However, if you set the display type of a elements to inline-block or block, you can then work with their box model properties. This is an especially useful technique when changing the background color of links with the :hover pseudo-class because it can be useful to create padding around the link text.

FIGURE F-11: Style rule for `:hover` pseudo-class

```
56    nav.sitenavigation p {
57        display: inline-block;
58        margin: 0.5em;
59    }
60    nav.sitenavigation a:hover {
61        color: ivory;
62    }
63
64    /* main content */
65    article {
```

Style rule for `:hover` pseudo-class of links in site nav bar

FIGURE F-12: Text color changed by `:hover` style rule

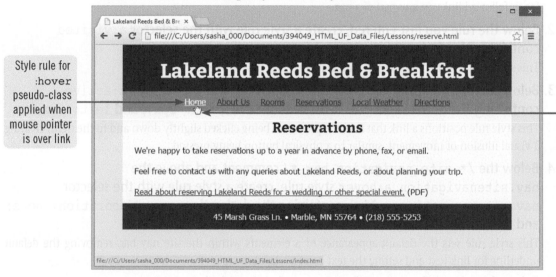

Style rule for `:hover` pseudo-class applied when mouse pointer is over link

Mouse pointer becomes a pointing hand when over a link

Understanding the difference between pseudo-elements and pseudo-classes

Both pseudo-elements and pseudo-classes are CSS selectors that you specify with a colon preceding them. However, there are a number of differences between these two features. You use a pseudo-element to work with part of an element, such as the first letter. As long as the base element exists in your HTML code, a style rule that uses a pseudo-element selector is always applied to the page. By contrast, you use a pseudo-class to style an element based on the status of user interaction with it. This means that styling for a pseudo-class can be applied to a web page at certain times and not at others—for example, only when the mouse pointer or focus is on a link. You can

think of a pseudo-element as a way to create or carve out an element using CSS; likewise, a pseudo-class is a way to assign a class value to an element based on its state.

Starting with CSS3, the language has standardized on using a single colon before a pseudo-class (such as `:focus`) and two colons before a pseudo-element (such as `::first-letter`) to distinguish between the two in code. However, older browsers do not recognize the double-colon versions of pseudo-elements, so it's best to continue to use a single colon for both features until older browsers, such as IE8, are no longer in wide use.

Style Multiple Link States

In addition to :hover, links have four other states that you can style with pseudo-classes—:link, :visited, :focus, and :active. TABLE F-3 summarizes the 5 pseudo-classes for links. While you are not required to use all five pseudo-classes for a link, you must specify any you do use in the order shown in the table (though :hover and :focus can be swapped or specified for the same rule). **CASE** *You implement additional pseudo-classes for the Lakeland Reeds nav bar to maximize contrast within the site's color scheme.*

STEPS

1. **Return to** styles.css **in your text editor, scroll to the** /* body */ **comment, then, after the** p **style rule, create a style rule with the selector** a:link **containing the declaration** color: black;

   The :link pseudo-class applies only when the other four do not. This style rule sets the text color to black for unfollowed links on any part of a page.

2. **Below the rule you just entered, create a style rule with the selector** a:visited **containing the declaration** color: #888;

   This style rule sets the text color to dark gray for a link that has been followed.

3. **Below the rule you just entered, create a style rule with the selector** a:active **containing the declarations** position: relative;, top: 1px;, **and** left: 1px;

   This style rule positions a link that is in the process of being clicked slightly down and to the right, creating a visual illusion of movement, similar to a physical button being pressed.

4. **Below the** /* site navigation bar */ **comment and above the** nav.sitenavigation a:hover **style rule, create a style rule with the selector** nav.sitenavigation a:link **containing the declarations** text-decoration: none; **and** color: #34180f;

   This style rule sets the default appearance of a elements within the site nav bar, removing the default underline for link text and setting the text color to dark brown.

5. **Below the rule you just entered, create a style rule with the selector** nav.sitenavigation a:visited **containing the declaration** color: #744f42;

   This style rule sets the text color of followed links within the site nav bar to a medium brown.

6. **In the** nav.sitenavigation a:hover **style rule, add the selector** nav.sitenavigation a:focus

   Adding the :focus pseudo-class to this selector ensures that the color change rollover effect is also applied when users navigate the page using a keyboard. **FIGURE F-13** shows the code for the additional pseudo-elements.

7. **Save your changes, return to your web browser, then clear your browsing history**

   The option varies among browsers but is commonly listed under privacy or safety settings.

8. **Refresh or reload reserve.html in your browser, then move your mouse pointer over the Home link on the nav bar**

   The link text appears ivory when the mouse pointer is over it, as it did previously. The link for the current page, which is open in the browser, is a medium brown based on the :visited style rule for the nav bar.

9. **Press and hold the mouse button**

   The link text moves slightly down and to the right, creating an illusion that simulates a physical key being pressed, as shown in **FIGURE F-14**.

10. **Release the mouse button, then let the target page load**

    The Home and Reservations links appear medium brown, indicating you've visited those pages.

FIGURE F-13: Global pseudo-class styles and styles for site nav bar added to style sheet

```
31    p {
32        font-size: 1.4em;
33        line-height: 1.6em;
34    }
35    a:link {
36        color: black;
37    }
38    a:visited {
39        color: #888;
40    }
41    a:active {
42        position: relative;
43        top: 1px;
44        left: 1px;
45    }
46
47    /* header section */
```

```
67    nav.sitenavigation p {
68        display: inline-block;
69        margin: 0.5em;
70    }
71    nav.sitenavigation a:link {
72        text-decoration: none;
73        color: #34180f;
74    }
75    nav.sitenavigation a:visited {
76        color: #744f42;
77    }
78    nav.sitenavigation a:hover, nav.sitenavigation a:focus {
79        color: ivory;
80    }
```

FIGURE F-14: Links styled using multiple pseudo-classes

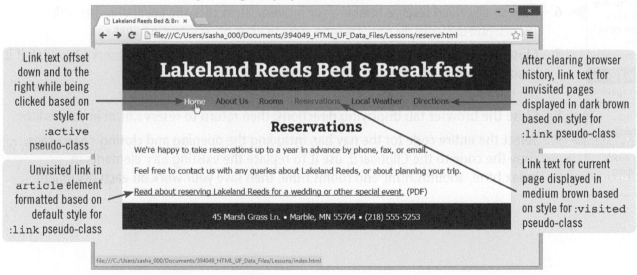

Link text offset down and to the right while being clicked based on style for :active pseudo-class

Unvisited link in article element formatted based on default style for :link pseudo-class

After clearing browser history, link text for unvisited pages displayed in dark brown based on style for :link pseudo-class

Link text for current page displayed in medium brown based on style for :visited pseudo-class

TABLE F-3: Pseudo-class states for linked elements

pseudo-class	provides styles for
:link	link that has not been visited, does not currently have the focus or the mouse pointer over it, and is not being clicked
:visited	link that has already been viewed
:focus	link that currently has the focus regardless of how it was selected, including via keyboard navigation
:hover	link that the mouse pointer is currently over
:active	link that is currently being clicked

Open Links in New Tabs

Learning Outcomes
• Create a link that opens in a new tab

By default, a link opens a new web page in the same tab as the source page. This enables users to revisit previous pages using the back buttons in their browsers. In certain situations, however, you want a link to open a web page in a new tab. For instance, some websites open target pages for links to external sites in new tabs so users can have both sites open at once. Opening a link in a new window or tab from a web page containing a lot of information allows a user to easily and quickly return to their place on the original page when they're done with the linked information. You can control where a link target opens by including the target attribute of the a element. A value of _blank specifies that the target page should open in a new tab. **TABLE F-4** details the commonly used values for the target attribute. **CASE** ▶ *In consultation with your contacts at Lakeland Reeds, you've decided that the Local Weather and Directions link targets should open in new tabs. You add the* target *attribute to these links.*

STEPS

1. **Return to reserve.html in your editor**

2. **Within the nav element, position the insertion point before the closing > in the opening <a> tag for the Local Weather link**

3. **Press [Spacebar], then type target="_blank"**

4. **Position the insertion point before the closing > in the opening <a> tag for the Directions link**

QUICK TIP
An older browser or a browser with custom settings may open the link in a new window instead of a new tab.

5. **Press [Spacebar], type target="_blank", then save your changes**
   FIGURE F-15 shows the web page code with the target attributes added.

6. **Refresh or reload reserve.html in your browser, then click the Local Weather link**
   The web page displaying the current weather opens in a new tab, as shown in **FIGURE F-16**.

7. **Close the browser tab displaying the weather information, click the reserve.html tab if it is not the active tab, then click the Directions link**
   Like the weather page, the web page displaying directions opens in a new tab.

QUICK TIP
Copying and pasting corrected code can be quicker than entering changes manually on multiple pages, and avoids potential typing mistakes.

8. **Close the browser tab displaying directions, then return to reserve.html in your editor**

9. **Select the entire code for the nav bar, including the opening and closing <nav> tags, copy the code to the Clipboard, use it to replace the existing nav elements in index.html, aboutus.html, and rooms.html, then save your work on each document**

TABLE F-4: Common values of the target property of the a element

value	description
_blank	Opens target document in a new tab
_self	Opens target document in same tab as source document (default value)

FIGURE F-15: `target` attribute added to external links

```
26          <nav class="sitenavigation">
27              <p><a href="index.html">Home</a></p>
28              <p><a href="aboutus.html">About Us</a></p>
29              <p><a href="rooms.html">Rooms</a></p>
30              <p><a href="reserve.html">Reservations</a></p>
31              <p><a href="http://wxug.us/lhn14" target="_blank">Local Weather</a></p>
32              <p><a href="https://goo.gl/maps/bwf5R" target="_blank">Directions</a></p>
33          </nav>
```

target attribute value set to `_blank` for both links to external sites

FIGURE F-16: Link target opened in new tab

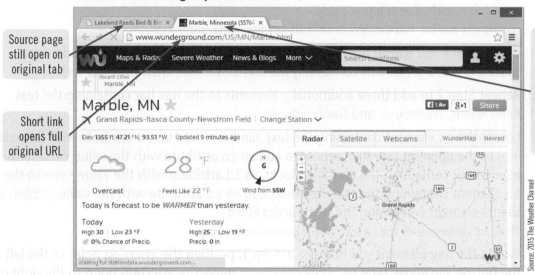

Source page still open on original tab

Short link opens full original URL

Weather page opens in a new tab because of the `_blank` value assigned to the link's `target` attribute

Source: 2015 The Weather Channel

Using short links

Especially long external links can clutter your web page code. To make your code easier to read, you can use **short links**, which are generated URLs that use especially short domain names and specially crafted paths to represent large, unwieldy links as short, manageable URLs. Many popular websites allow you to share links to their content using custom short links with domain names specific to the company. For instance, Google generates short links that use the goo.gl domain name, and the New York Times uses the domain nyti.ms for its short links. Even without access to a custom domain, you can generate your own short links using a web-based service such as bit.ly or tinyurl.com. To use these services, you start by copying the full URL of the web page you want to link to, then navigating to the website of whichever link shortener you choose. Next, you paste your long link into the text box

for that purpose, then click the associated button, which is often labeled "shorten" or something similar. The service processes your link and returns a new short link that starts with the link shortener's name. You then copy the new link to the Clipboard and paste it into your web page.

One drawback of using short links in your website is that users are unable to tell from inspecting the URL what domain the link targets, which could be unsettling to some people. Short links make more sense on websites for large, well-established businesses and organizations and for websites that target people likely to have experience using such links. You may want to consider avoiding using short links on a website for a person or organization that's not well known, or on a site that targets more security-focused users.

Link Within a Document

Learning
Outcomes
• Create links to
elements within a
web page

You can link to locations within the current web page using the same elements and attributes as other links you've created. However, instead of linking to URLs or filenames, you link to elements within the current document that have specific values for the id attribute. To reference an id value using the href attribute of the a element, you simply precede the id value with a pound sign (#). Because this symbol is also known as a hash mark, links to id values are known as **hash links**. **CASE** ▸ *You add an id value to the h3 element for each room heading on the Rooms page, then add a second nav bar to the page containing a hash link to each room heading.*

STEPS

1. **Return to rooms.html in your editor, add a blank line before the h3 element containing the text** *Sun Room*, **indent and type** `<nav class="pagenavigation">`, **press** [Enter] **twice, then indent and type** `</nav>`

   Like the site nav bar, you use the nav element for the page nav bar.

2. **On the blank line within the nav element you created in Step 1, indent 3 additional spaces, create a p element containing the text** Sun Room, **then press** [Enter]

3. **Repeat Step 2 to add three additional p elements to the nav bar containing the text** Reed Room, Treehouse, **and** Garden Room

QUICK TIP
Another common use
of hash links involves
adding an id value to
a page's main head-
ing, then creating
links to that heading
at the bottom of each
section of the page,
allowing users to
easily return to the
top of the page.

4. **Locate the h3 element containing the text** *Sun Room*, **add an id attribute with the value** sun **to the opening tag, then repeat to add an id attribute with the value** reed **to the h3 element containing the text** *Reed Room*, **an id attribute with the value** tree **to the h3 element containing the text** *Treehouse*, **and an id attribute with the value** garden **to the h3 element containing the text** *Garden Room*

   These id values provide the values for hash links to the headings.

5. **Within the nav element you inserted in Step 1, position the insertion point to the left of the phrase** *Sun Room*, **type** `<a href="#sun">`, **move the insertion point to the right of the phrase** *Sun Room*, **then type** `</a>`

6. **Repeat Step 5 to create the following three links, as shown in FIGURE F-17:**

   ```
   <p><a href="#reed">Reed Room</a></p>

   <p><a href="#tree">Treehouse</a></p>

   <p><a href="#garden">Garden Room</a></p>
   ```

TROUBLE
If the web page is not
long enough to place
the element with the
target id value at the
top of the window,
the element may
remain in the middle
or at the bottom of
the window.

7. **Save your work, return to styles.css in your editor, then below the** `/* main content */` **comment and after the** `.title` **rule, enter the style rules shown in FIGURE F-18**

   The first two new style rules shown in **FIGURE F-18** style the nav element with the class value pagenavigation and p elements within that nav element. The final three new style rules set properties for the :link, :visited, :hover, and :focus pseudo-classes for links within the new nav element.

8. **Save your work, open rooms.html in your browser, click the Sun Room link in the page nav bar, scroll back up, then repeat to test the remaining links in the page nav bar**

Linking to id values in other documents

You can combine a relative or absolute link with a hash value to link to a specific element in a different document. When specifying the href value for the link, simply enter the URL or filename for the target document, add a pound sign (#) to the end, then add the id value. When the target page opens in a user's browser, the page scrolls to the element with the specified id value.

```
34              <article>
35                  <h2>Rooms</h2>
36                  <p>All rooms include down comforters, air conditioning, and DVD players, and
37                  each can accommodate an additional twin fold-out bed.</p>
38                  <nav class="pagenavigation">
39                      <p><a href="#sun">Sun Room</a></p>
40                      <p><a href="#reed">Reed Room</a></p>
41                      <p><a href="#tree">Treehouse</a></p>
42                      <p><a href="#garden">Garden Room</a></p>
43                  </nav>
44                  <h3 id="sun">Sun Room</h3>
45                  <p>With windows on three sides, the sunlight in this second-floor room
46                  supports a large selection of houseplants.</p>
47                  <p>1 queen bed.</p>
48                  <h3 id="reed">Reed Room</h3>
49                  <p>This first-floor room looks out over the reeds on the edge of the lake and
50                  the water beyond.</p>
51                  <p>1 queen bed and 1 twin bed.</p>
52                  <h3 id="tree">Treehouse</h3>
53                  <p>A winding staircase takes you to your own private getaway at the top of
54                  the house, with view of the surrounding trees and meadows and the lake.</p>
55                  <p>1 queen bed.</p>
56                  <h3 id="garden">Garden Room</h3>
57                  <p>This room's French doors open onto our stone patio and flower garden.</p>
58                  <p>1 queen bed and 2 twin beds.</p>
59              </article>
```

New nav element created for navigating within the page

id values added to h3 elements as targets for hash links

```
105   .title {
106       font-style: italic;
107   }
108   nav.pagenavigation {
109       margin-top: 1em;
110       text-align: center;
111       color: white;
112       background-color: #422100;
113   }
114   nav.pagenavigation p {
115       display: inline-block;
116       margin: 0.5em;
117       padding: 0;
118   }
119   nav.pagenavigation a:link {
120       text-decoration: none;
121       color: #cbb58b;
122   }
123   nav.pagenavigation a:visited {
124       color: #dee9f9;
125   }
126   nav.pagenavigation a:hover, nav.pagenavigation a:focus {
127       color: ivory;
128   }
129
130   /* footer section */
```

Style rules for appearance of page nav bar and p elements within it

Style rules for :link, :visited, :hover, and :focus states of links within page nav bar

Clearing browser history to retest link states

When changing properties for link pseudo-classes, you may find that all links in a page are formatted as :visited due to earlier testing. To reset the appearance of links to their default :link state, you need to clear your **browser history**, which is the log your browser maintains of URLs that you've visited. Browsers use browser history to enable features such as autocompleting addresses that you type in the Address bar. In addition, browsers render a link using declarations for the :visited pseudo-class if the link target appears in the browser history. Every browser enables you to clear the history list. Consult your browser documentation or search the web if you need help clearing your browser history.

HTML5 & CSS3

Aid Navigational Accessibility

Learning Outcomes
• Create a skip link
• Test accessibility with keyboard navigation

Users of screen readers and other users who navigate using a keyboard often experience a web page element-by-element in sequence from top to bottom. These users encounter the heading followed by each link in a nav bar before getting to the main content of the page. To allow users to skip straight to the main page content, it's good practice to include a **skip link**, which targets an id value at the start of the main page content and allows users to bypass navigation. **CASE** ▶ *You add a skip link to each web page in the Lakeland Reeds site, and you test the link using keyboard navigation.*

STEPS

1. **Return to** index.html **in your editor, place the insertion point just after the** p **in the opening** <p> **tag just below the opening** <article> **tag, press [Spacebar], then type** id="contentstart"
   This id value marks the start of the main page content.

2. **Add a blank line beneath the opening** <div> **tag for the** container **class, indent to align with the** <header> **tag that follows, then type** <p class="skipnavigation"> <a href="#contentstart">Skip navigation</a></p>
   FIGURE F-19 shows the code for the target id attribute and the skip link.

3. **Save your changes, open** index.html **in a browser, drag the bottom border of your browser up so only the skip link and the** h1 **heading are visible, then click** Skip navigation
   The skip link is displayed at the top of the browser window when the page opens, and when you click the link the browser displays the beginning of the main page content.

4. **Repeat Steps 1–3 for** aboutus.html, rooms.html, **and** reserve.html, **adding the** id **attribute in Step 1 to the** h2 **element in each document**

5. **Return to** styles.css **in your editor, above the** /* header section */ **comment, add the comment** /* skip navigation link */, **then create a style rule with the selector** p.skipnavigation a **containing the declarations** position: absolute; **and** left: -10000px;
   It's common to use absolute position to take a skip link out of the normal flow and then position it far outside the visible area of the page so users navigating by sight with a touch device don't see the link.

6. **Below the style rule you created in Step 5, create a new style rule with the selector** p.skipnavigation a:focus **containing the declarations** color: #34180f;, background-color: ivory;, top: 0.2em;, left: 0.4em;, **and** z-index: 2;
   This rule makes the link visible on the screen and highlights it when it has the focus so a user navigating with a keyboard can view and select the link when interacting with the page. **FIGURE F-20** shows the CSS code.

7. **Save your changes, refresh or reload** index.html **in your browser, then press [Tab] one or more times until the text** Skip Navigation **is displayed at the top of the page, as shown in FIGURE F-21**
   The skip link is not displayed when the page first opens, but becomes visible when it receives the focus while you navigate through the links on the page with the [Tab] key.

8. **Press the [Tab] key to select each of the remaining links on the page**
   When the skip link no longer has the focus, it is no longer displayed.

9. **Press [Enter]**
   Pressing [Enter] selects the element with focus. Selecting the skip link scrolls the page to the h2 heading.

10. **Validate the code for all your web pages and your style sheet**

FIGURE F-19: Skip link and target `id` value added to index.html

```
22          <div class="container">
23              <p class="skipnavigation"><a href="#contentstart">Skip navigation</a></p>
24              <header>
25                  <h1>Lakeland Reeds Bed &amp; Breakfast</h1>
26              </header>
27              <nav class="sitenavigation">
28                  <p><a href="index.html">Home</a></p>
29                  <p><a href="aboutus.html">About Us</a></p>
30                  <p><a href="rooms.html">Rooms</a></p>
                    <p><a href="reserve.html">Reservations</a></p>
                    <p><a href="http://wxug.us/1hn14" target="_blank">Local Weather</a></p>
                    <p><a href="https://goo.gl/maps/bwf5R" target="_blank">Directions</a></p>
                </nav>
                <article>
                    <p id="contentstart">Lakeland Reeds is a rustic bed and breakfast on Twin
37                  Lakes near rural Marble, Minnesota. Convenient to US 2 and 169, the fresh air
38                  and quiet make for an ideal weekend escape from the rush of city life.</p>
39              </article>
```

Target of skip link is the element with the id value `contentstart`

id value added to element at start of main page content

FIGURE F-20: CSS code to style skip link

```
47      /* skip navigation link */
48      p.skipnavigation a {
49          position: absolute;
50          left: -10000px;
51      }
52      p.skipnavigation a:focus {
53          color: #34180f;
54          background-color: ivory;
55          top: 0.2em;
56          left: 0.4em;
57          z-index: 2;
58      }
59
60      /* header section */
```

FIGURE F-21: Skip link displayed in response to keyboard navigation

Skip link displayed when element receives focus

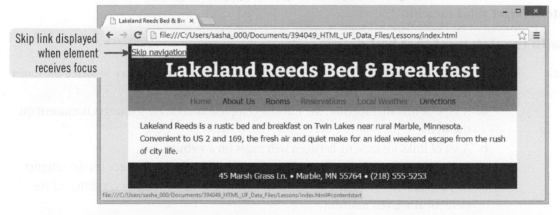

Testing web pages with a screen reader

In addition to the keyboard, a screen reader is another common means of navigating a web page for people with certain disabilities. A screen reader is software that reads content on a computer, including web pages, out loud. Screen readers are commonly used by people with low vision and by blind people. As a developer, it can be useful to test your pages on screen readers to identify any issues with your documents that might prevent screen reader users from accessing all of your content.

Free, full-featured screen readers are available for both Windows and Mac computers. For Windows, you can download the free NVDA screen reader from nvaccess.org. For Mac, VoiceOver is a screen reader that's installed by default as part of the operating system; to enable and customize VoiceOver, open System Preferences, click Accessibility, then click VoiceOver. For more information on VoiceOver, see apple.com/accessibility/osx/voiceover/.

Practice

Concepts Review

Refer to FIGURE F-22 to answer the questions that follow.

FIGURE F-22

```
23      <p class="skipnavigation"><a href="#contentstart">Skip navigation</a></p>
24      <header>
25          <h1>Lakeland Reeds Bed &amp; Breakfast</h1>          f
26      </header>
27      <nav class="sitenavigation">                              e
28          <p><a href="index.html">Home</a></p>
29          <p><a href="aboutus.html">About Us</a></p>
30  a       <p><a href="rooms.html">Rooms</a></p>
31          <p><a href="reserve.html">Reservations</a></p>
32          <p><a href="http://wxug.us/1hn14" target="_blank">Local Weather</a></p>
33          <p><a href="https://goo.gl/maps/bwf5R" target="_blank">Directions</a></p>
34      </nav>
35      <article>
36          <h2 id="contentstart">Reservations</h2>
                    b           c                   d
```

1. Which item marks a nav bar?
2. Which item is an absolute link?
3. Which item is a relative link?
4. Which item opens a link in a new tab?
5. Which item is a hash link?
6. Which item creates a target value for a link?

Match each term with the statement that best describes it.

7. Uniform resource locator (URL)

8. Relative link

9. Nav bar

10. Absolute link

11. Skip link

12. Pseudo-class

a. A link that gives only the path and filename information necessary to locate the target document based on the location of the current web page

b. A type of link that specifies the full and complete address for the target document on the web

c. A set of links for moving between web pages on a website

d. A standard format for specifying how and where to access a resource on the Internet

e. A categorization of a web page element based on a relationship or condition of the element at a given moment

f. A link that targets an anchor at the start of the main page content and allows users to bypass navigation

Select the best answer from the list of choices.

13. When creating a link, the web page or other document you link to is known as the _____ .
    a. relative link
    b. hash
    c. absolute link
    d. target

14. Which type of web reference contains a scheme, a server name, and a path?
    a. hash
    b. relative link
    c. URL
    d. nav element

15. **Web servers make documents available using which protocol?**
    a. http
    b. ftp
    c. mailto
    d. telnet

16. **What does the value #section3 for the href attribute target?**
    a. a URI
    b. a PDF file
    c. an id value
    d. a filename

17. **When you enter a URL, which of the following are you creating?**
    a. a hash link
    b. a skip link
    c. a relative link
    d. an absolute link

18. **Because web pages on a small website almost always share the same folder on a web server, it's most efficient to create which type of links when creating a nav bar?**
    a. relative
    b. absolute
    c. hash
    d. skip

19. **Which pseudo-class is applied when a user's mouse pointer is over the affected link?**
    a. a:link
    b. a:visited
    c. a:hover
    d. a:active

20. **You specify that a link should open in a new tab using which attribute?**
    a. href
    b. target
    c. class
    d. id

Skills Review

1. **Create relative links.**
    a. In your editor, open the file HTM_F-6.html from the SR folder where you store your Data Files for this unit, save it as **index.html**, then repeat to save the file HTM_F-7.html as **history.html**, HTM_F-8.html as **location.html**, and HTM_F-9.css as **styles.css**.
    b. Within the comment section at the top of each file, enter your first and last names and today's date, then save your changes.
    c. Return to index.html in your editor, then below the header element add a nav element with a class value of sitenavigation.
    d. Within the nav element, enter 4 p elements containing the text **Home**, **History**, **Menu**, and **Locations**.
    e. Create a relative link on the word **Home** that opens the page index.html, then repeat to add relative links to the text History to open the page history.html, Menu to open the file bigjmenu.pdf, and Locations to open location.html.
    f. Save your changes, return to styles.css in your editor, then above the main content section create a comment with the text **site navigation**.
    g. Below the comment you entered in the previous step, create a style rule for nav elements with the class value sitenavigation that sets the width to 19%, margins to 1em 0 0 2%, padding to 2%, float to left, and background color to #ddd.
    h. Save your changes, open index.html in your browser, then click the Locations link to test it.
    i. Return to index.html in your editor, copy the nav element including the opening and closing <nav> tags to the Clipboard, then paste the copied code after the header elements in history.html and in location.html.
    j. Save your changes to both documents, open index.html in your browser, then test the nav bar links on all 3 pages to ensure that all links work.

2. **Create absolute links.**
    a. Return to location.html in your editor, then copy the full address of the first location from the p element to the Clipboard. (*Hint*: Do not copy [Map].)
    b. Open a website that provides maps, such as maps.google.com or mapquest.com, paste the contents of the Clipboard into the location box on the web page, then press [Enter].

Skills Review (continued)

   c. Copy the URL from the Address bar (or a short link if available).

   d. Return to location.html in your editor, then add an absolute link on the word *Map* at the end of the first address, pasting the URL from the Clipboard as the `href` value. Be sure to add the closing tag for the a element just before the closing]. (*Hint*: If the URL you paste contains the ampersand (&) symbol, replace each occurrence with & to ensure your code validates.)

   e. Repeat Steps a–d for the remaining two locations, save your work, then open location.html in your web browser and test each of the Map links.

3. Change CSS display type.

   a. Return to styles.css in your editor, then in the `nav.sitenavigation` rule, comment out the declarations for the `width`, `padding`, and `float` properties.

   b. Repeat Step a to comment out the `width` and `float` declarations in the `article` style rule and the `clear` declaration in the `footer` style rule.

   c. Below the `nav.sitenavigation` rule, add a new style rule for p elements within the nav element with the `class` value `sitenavigation`, setting the display type to `inline-block` and the top and bottom padding to 0.3em.

   d. Below the style rule you created in the previous step, add a new style rule for a elements within p elements within the nav element with the `class` value `sitenavigation`, setting the padding to 0.2em 0.6em and the display type to `inline-block`.

   e. In the `nav.sitenavigation` rule, change the margins to 1em 1em 0 and the background color to `black`, then add a declaration to center-align text.

   f. In the `article` rule in the main content section, change the margins to 0 1em 1em and the padding to 1em 1em 0.5em.

   g. Save your changes, refresh or reload index.html in your browser, then use the nav bar links to view all the pages on the site and verify that the layout changes have been applied to all documents.

   h. Return to styles.css in your editor, then in the media query at the end of the document, create a new style rule above the `@page` rule that sets the display type for nav elements to none.

   i. Save your changes, refresh or reload index.html in your browser, open a print preview, then verify that the nav element is not part of the layout.

4. Style links with a pseudo-class and style multiple link states.

   a. Return to styles.css in your editor, then in the body and container section below the rule for the p element, add a new style rule that formats the font color of a default link as `black`.

   b. Below the rule you created in the previous step, add a rule to format the font colors of visited links with the color `#888`, then add another rule to relatively position active links 1px down from the top and 1px over from the left.

   c. At the bottom of the site navigation section, add a rule that sets the font color of a default link to white and removes the link's underline, then add another rule that sets the font color for visited links to the value `#ccc`.

   d. Below the rules you created in the previous step, add a rule that sets the font color of links that the mouse pointer is over and links that have the focus to `red` and sets the background color to `white`.

   e. In the `nav.sitenavigation` rule, change the background color value to `black`.

   f. Save your changes, return to your browser, then clear your browsing history.

   g. Refresh or reload index.html in your browser, verify that the font and background colors change for links on the nav bar when the mouse pointer is over them and when the target pages have been viewed, verify that the position of links changes while they are being clicked, then repeat for history.html and location.html.

5. Open links in new tabs.

   a. Return to location.html in your text editor, then in the opening `<a>` tag for the first Map link, add an attribute and value that opens the link in a new browser tab.

   b. Repeat the previous step for the remaining two Map links.

   c. Save your work, refresh or reload location.html in your browser, then test each Map link, verifying that it opens in a new tab.

Skills Review (continued)

6. Link within a document.

a. Return to location.html in your editor.

b. In the opening tag for the h3 element containing the text Queen’s Park, add an id attribute with the value queen.

c. Repeat Step b to add an id attribute with the value stclair to the h3 element containing the text St. Clair, and an id attribute with the value dundas to the h3 element containing the text Dundas.

d. Below the h2 element, enter a nav element with the class value pagenavigation.

e. Within the new nav element, add 3 p elements containing the text **Queen’s Park/UT**, **St. Clair**, and **Dundas**.

f. Link the text in the first p element to the element with the id value queen, the second to the element with the id value stclair, and the third to the element with the id value dundas.

g. Save your changes, then return to styles.css in your editor.

h. Above the main content section, add a comment with the text **page navigation**, then below the comment enter the following style rules:

- For the nav element with the class value pagenavigation, set the margin to 0 1em and center-align text
- For p elements within the nav element with the class value pagenavigation, set margins to 0 0.2em, display type to inline-block, and the background color to #ffcc66
- For a elements within p elements within the nav element with the class value pagenavigation, set padding to 0.2em 0.6em and display type to inline-block
- For default links within the nav element with the class value pagenavigation, create a 2px solid white border and remove the underline
- For visited links within the nav element with the class value pagenavigation, create a 2px solid white border and set the text color to #999
- For links that have the mouse pointer over them or that have the focus and that are within the nav element with the class value pagenavigation, create a 2px solid border with the color #ffcc66, set the text color to red, and set the background color to white

i. Save your changes, open location.html in your browser, then test each of the links in the page navigation bar. (*Hint*: Reduce the height of your browser window if necessary to verify that all of the links work.) Your document should match **FIGURE F-23**.

FIGURE F-23

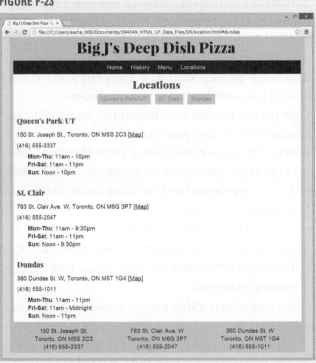

7. Aid navigational accessibility.

a. Return to index.html in your editor, then add an id attribute with a value of contentstart to the first p element within the article element.

b. Above the header element, add a p element with the class value skipnavigation containing the text **Skip navigation**, then link the text Skip navigation to the id value contentstart.

c. Save your changes, return to styles.css in your editor, then above the header section add a comment containing the text **skip navigation link**.

d. Below the new comment, add a style rule for a elements within the p element with the class value skipnavigation that absolutely positions the elements -10000px from the left.

Skills Review (continued)

e. Below the rule you added in the previous step, create a rule for a elements that have the focus and that are within the p element with the `class` value `skipnavigation` that sets the text color to `#34180f`, the background color to `white`, positions the elements 0.4em from the top and 0.4em from the right, sets the `left` value to `auto`, and assigns a z-index of 2.

f. Save your changes, refresh or reload index.html in your browser, then use the keyboard to verify that the Skip navigation link is displayed when it has the focus.

g. Repeat Steps a–b for history.html and location.html, adding the `id` attribute in Step a to the `h2` element in each file, then repeat Step f to test each file.

h. Validate the code for your web pages and style sheet.

Independent Challenge 1

As you continue your work on the website for the Spotted Wren Garden Center, you add a nav bar and links to gardening resources, along with navigational accessibility features.

a. In your editor, open the file HTM_F-10.html from the IC1 folder where you store your Data Files for this unit, save it as **index.html**, then repeat to save the file HTM_F-11.html as **hours.html**, and HTM_F-12.css as **styles.css**.

b. Within the comment section at the top of each file, enter your first and last names and today's date, then save your changes.

c. Return to index.html in your editor, then below the `header` element add a `nav` element with a `class` value of `sitenavigation`.

d. Within the nav element, create 4 p elements containing the text **Home, Hours, Location,** and **Tips**. Link the text Home to index.html, Hours to hours.html, and Tips to tipsheet.pdf.

e. In your browser, navigate to a map service, then using the address in the `footer` element of index.html, open a map showing that location. Copy the URL (or a short link) to the Clipboard, return to index.html in your editor, then, using the URL you copied, add a link to the word **Location** on the nav bar, specifying that the file should open in a new browser tab. Save your changes.

f. Copy the nav element from index.html, return to hours.html in your editor, then paste the nav element below the `header` element. Save your changes.

g. Return to styles.css in your editor, above the main content section add a comment containing the text **site navigation**, then below the comment, create the following style rules:

- For the `nav` element with the `class` value `sitenavigation`, set the background color to rgb(241,90,36) and center-align the text.
- For p elements within the `nav` element with the `class` value `sitenavigation`, set the display type to `inline-block`, the margins to 0.4em 0.6em, and the font size to 1.6em.
- For default links within the `nav` element with the `class` value `sitenavigation`, set text color to `yellow` and remove underlines.
- For visited links within the `nav` element with the `class` value `sitenavigation`, set text color to `white`.
- For links that the mouse pointer is over or that have the focus and that are within the `nav` element with the `class` value `sitenavigation`, set text color to `yellow` and create a text shadow with 1px horizontal offset, -1px vertical offset, 0 blur, and a color of `black`.
- For links that are being clicked and that are within the `nav` element with the `class` value `sitenavigation`, set a relative position 1px down from the top and 1px over from the left.

h. Save your changes to styles.css, return to index.html in your editor, then in the opening `<h2>` tag in the `article` element, add an `id` value of `contentstart`.

i. Below the opening `<div>` tag with the `class` value `container`, add a p element with the `class` value `skipnavigation`. Within the p element, add the text **Skip navigation** and link it to the element with the `id` value `contentstart`. Save your changes, then repeat Steps h and i for hours.html.

Independent Challenge 1 (continued)

j. Return to styles.css in your editor, then above the header section, add a comment containing the text **skip navigation link**. Below it, add the following style rules:

- For the p element with the class value skipnavigation, set margins to 0.
- For a elements within the p element with the class value skipnavigation, set an absolute position -10000px from the left.
- For a elements with the focus that are within the p element with the class value skipnavigation, set text color to black, background color to white, set a relative position 0.4em from the top and right, set the left value to auto, and set a z-index of 2.

k. In the print styles section, add a style rule before the @page rule that removes nav elements from the layout for printed output.

l. Save your changes, open index.html in a browser, then compare it to **FIGURE F-24**.

m. Test all the links on both index.html and hours.html, test the Skip navigation link using a keyboard, then create a print preview and verify that the nav bar is not displayed and the content is displayed as black text on a white background.

n. Validate the code for your web pages and style sheet.

FIGURE F-24

Independent Challenge 2

As you continue developing the website for the Murfreesboro Regional Soccer League, you create links between pages as well as links to anchors. You also incorporate features to make the site navigation more accessible.

a. In your editor, open the file HTM_F-13.html from the IC2 folder where you store your Data Files for this unit, save it as **index.html**, then repeat to save the file HTM_F-14.html as **started.html**, HTM_F-15.html as **schedule.html**, and HTM_F-16.css as **styles.css**.

b. Within the comment section at the top of each file, enter your first and last names and today's date, then save your changes.

c. Return to index.html in your editor, then below the header element add a nav element with a class value of sitenavigation.

d. Within the nav element, create 4 p elements containing the text **Home, Getting Started**, **Schedules**, and **Field Location**. Link the text Home to index.html, Getting Started to started.html, and Schedules to schedule.html.

e. In your browser, navigate to a map service, then open a map showing 515 Cherry Lane Drive, Murfreesboro, Tennessee. Copy the URL (or a short link) to the Clipboard, return to index.html in your editor, then add a link to the phrase Field Location on the nav bar using the URL you copied, specifying that the file should open in a new browser tab. Save your changes.

f. Copy the nav element from index.html, then paste it below the header element in started.html and schedule.html. Save your changes to both files.

g. Return to styles.css in your editor, above the main content section add a comment containing the text **site navigation**, then below the comment, create the following style rules:

- For the nav element with the class value sitenavigation, set padding to 2%, width to 25%, position to absolute, left to 0, and the background color to #c8f098.
- For p elements within the nav element with the class value sitenavigation, set the bottom margin to 0.6em, the padding to 0.2em, the background color to black, and the font weight to bold.

Independent Challenge 2 (continued)

- For default links within the nav element with the class value sitenavigation, set text color to white and remove underlines.
- For visited links within the nav element with the class value sitenavigation, set text color to #c8f098.
- For links that the mouse pointer is over or that have the focus and that are within the nav element with the class value sitenavigation, set text color to yellow.
- For links that are being clicked and that are within the nav element with the class value sitenavigation, set a relative position 1px down from the top and 1px over from the left.

h. Save your changes to styles.css, return to schedule.html, add the id value red to the first h3 element, then repeat for the remaining 3 h3 elements using the id values blue, green, and yellow.

i. Above the first h3 element, create a nav element with the class value pagenavigation.

j. Within the new nav element, add 4 p elements containing the text **Red**, **Blue**, **Green**, and **Yellow**. Link the text of each p element to the corresponding h3 element using its id value.

k. Save your changes, return to styles.css, then above the footer section create a comment containing the text page navigation. Below the comment, add the following style rules:

- For the nav element with the class value pagenavigation, set the left margin to 1em and the left padding to 7%.
- For p elements within the nav element with the class value pagenavigation, set display type to inline-block, margins to 0.4em 0.4em 1em, padding to 0.4em, the background color to #c8f098 and add a 1px solid black border.
- For default links within the nav element with the class value pagenavigation, remove the underline and set the text color to black.
- For links that have the mouse pointer over them or that have the focus and that are within the nav element with the class value pagenavigation, set the text color to red.

l. Return to index.html in your editor, then in the opening <h2> tag in the article element, add an id value of contentstart.

m. Below the opening <div> tag with the class value container, add a p element with the class value skipnavigation. Within the p element, add the text **Skip navigation** and link it to the element with the id value contentstart. Save your changes.

n. Repeat Steps l and m for started.html and for schedule.html.

o. Return to styles.css in your editor, then above the header section, add a comment containing the text **skip navigation link**. Below it, add the following style rules:

- For the a element within the p element with the class value skipnavigation, set an absolute position -10000px from the left.
- For the a element with the focus that is within the p element with the class value skipnavigation, set the left value to auto, position the element 0.2em from the top and right, set text color to black, background color to white, and set a z-index of 2.

p. In the print styles section, add a style rule before the first existing rule that positions the article element 0px from the left, then add a style rule before the @page rule that removes nav elements from the layout for printed output.

q. Save your changes, open schedule.html in a browser, then compare it to **FIGURE F-25**.

r. Test all the links on index.html, started.html, and schedule.html, test the Skip navigation link using a keyboard, then create a print preview and verify that the nav bar is not displayed, the article element is positioned at the left edge of the container, and all content is displayed as black text on a white background.

s. Validate the code for your web pages and style sheet.

FIGURE F-25

Independent Challenge 3

As you continue your work on the website for Hotel Natoma, you incorporate links between pages as well as to external websites, and incorporate navigational accessibility features.

a. In your editor, open the file HTM_F-17.html from the IC3 folder where you store your Data Files for this unit, save it as **index.html**, then repeat to save the file HTM_F-18.html as **nearby.html**, and HTM_F-19.css as **styles.css**.

b. Within the comment section at the top of each file, enter your first and last names and today's date, then save your changes.

c. Return to index.html in your editor, then below the `header` element add a `nav` element with a `class` value of `sitenavigation`.

d. Within the `nav` element, create 3 p elements containing the text **Home**, **What's Nearby**, and **Location**. Link the text Home to index.html and What's Nearby to nearby.html. (*Hint*: Replace the curly apostrophe in What's Nearby with the character reference `&rsquo;`.)

e. In your browser, navigate to a map service, then, using the address in the `footer` element of index.html, open a map showing that location. Copy the URL (or a short link) to the Clipboard, return to index.html in your editor, then, using the URL you copied, add a link to the word **Location** on the nav bar, specifying that the file should open in a new browser tab. Save your changes.

f. Copy the `nav` element from index.html, return to nearby.html in your editor, then paste the `nav` element below the `header` element. Save your changes.

g. Return to styles.css in your editor, above the main content section add a comment containing the text **site navigation**, then below the comment, create the following style rules:

- For the `nav` element with the `class` value `sitenavigation`, set the width to 20%, padding to 2%, and float the element on the left.
- For p elements within the `nav` element with the `class` value `sitenavigation`, set the bottom margin to 0.5em.
- For default links within the `nav` element with the `class` value `sitenavigation`, set text color to `white`, the font weight to bold, and remove underlines.
- For visited links within the `nav` element with the `class` value `sitenavigation`, set text color to `#ddd`.
- For links that the mouse pointer is over or that have the focus and that are within the `nav` element with the `class` value `sitenavigation`, create a text shadow with 0 horizontal offset, 0 vertical offset, 5px blur, and a color of `#082008`.
- For links that are being clicked and that are within the `nav` element with the `class` value `sitenavigation`, set a relative position 1px down from the top and 1px over from the left.

h. Save your changes to styles.css, return to index.html in your editor, then in the opening `<p>` tag in the `article` element, add an `id` value of `contentstart`.

i. Below the opening `<div>` tag with the `class` value `container`, add a p element with the `class` value `skipnavigation`. Within the p element, add the text **Skip navigation** and link it to the element with the `id` value `contentstart`. Save your changes.

j. Repeat Steps h and i for nearby.html, adding the id value to the `h2` element.

k. Return to styles.css in your editor, then above the `header` section, add a comment containing the text **skip navigation** link. Below it, add the following style rules:

- For a elements within the p element with the `class` value `skipnavigation`, set an absolute position -10000px from the left.
- For a elements with the focus that are within the p element with the `class` value `skipnavigation`, set the position 0.2em from the left and 0.2em from the top, set the background color to `linen`, set the text color to `#082008`, and set a z-index of 2.

l. In the print styles section, add a style rule before the existing first style rule that sets `float` to `none` for the `article` element and sets its width to 100%, then add another style rule before the `@page` rule that removes `nav` elements from the layout for printed output.

Independent Challenge 3 (continued)

m. Save your changes, open nearby.html in a browser, then compare it to **FIGURE F-26**.

n. Test all the links on both index.html and nearby.html, test the Skip navigation link using a keyboard, then create a print preview and verify that the nav bar is not displayed, the article element is positioned at the left edge of the container, and all content is displayed as black text on a white background.

o. Validate the code for your web pages and style sheet.

FIGURE F-26

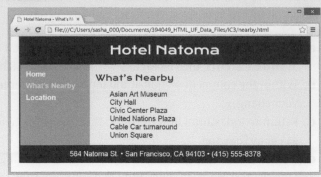

Independent Challenge 4—Explore

You continue your work building the website for Eating Well in Season by adding site navigation and accessibility features to existing pages.

a. In your editor, open the file HTM_F-20.html from the IC4 folder where you store your Data Files for this unit, save it as **index.html**, then repeat to save the file HTM_F-21.html as **sources.html**, HTM_F-22.html as **menus.html**, and HTM_F-23.css as **styles.css**.

b. Within the comment section at the top of each file, enter your first and last names and today's date, then save your changes.

c. Return to index.html in your editor, then below the `header` element create a `nav` element with links to the files index.html, sources.html, and menus.html. Copy the `nav` element to sources.html and menus.html, then save your changes to all 3 files.

d. Return to styles.css in your editor, above the main content section add a comment containing the text **site navigation**, then below the comment, create style rules to do the following:
- Set the background color of the `nav` element to black and center text within it.
- Use the inline-block display type for p elements within the nav element and add a 4px solid black border to each p element.
- Use the inline-block display type for each a element within the nav element and set the padding to 0.2em 0.8em.
- Set the default text color for links to `rgb(246,224,65)` and remove underlines from links.
- Set the text color for visited links to `#eee`.
- Set the text color for links with the mouse pointer over them or for links with the focus to black, with a background color of `rgb(246,224,65)`.
- Add the visual effect of a button being pushed to links that are being clicked.

e. Save your changes, then return to index.html in your editor. Below the opening `<div>` tag with the `class` value `container`, create a link with the text **Skip navigation** and link it to the first element nested within the article element. Save your changes, then repeat for sources.html and menus.html.

f. Return to styles.css in your editor, then above the `header` section, add a comment containing the text **skip navigation link**. Below it, add the following style rules for the skip navigation link you created:
- Position the link absolutely and out of the visible range of the page.
- When the link has the focus, give it a 2px solid black border, position it 0.2em from the left and 0.2em from the top of the containing element, set the background color to `white`, set the text color to `black`, and set a z-index of 2.

g. In the print styles section, add a style rule before the `@page` rule that removes `nav` elements from the layout for printed output.

Independent Challenge 4—Explore (continued)

h. Save your changes, open index.html in a browser, then compare it to **FIGURE F-27**.

i. Test all the links on index.html, sources.html, and menus.html, test the Skip navigation link using a keyboard, then create a print preview and verify that the nav bar is not displayed, the article element is positioned at the left edge of the container, and all content is displayed as black text on a white background.

j. Validate the code for your web pages and style sheet.

k. Install screen reader software and learn to use it.

- **Windows:** Download the free NVDA screen reader from nvaccess.org, then follow the instructions at http://community.nvda-project.org/documentation/userGuide.html to install and learn to use it. You do not have to make a donation to use the software for a trial run, although if you plan to use the software on a regular basis, you should consider donating. To turn off the program if it starts automatically, press [Insert] or [Caps Lock] + Q, then when you are prompted whether to end the program, select Yes, then Enter.

- **Mac:** Open System Preferences, click Accessibility, click VoiceOver, click the Enable VoiceOver box. In the dialog box that opens, click Learn More or Learn VoiceOver, then complete the tutorial to learn to use it.

l. Navigate index.html using your screen reader software, moving up and down within the page, and activating each link in the page. Open a new document in a word processor, then save it with the name **ScreenReaderSummary** to the IC4 folder where you save your files for this unit. Enter your name and today's date in the document, then write descriptions of 3 aspects of navigating the web with a screen reader that surprised you. For each aspect, describe what you were trying to do, how you would do that using a mouse, the steps required to complete it with a screen reader, and what part of the experience you found most surprising. Save your changes.

FIGURE F-27

Visual Workshop

In your text editor, open the file HTM_F-24.html from the VW directory where you store your Data Files for this unit and save it as **index.html**. Repeat to save HTM_F-25.html as **events.html**, HTM_F-26.html as **releases.html**, and HTM_F-27.css as **styles.css**. Add your first and last names and today's date to the comment section at the top of each file, then save your changes. Add a nav bar to all 3 web pages, formatting the default, visited, hover, and focus states as shown in **FIGURE F-28**, and adding a simulated push button effect for the active state. Link the first 3 nav bar links to the relevant pages in the website, and link the text *Location* to a map showing the business location listed at the bottom of the page that opens in a new tab. Create a skip navigation link for each document that is visible only when it has the focus and takes users to the first element in the main page content when selected. Edit the media query for printed output to exclude the navigation bars from printed output. Validate your HTML and CSS code. **FIGURE F-28** shows the completed version of events.html.

FIGURE F-28

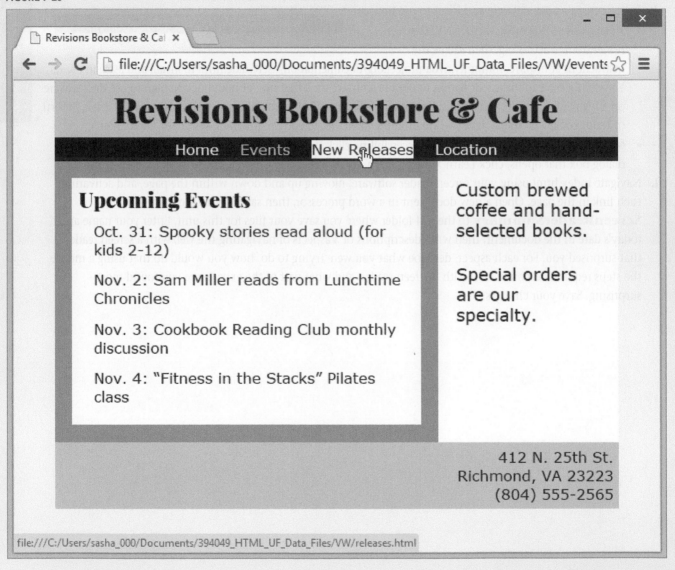

Inserting and Working with Images

CASE ▶ Your design colleagues at Lakeland Reed Bed & Breakfast have provided a logo image and several other graphics for the website you are creating. In this unit, you add the HTML and CSS code to incorporate these images into the site.

Unit Objectives

After completing this unit, you will be able to:

- Evaluate image file types
- Insert images
- Insert a background image
- Mark images as figures
- Create a figure caption

- Use images as links
- Create an image map
- Define additional hotspots
- Add a favicon and touch icons

Files You Will Need

 L   14 files   IC3   16 files

 SR   13 files   IC4   12 files

 IC1   11 files   VW   9 files

 IC2   11 files

For specific filenames, see Filenames_G.pdf in the Unit G Data Files folder.

Evaluate Image File Types

Learning
Outcomes
• Describe graphics
 file types
• Describe image
 sizing
 considerations

You can use HTML to incorporate images into your web pages and specify CSS properties to affect the way user agents display the images. Just as you can link to an external style sheet, you can add an image to a web page by linking to a separate image file, as illustrated in **FIGURE G-1**. **CASE** ▶ *As you prepare to incorporate graphics into the website for Lakeland Reeds Bed & Breakfast, you review the basics of images in HTML documents.*

DETAILS

To create optimal graphics for the web, it's important to understand a few concepts:

QUICK TIP

Both PNG and GIF
support transparent
pixels, allowing the
page background or
other elements to
show through parts
of an image. JPEG
does not support
transparency.

• **File types**

Images can be represented electronically in two ways: as bitmaps or as vectors. While a **bitmap image** represents an image as a grid of dots and specifies the color of each dot, a **vector graphic** encodes the appearance of a graphic as geometric shapes. Many file formats are available that render bitmap or vector representations in different ways. The three most widely used formats on the web are all different types of bitmap encoding. The **JPEG** or **JPG** format, named for the Joint Photographic Experts Group that created it, is optimized for images that contain many colors, such as photographs. **PNG**, short for portable network graphics, works best for art that contains a limited number of colors and areas with defined borders between areas. **GIF**, an abbreviation for graphics interchange format, is an older format with similar uses to PNG. An image in GIF format is generally larger than the same image in PNG format, and the GIF format supports fewer features than PNG, so PNG is generally preferred over GIF.

Browsers have long supported bitmap formats, but not vector graphics. However, all modern browsers support the **Scalable Vector Graphics (SVG)** format, which is optimal for encoding line art. Unlike bitmap formats like JPEG, which encode graphics at specific dimensions, an SVG file can be displayed at different dimensions with no decrease in quality. The only major browser that does not support SVG is IE8, so, if you need to maintain support for IE8 users, you should avoid use of SVG images.

• **Resolution and size**

When using any bitmap file formats, including JPEG, PNG, and GIF, it's important that an image is created and formatted with its use on the website in mind. All bitmap images are created to be displayed at a set resolution and size. **Resolution**, measured in **dots per inch (dpi)**, specifies how close the dots in the bitmap should appear on the output. While the standard for display on a monitor is 72 dpi, other media have different standards: for example, many home and office printers can print at 2400 dpi or greater. While a higher dpi image provides more detail, it also creates a file with a greater file size and takes up extra room on a web page. For this reason, it's important to save an image specifically for use on the web in a format and size that minimizes download time and ensures that the image fits in the page layout.

The size of a bitmap image is measured in **pixels**, which are the individual dots that make up the image. Every bitmap image is created with a specific length and width. While a vector graphic can be scaled larger or smaller with no change in quality, bitmap graphics display optimally only at their original, or **native**, length and width. As **FIGURE G-2** illustrates, scaling a larger bitmap to a smaller size unnecessarily increases the amount of data users have to download. While scaling a smaller image to a larger size decreases the amount of data that users have to download, it also results in markedly poor image quality. For this reason, it's important that designers create graphics at the precise dimensions required for a layout, in addition to generating them with the correct resolution for the web.

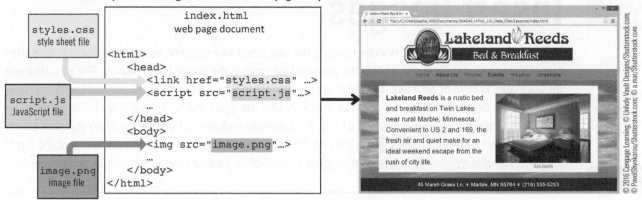

FIGURE G-2: Balancing bitmap file size and resolution

© Courtesy Sasha Vodnik

500px x 375px, 125 KB

Shrunk to 350px x 262px

350px x 262px, 40 KB

Displayed at same size

100px x 75px, 6 KB

Enlarged to 350px x 262px

3 image files with different native dimensions

Result of displaying all 3 images on a web page at 350px x 262px

Not optimal: Use of largest file requires users to download 85 KB more data but largest file is no clearer than medium file when displayed at medium file size

Optimal: Use of file displayed at its native dimensions results in best balance of file size and clarity

Not optimal: Use of smallest file saves 34 KB of data but results in fuzzier image when enlarged to medium file size

Assessing the future of SVG

The most widely supported graphics formats—GIF, JPEG, and PNG—require external files created with image editors. SVG graphics, however, are written in a markup language similar to XML. As support for the format grows, you will be able to create simple graphics like you create style sheets—that is, by creating external documents in a text editor and linking them to your web pages. Browser makers are also beginning to incorporate support for SVG code within HTML documents, meaning that eventually you will have the option to embed graphics like you embed CSS. SVG is supported by all major browsers, but not IE8, so if it's important that your site be compatible with IE8, you should use other graphics formats instead.

Insert Images

Learning Outcomes
• Add an image to a web page
• Specify alt text for an image

You add an image to an HTML document using the one-sided `img` element, which must include two attributes. The value of the `src` attribute is the path and filename of the image file to display. The `alt` attribute specifies text, known as **alt text**, to display in case the image is unavailable or is to be read by screen readers. **TABLE G-1** details attributes for the `img` element. Like the `span` element, `img` is an inline element by default. You can nest an `img` element in a block-level element and align it horizontally using standard block-level alignment techniques. **CASE** ▸ *You add the Lakeland Reeds logo in place of the heading at the top of the page. You also replace the bullets separating the sections of the contact information with decorative graphics.*

STEPS

1. **In your text editor, open HTM_G-1.html from the Lessons folder where you store your Data Files for this unit, save it as index.html, then repeat to save HTM_G-2.html as rooms.html, and HTM_G-3.css as styles.css**

2. **In the comment at the top of each file, enter your name and today's date where indicated, then save the files**

3. **In index.html, locate the `h1` element, delete the text Lakeland Reeds Bed & Breakfast, leaving the `<h1>` and `</h1>` tags, then between the `<h1>` tags, type**
   `<img src="images/lakeland.gif" width="659" height="165" alt="Lakeland Reeds Bed and Breakfast">`
   Image files for a website are commonly stored in a separate folder to keep the files organized.

4. **In the `footer` element, select the first occurrence of the character code `&bull;`, replace it with `<img src="images/flourish.gif" width="16" height="16" alt="">`, then repeat to replace the second occurrence of the character code with the same HTML code**
   Because these images are merely decorative and do not add information to the page, you use an empty value for the `alt` attribute to let screen readers know that they can skip these elements. **FIGURE G-3** shows the code containing the `img` elements you added.

5. **Save your changes, then open index.html in a browser**
   The logo image replaces the main heading text at the top of the page and the decorative graphic images replace the bullets in the footer, as shown in **FIGURE G-4**.

6. **Open index.html on a handheld device**
   The layout is narrowed to fit the device width, and then is narrowed further to fit the width of the logo.

7. **Return to styles.css in your editor, create a new style rule for the `img` element at the end of the reset styles section, then add the declarations `max-width: 100%;`, `height: auto;`, and `width: auto;`**
   The first declaration ensures that all images, including the logo image, are displayed no wider than the browser width, and the second declaration tells browsers to proportionally resize the height of an image if the width is resized. The third declaration is required for compatibility with IE8.

8. **In the style rule that sets border, padding, and margin to 0 in the reset styles section, add the `img` selector to the list of selectors**
   FIGURE G-5 shows the changes to the reset styles section of the style sheet.

9. **Save your changes, then refresh or reload index.html on your handheld device**
   The logo image is resized to fit the screen width, and the remaining page content fits the screen.

10. **Repeat Steps 3-6 to add the logo and decorative graphic to the corresponding elements in rooms.html, then preview your changes on desktop and mobile browsers**

FIGURE G-3: `img` elements added to index.html

```
23              <header>
24                  <h1><img src="images/lakeland.gif" width="659" height="165" alt="Lakeland
25                  Reeds Bed and Breakfast"></h1>
26              </header>
```

```
43              <footer>
44                  <p>45 Marsh Grass Ln. <img src="images/flourish.gif" width="16" height="16"
45                  alt=""> Marble, MN 55764 <img src="images/flourish.gif" width="16"
46                  height="16" alt=""> (218) 555-5253</p>
47              </footer>
```

FIGURE G-4: Main web page with images inserted

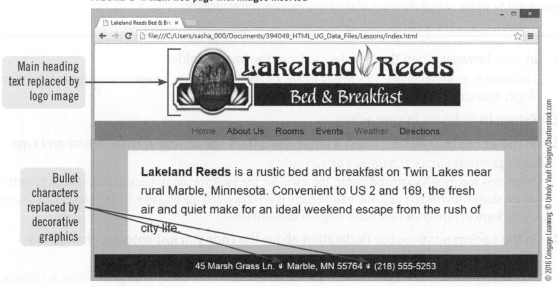

Main heading text replaced by logo image

Bullet characters replaced by decorative graphics

© 2016 Cengage Learning; © Unholy Vault Designs/Shutterstock.com

FIGURE G-5: Reset styles for `img` element

```
10      /* reset styles */
11      html {
12          font-size: 16px;
13      }
14      a, article, body, div, footer, header, h1, h2, h3, img, nav, p {
15          border: 0;
16          padding: 0;
17          margin: 0;
18      }
19      img {
20          max-width: 100%;
21          height: auto;
22          width: auto;
23      }
```

TABLE G-1: Attributes for the `img` element

attribute	value
src	path and filename for image file to display
alt	text to display or read in place of image
height width	native height and width of image file in pixels

© 2016 Cengage Learning

Insert a Background Image

Learning Outcomes
- Specify a background image
- Specify a fallback background color

In addition to specifying a color as the background for a web page or web page element, you can provide a path and filename for a background image using the background-image property. As with background colors, it's important to choose a background image that provides contrast with other web page elements, especially text. If a background image does not fill the entire element, by default browsers **tile** it, meaning that, like tiles on a floor or wall, the image is displayed repeatedly both across and down the element to fill it up. **TABLE G-2** describes additional properties you can use to change the way a background image is displayed. **CASE** *The designers have provided a background image for the article element. Because the article element's content is within a separate div element with its own background color, the background image will be visible only at the edges of the page, maintaining readability.*

STEPS

1. **In your browser, open the file lake.jpg from the images folder**

   The image is small and square. This type of image, known as a **seamless image**, is designed to look like a single, uninterrupted image when tiled.

2. **Return to styles.css in your editor**

3. **In the article style rule, insert a blank line before the closing }, then indent and type** background: url("images/lake.jpg");

   When you specify a background image, the value for the background or background-image property always starts with the text url. The relative path, if necessary, and the filename for the background image are enclosed in parentheses and either single or double quotes.

4. **In the background-color declaration above the code you just entered, change the property name background-color to background**

   Even when you specify a background image, you should also continue to specify a background color as a fallback for user agents that don't display images, or for situations where the background image file is unavailable. When declarations conflict, the one that occurs later in the rule takes precedence. For example, when you specify both background color and background image using the shorthand background property, the final property that a browser can render is used, and the other is ignored. If a user agent is unable to load the image specified by the second background property, it falls back to the preceding background declaration and displays the background color instead. **FIGURE G-6** shows the code for the background color and image.

5. **Save your work, then reload index.html in your browser**

   As **FIGURE G-7** shows, the background image appears behind the article element. The image is repeated vertically and horizontally to fill the entire length and height of the element. The element contents are within a div element that has a background color of ivory; this prevents the background image from appearing behind the text and preserves readability.

6. **Return to styles.css in your editor, then in the print styles section at the end of the document and in the** body, h1, article, footer **style rule, replace the** background-color **property with** background

   FIGURE G-8 shows the edited code.

7. **Save your work, reload index.html in your browser, then open a print preview**

   The article element is displayed with a white background instead of a background image.

FIGURE G-6: Code for background color and background image

```
85    /* main content */
86    article {
87        margin: 0 auto;
88        padding: 1.4em;
89        background: #7eccec;
90        background: url("images/lake.jpg");
91    }
```

background-color property name changed to background to serve as fallback for declaration that follows

background declaration added for background image

FIGURE G-7: Main web page with tiled background image

Nested div element has a background color of ivory to provide contrast for text

Background image repeated vertically and horizontally to cover entire article element

Home   About Us   Rooms   Events   Weather   Directions

Lakeland Reeds is a rustic bed and breakfast on Twin Lakes near rural Marble, Minnesota. Convenient to US 2 and 169, the fresh air and quiet make for an ideal weekend escape from the rush of city life.

45 Marsh Grass Ln. ⚜ Marble, MN 55764 ⚜ (218) 555-5253

© 2016 Cengage Learning; © a.mar/Shutterstock.com

FIGURE G-8: `background-color` declaration changed to `background` in print styles section

```
147    /* print styles */
148    @media print {
149        body, h1, article, footer {
150            color: rgb(0,0,0);
151            background: rgb(255,255,255);
152        }
```

TABLE G-2: Properties that affect an element's background

property	specifies
background-attachment	whether a background image scrolls with document content (scroll, the default), scrolls only with element content (local), or does not scroll (fixed)
background-blend-mode	how overlapping background images blend with each other and with background color, using one or more keywords
background-clip	whether a background image extends only behind element content (content-box), up to the inner edge of the border (padding-box), or to the outer edge of the border (border-box, the default)
background-color	a background color using a color keyword or a hex, RGB, RGBa, HSL, or HSLa value
background-image	an image file to use as the background for an element with the syntax url("path/filename")
background-origin	whether a background image starts only behind element content (content-box), at the inner edge of the border (padding-box), or at the outer edge of the border (border-box, the default)
background-position	the position within an element of the edges of a background image using a combination of values and keywords
background-repeat	whether a background image is repeated horizontally, vertically, both, or neither, using one or more keywords
background-size	the size of a background image with keywords, lengths, or percentages
background	values for one or more properties related to background listed in a specific order

© 2016 Cengage Learning

Mark Images as Figures

HTML5 includes the semantic `figure` element to mark images that add information to a web page. To decide whether an image should be marked as a `figure`, think about whether the basic information conveyed by the page would still be complete if the image were not shown. If so, the image should be marked as a `figure`. For instance, a picture, chart, or map illustrating the topic of a paragraph would be marked as a figure because, while it illustrates the paragraph content, it isn't absolutely necessary for a user to understand the information. However, a logo image would not be marked as a `figure` because it's integral to conveying the overall subject of a page. **CASE** ▶ *You add a* `figure` *element for each room on the Rooms page.*

STEPS

1. **Return to rooms.html in your editor, on a new line below the opening tag for the h3 element containing the text** *Reed Room,* **indent and type** `<figure>`, **press [Enter] twice, then indent and type** `</figure>`

2. **On the blank line between the opening and closing `<figure>` tags, indent and then type** `<img src="images/reed.jpg" width="370" height="392" alt="a carpeted room with a high sloping ceiling, two small bright windows, and a two-person bed with a bedside table and lamp on each side">`

3. **Repeat Steps 1 and 2 to add opening and closing `<figure>` tags below the h3 headings** *Sun Room* **and** *Treehouse,* **then on the blank line in each element, add the img elements shown in FIGURE G-9**

   FIGURE G-9 shows the code for the `figure` and `img` elements added to rooms.html.

QUICK TIP

If the width of a `figure` element is not specified with a percentage value, you use the declaration `max-width: 100%;` to ensure that the element automatically scales to fit smaller screens.

4. **Save your changes, return to styles.css in your editor, then, at the bottom of the main content section, add a style rule that uses the `article figure` selector with the declarations** `max-width: 100%;`, `margin-left: 2em;`, **and** `float:right;`

5. **Scroll to the reset styles section, then add the `figure` selector to the list of selectors in the style rule that sets border, padding, and margin to 0**

6. **Scroll to the main content section, add the declaration** `overflow: auto;` **to the `article div` style rule**

   Because a floated element is not used in calculating the height of its parent element and the Treehouse image is taller than the text content it floats next to, the bottom of the parent element comes before the bottom of the image. Setting the `overflow` property to `auto` extends the height of the parent element to include the entire floated element, which will cause the ivory background of the `article` element to extend the entire length of the image. **FIGURE G-10** shows the changes to the style sheet.

7. **Save your changes, then refresh or reload rooms.html in your browser**

   The three images you added within `figure` elements are floated to the right below the h3 elements. **FIGURE G-11** shows one image as rendered by a browser.

Obtaining permission for image use

Although it's possible to find and copy images from the web for use on your own web pages, it's important to make sure you have permission to use a given image before incorporating it into your designs. In addition to avoiding potential legal action for unauthorized use of someone else's work, it's a show of respect to photographers and designers to ask for permission to use their work. For small projects, a photographer or designer may allow use in return for credit and a link to their site; for larger professional sites, a photographer or designer usually requires a use fee and agreed-on terms of use. If you're hiring a designer to create artwork for your website, make sure your agreement specifies how long and in what context you or your organization may use the work.

FIGURE G-9: `figure` and `img` elements added to rooms.html

```
38            <h3 id="reed">Reed Room</h3>
39            <figure>
40               <img src="images/reed.jpg" width="370" height="392" alt="a carpeted room
41               with a high sloping ceiling, two small bright windows, and a two-person
42               bed with a bedside table and lamp on each side">
43            </figure>
44            <p>This first-floor room looks out over the reeds on the edge of the lake and
45            the water beyond.</p>
46            <p>1 queen bed and 1 twin bed.</p>
47            <h3 id="sun">Sun Room</h3>
48            <figure>
49               <img src="images/sun.jpg" width="370" height="278" alt="room with a
50               hardwood floor, bright windows on two sides, and a two-person bed with a
51               bedside table and lamp on each side">
52            </figure>
53            <p>With windows on three sides, the sunlight in this second-floor room
54            supports a large selection of houseplants.</p>
55            <p>1 full bed.</p>
56            <h3 id="tree">Treehouse</h3>
57            <figure>
58               <img src="images/tree.jpg" width="370" height="247" alt="a large room with
59               a hardwood floor, a tall window overlooking trees, a two-person bed with a
60               single bedside table, and a padded chair next to the window">
61            </figure>
62            <p>A winding staircase takes you to your own private getaway at the top of
```

FIGURE G-10: Style rules for `figure` elements

```
14  a, article, body, div, figure, footer, header, h1, h2, h3, img, nav, p {
15     border: 0;
16     padding: 0;
17     margin: 0;
18  }
```

```
92  article div {
93     max-width: 800px;
94     margin: 0 auto;
95     padding: 0 3% 1em;
96     background-color: ivory;
97     overflow: auto;
98  }
```

```
116  article p.pullquote {
117     font-size: 1.7em;
118  }
119  article figure {
120     max-width: 100%;
121     margin-left: 2em;
122     float: right;
123  }
```

FIGURE G-11: Style rules applied to `figure` elements

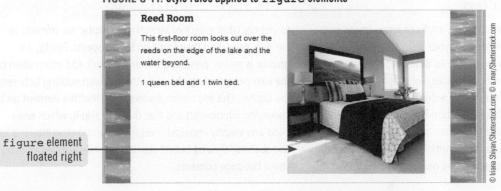

figure element floated right

© Inana Shiyan/Shutterstock.com; © a.mar/Shutterstock.com

Create a Figure Caption

In addition to providing alternative text for an image using the alt attribute, you can associate other types of text with an image. Many images benefit from a text caption that provides context, explanation, or credit. To associate caption text with an img element, you place the text in a figcaption element that is nested within the figure element for the image. **CASE** *Because the images on the Rooms web page are already explained by the surrounding content, you decide not to add captions to them. However, you add an image with a caption on the main page of the website.*

STEPS

1. **Return to index.html in your editor, insert a new line below the opening tag for the div element with the id value contentstart, indent and type <figure class="example">, press [Enter] twice, then indent and type </figure>**

2. **On the blank line between the opening and closing <figure> tags, indent and then type** `<img src="images/sun.jpg" width="370" height="278" alt="room with a hardwood floor, bright windows on two sides, and a two-person bed with a bedside table and lamp on each side">`

3. **Insert a new line beneath the <img> tag you entered in the previous step, then indent and type** `<figcaption><a href="rooms.html#sun">Sun Room</a></figcaption>`
   The figcaption element marks the text it contains as a caption for the associated image within the figure element. **FIGURE G-12** shows the code for the figure, img, and figcaption elements added to index.html.

4. **Save your changes, then return to styles.css in your editor**

5. **At the bottom of the main content section, add a style rule that uses the** `article figure.example` **selector with the declaration** `margin-top: 2em;`**, then add another style rule with the** `article figcaption` **selector and the declaration** `text-align: center;`

6. **Scroll to the reset styles section, then add the** figcaption **selector to the list of selectors in the style rule that sets border, padding, and margin to 0**
   FIGURE G-13 shows the changes to the style sheet.

7. **Save your changes, then refresh or reload index.html in your browser**
   The text *Sun Room* is centered beneath the image, as shown in **FIGURE G-14**.

Creating useful alt text

The text you provide using the alt attribute for an image is an important accessibility element for your website. It's also significant for users who are unable to download the image or who choose to browse without images. For graphics that include text, that text should be included in the value of the alt attribute, along with a description if it adds useful information. The alt value for photos and other graphics without text should include a description of the image. Because there are many ways to describe any given image, it's important to identify what aspect or aspects of a graphic are relevant to the web page, and then focus on those aspects. Finally, if a graphic is merely presentational and doesn't add information to the web page, include the alt attribute with nothing between the quotes. This lets screen readers know that the element isn't conveying information and that they can skip it, which saves blind and visually impaired users from wasting time listening to text such as "stylized bullet" repeatedly while learning nothing about the page contents.

```
34              <article>
                <div id="contentstart">
                    <figure class="example">
                        <img src="images/sun.jpg" width="370" height="278" alt="room with a
                        hardwood floor, bright windows on two sides, and a two-person bed with a
                        bedside table and lamp on each side">
                        <figcaption><a href="rooms.html#sun">Sun Room</a></figcaption>
                    </figure>
                    <p class="pullquote"><span class="accent">Lakeland Reeds</span> is a rustic
```

`figcaption` element nested within `figure` element to provide caption for sibling `img` element

FIGURE G-13: Style rules for `figure` element with example `class` value and for `figcaption` element

```
14  a, article, body, div, figcaption, figure, footer, header, h1, h2, h3, img, nav, p {
15      border: 0;
16      padding: 0;
17      margin: 0;
18  }
```

```
118  article figure {
119      max-width: 100%;
120      margin-left: 2em;
121      float: right;
122  }
123  article figure.example {
124      margin-top: 2em;
125  }
126  article figcaption {
127      text-align: center;
128  }
```

FIGURE G-14: Figure caption in main web page

Lakeland Reeds is a rustic bed and breakfast on Twin Lakes near rural Marble, Minnesota. Convenient to US 2 and 169, the fresh air and quiet make for an ideal weekend escape from the rush of city life.

Content of `figcaption` element displayed below `img` element

© PavelShynkarou/Shutterstock.com; © a.mar/Shutterstock.com

HTML5 & CSS3

Understanding the `title` attribute

You can also specify additional information about an image using the `title` attribute, which is supported by the `img` and `figure` elements as well as most other HTML elements. Most visual user agents display the value of the `title` attribute as floating text when a user moves the mouse pointer over the associated element. However, modern desktop browsers do not provide access to the `title` value when navigating with a keyboard. In addition, mobile browsers do not support the display of the `title` attribute on touchscreen devices. For this reason, the W3C does not recommend that web developers use the `title` attribute until browser makers provide access for all users.

Use Images as Links

You can add a link to an image in an HTML document by nesting the img element in an a element. Many websites add a link to the logo image on each page that returns the user to the main page of the site when the logo is clicked or touched. **CASE** ▶ *You link the logo image on the Rooms page back to index.html to provide a shortcut for visitors to the site. You also link the image of the Sun Room on the main web page to the information about that room on rooms.html.*

STEPS

1. **Return to rooms.html in your editor**

2. **Position the insertion point after the opening `<h1>` tag and before the `<img>` tag in the header element, then type `<a href="index.html">`**

3. **Position the insertion point between the closing `>` of the `<img>` tag and the closing `</h1>` tag, type `</a>`, then save your changes**
   FIGURE G-15 shows the added code.

4. **Return to index.html in your editor**

5. **Position the insertion point before the opening `<` of the `<img>` tag for the sun.jpg image in the article element, then type `<a href="rooms.html#sun">`**

6. **Position the insertion point after the closing `>` of the `<img>` tag, type `</a>`, then save your changes**
   FIGURE G-16 shows the added code.

TROUBLE
If the Rooms page opens but the Sun Room information is not at the top of the window, the window may be too tall for that section to scroll to the top. Reduce the height of your browser window, click your browser's Back button, then repeat Step 9.

7. **Refresh or reload rooms.html in your browser, then move the mouse pointer over the logo image**
   The pointer becomes a pointing hand when it moves over the image as shown in **FIGURE G-17**, indicating that the image is a link.

8. **Click the logo image at the top of the page**
   The main page opens.

9. **Click the Sun Room image**
   The Rooms page opens, with the Sun Room information at the top of the browser window.

Styling an image with opacity

Recent versions of all major browsers support the CSS opacity property for img elements. The opacity property sets how transparent an element is, from 0 (fully transparent) to 1 (fully opaque, which is the default). For instance, to set 50% opacity, you use the code

```
opacity: 0.5;
```

IE8 and older versions of Internet Explorer don't support this syntax, however, and require an additional declaration using a Microsoft-specific property:

```
filter: alpha(opacity=number);
```

where *number* is a percentage from 0 (fully transparent) to 100 (fully opaque). When you decrease the opacity of an image, you make it partially transparent. This can be useful if you want to increase the contrast between the image and other page elements or simply to alter the image to more closely match a site's design.

FIGURE G-15: a element enclosing `img` element for logo

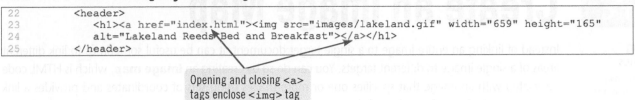

```
22          <header>
23              <h1><a href="index.html"><img src="images/lakeland.gif" width="659" height="165"
24              alt="Lakeland Reeds Bed and Breakfast"></a></h1>
25          </header>
```

Opening and closing `<a>` tags enclose `<img>` tag

FIGURE G-16: a element enclosing `img` element for Sun Room photo

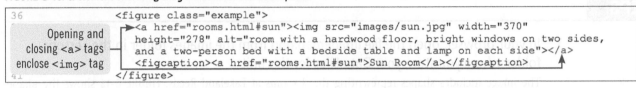

```
36              <figure class="example">
                <a href="rooms.html#sun"><img src="images/sun.jpg" width="370"
                height="278" alt="room with a hardwood floor, bright windows on two sides,
                and a two-person bed with a bedside table and lamp on each side"></a>
                <figcaption><a href="rooms.html#sun">Sun Room</a></figcaption>
41              </figure>
```

Opening and closing `<a>` tags enclose `<img>` tag

FIGURE G-17: Link added to logo image

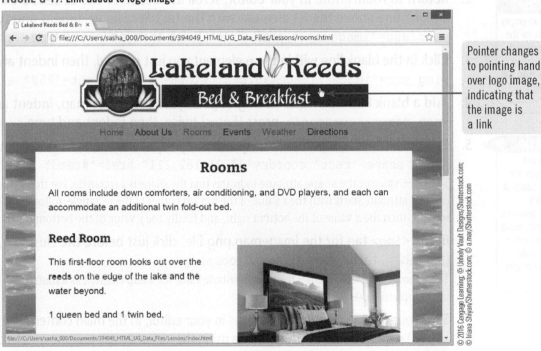

Pointer changes to pointing hand over logo image, indicating that the image is a link

---

Using a background image and a background color together

When you specify a background color and a background image in separate declarations using the `background` property, only one of the declarations is rendered by browsers. However, in some cases you want to apply both a background color and a background image at the same time. This is most common when your background image has some transparent pixels and you want to control the color that's visible behind the image. To apply both a background color and a background image, you use a single shorthand `background` property and specify the background image name followed by the background color, separated by a space. For instance, to use the background image sky.jpg with a background color of #001848, you would use the declaration `background: url("sky.jpg") #001848;`. In this case, there's no need to create a second `background` declaration, as the specified color automatically serves as a fallback for the background image.

Create an Image Map

Learning Outcomes
- Apply an image map to an image
- Create a rectangu-lar hotspot

Instead of linking an entire image to a single target document, it can be useful sometimes to link different areas of a single image to different targets. You can do so by creating an **image map**, which is HTML code associated with an image that specifies one or more shapes using sets of coordinates and provides a link target for each shape. Each shape is known as a **hotspot**. You create an image map with a single map element, in which you nest an area element for each hotspot. TABLE G-3 describes commonly used attributes of the area element. **CASE** ▸ *You add an image showing room sizes to the Rooms page, then create an image map containing a rectangular hotspot for the Reed room.*

STEPS

1. **In your browser, open the file imagemap.png from the images folder in the Lessons folder where you store your Data Files for this unit**

   The image includes shapes representing the 3 rooms at Lakeland Reeds. **FIGURE G-18** shows the shape attribute value and the coords attribute for the rectangular Reed Room shape and illustrates the measurement of the coordinates from the top left corner of the image.

2. **Return to rooms.html in your editor, scroll as needed to the article element, add a blank line above the h3 element with the text *Reed Room*, indent and type `<p class="imagemap">`, press [Enter] twice, then indent and type `</p>`**

3. **Click in the blank line within the p element you just created, then indent and type `<img src="images/imagemap.png" width="500" height="250" alt="">`**

4. **Add a blank line below the closing `</p>` tag for the image map, indent and type `<map name="roomsmap">`, press [Enter] twice, then indent and type `</map>`**

5. **Click in the blank line within the map element you just created, then indent and type `<area shape="rect" coords="33,21,162,211" href="#reed" alt="Reed Room">`**

   The rect value of the shape attribute indicates that the shape is a rectangle. For this shape, the value of the coords attribute starts with the *x* value of the top left corner of the rectangle, followed by the *y* value of the top left, then the *x* value of the bottom right, and finally the *y* value of the bottom right.

6. **In the `<img>` tag for the imagemap.png file, click just before the closing `>`, press [Spacebar], then type `usemap="#roomsmap"`**

   The usemap attribute specifies the name attribute value for a map element as a hash link. **FIGURE G-19** shows the completed code for the image map.

7. **Save your changes, return to styles.css in your editor, in the main content section, below the article p style rule, add a style rule using the `article p.imagemap` selector with the declaration `text-align: center;`, then add a style rule using the `article p.imagemap img` selector with the declarations `border: 1px solid black;` and `max-width: none;`**

   Setting the max-width property to none prevents browsers from resizing the image, which would mean the coordinates no longer correspond to the intended parts of the image. **FIGURE G-20** shows the rules added to the style sheet.

8. **Save your changes, refresh or reload rooms.html in your browser, move the mouse pointer over the rectangle labeled Reed Room in the map graphic**

   The mouse pointer changes to a pointing hand when it is over the rectangle, indicating that the rectangle is a link. Notice that when the mouse pointer moves off of the rectangle, it turns back to a pointing arrow.

9. **Click the rectangle**

   The browser scrolls the page down to the Reed Room section.

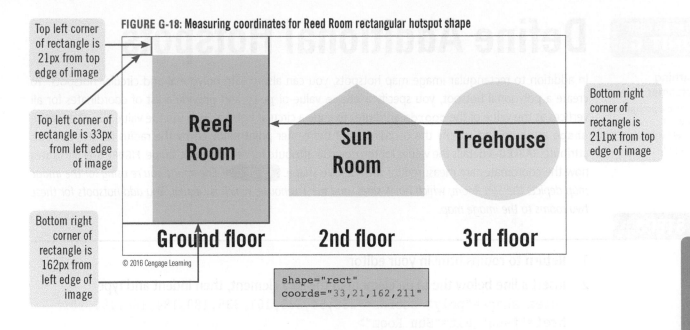

FIGURE G-18: Measuring coordinates for Reed Room rectangular hotspot shape

Top left corner of rectangle is 21px from top edge of image

Top left corner of rectangle is 33px from left edge of image

Bottom right corner of rectangle is 211px from top edge of image

Bottom right corner of rectangle is 162px from left edge of image

© 2016 Cengage Learning

```
shape="rect"
coords="33,21,162,211"
```

FIGURE G-19: `img`, `map`, and `area` elements for image map

```
38                     each can accommodate an additional twin fold-out bed.</p>
39     usemap          <p class="imagemap">
40     attribute of       <img src="images/imagemap.png" width="500" height="250" alt=""
41     img element     usemap="#roomsmap">
42     specifies name  </p>
43     value of map    <map name="roomsmap">
44     element to use     <area shape="rect" coords="33,21,162,211" href="#reed" alt="Reed Room">
45                     </map>
46     as image map    <h3 id="reed">Reed Room</h3>
```

map element contains one or more `area` elements for hotspots

`area` element with `shape` value of `rect` creates a rectangular hotspot

FIGURE G-20: Style rules for image map components

```
113    article p {
114        padding-top: 1em;
115    }
116    article p.imagemap {
117        text-align: center;
118    }
119    article p.imagemap img {
120        border: 1px solid black;
121        max-width: none;
122    }
```

Prevents image from resizing by causing browsers to use the `width` and `height` attribute values as fixed dimensions

TABLE G-3: Attributes of the area element

attribute	value
alt	Alternate text that describes the hotspot for users of screen readers or if the image doesn't load
coords	A comma-separated list of coordinates for the specified `shape` value measured from the top and left edges of the image
href	A URL, local filename, or hash link to the target document or location opened by the hotspot
shape	The value `circle` to create a circle, `poly` to create a polygon, or `rect` to create a rectangle

© 2016 Cengage Learning

Define Additional Hotspots

In addition to rectangular image map hotspots, you can also create polygonal and circular hotspots. To create a polygonal hotspot, you specify a `shape` value of `poly` and provide a list of coordinates for all vertices as the value of the `coords` attribute. To code a circular hotspot, you use the value `circle` for the `shape` attribute and specify the coordinates of the center point followed by the radius for the `coords` attribute. **TABLE G-4** details the values for the `coords` attribute for each hotspot shape. **FIGURE G-21** illustrates how the coordinates are measured for the `circle` shape. **CASE ▶** *The image you're using for the image map depicts the Sun Room, which has 5 sides, and the Treehouse, which is circular. You add hotspots for these two rooms to the image map.*

STEPS

1. **Return to rooms.html in your editor**

2. **Insert a line below the `area` element in the `map` element, then indent and type**
   ```
   <area shape="poly" coords="258,54,335,101,335,180,184,180,184,101"
   href="#sun" alt="Sun Room">
   ```
   The `poly` value of the `shape` attribute indicates that the shape is a polygon, which allows you to create a triangle or a shape with more than 4 sides. For this shape, the value of the `coords` attribute starts with the *x* value of any vertex of the shape, followed by the *y* value of that vertex, then the *x* value of the next vertex in either direction, the *y* value of that vertex, and so on until all vertices have been specified in order.

3. **Insert a line below the `area` element you just created, then indent and type**
   ```
   <area shape="circle" coords="419,116,65" href="#tree"
   alt="Treehouse">
   ```
   The `circle` value of the `shape` attribute indicates that the shape is a circle. For this shape, the value of the `coords` attribute starts with the *x* value of the center of the circle, followed by the *y* value of the center, then the length of the circle's radius. **FIGURE G-22** shows the final code for the image map.

4. **Save your changes, then refresh or reload rooms.html in your browser**

5. **Move the mouse pointer over the polygon labeled Sun Room in the map graphic, move the mouse pointer around the shape and on both sides of the shape border, then repeat for the circle labeled Treehouse**
   As with the Reed Room rectangle, the pointer is a pointing hand when it is over one of the shapes, as shown in **FIGURE G-23**, and returns to a default arrow pointer when it moves off of a shape.

6. **Click the Sun Room polygon**
   The browser scrolls the page down to the Sun Room section.

7. **Scroll back up to the image map graphic, then click the Treehouse circle**
   The browser scrolls the page down to the Treehouse section.

TABLE G-4: Values of the `coords` attribute for different hotspot shapes

shape value	coords value
circle	*x, y, r* where *x* and *y* are the *x* and *y* coordinates of the center point of the circle, and *r* is the radius
poly	*x1, y1, x2, y2, ...* where *x1, y1, x2, y2*, and so on are the *x* and *y* coordinates of the vertices of the polygon
rect	*x1, y1, x2, y2* where *x1* and *y1* are the *x* and *y* coordinates of the top left corner of the rectangle and *x2* and *y2* are the *x* and *y* coordinates of the bottom right corner of the rectangle

FIGURE G-21: Measuring coordinates for hotspot shapes

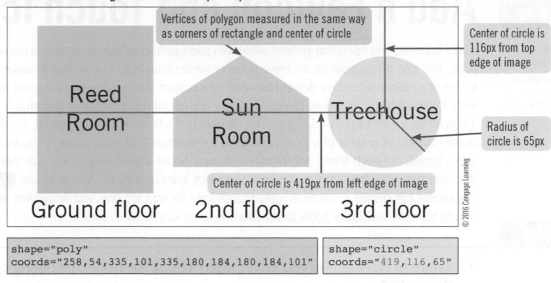

Vertices of polygon measured in the same way as corners of rectangle and center of circle

Center of circle is 116px from top edge of image

Radius of circle is 65px

Center of circle is 419px from left edge of image

© 2016 Cengage Learning

```
shape="poly"
coords="258,54,335,101,335,180,184,180,184,101"
```

```
shape="circle"
coords="419,116,65"
```

FIGURE G-22: `area` elements for polygonal and circular hotspots added

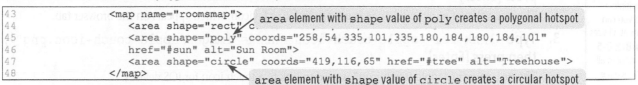

```
43    <map name="roomsmap">
44        <area shape="rect" c...
45        <area shape="poly" coords="258,54,335,101,335,180,184,180,184,101"
46        href="#sun" alt="Sun Room">
47        <area shape="circle" coords="419,116,65" href="#tree" alt="Treehouse">
48    </map>
```

area element with `shape` value of `poly` creates a polygonal hotspot

area element with `shape` value of `circle` creates a circular hotspot

FIGURE G-23: Testing link on Sun Room hotspot

Pointer changes to pointing hand over Sun Room shape, indicating that the shape is a link

© 2016 Cengage Learning; © a.mar/Shutterstock.com

Generating hotspot coordinates

Identifying the precise coordinates for a hotspot shape can be the most challenging part of creating an image map. Using graphic design software such as Adobe Photoshop, you can identify the coordinates of any point in an image. By looking up the coordinates for each point in your image, you can create the area element for each hotspot manually. However, many tools are available that let you point and drag and identify shapes and then provide you with the shape's coordinates. GIMP, a free graphic design application, lets you generate an image map in this way. Adobe Fireworks, a paid application, supports this method as well. Additionally, some websites provide image map generation utilities for free. To locate them, use a search engine to search on the terms *free image map generator*.

Add a Favicon and Touch Icons

Learning Outcomes
- Specify a favicon
- Specify touch icons for iOS and Android devices

Major browsers and operating systems allow web page authors to specify the icon associated with a web page. This icon may appear on the browser tab or the bookmarks list in a desktop browser or on the home screen of a mobile device. For desktop browsers, this custom icon is a graphic file known as a **favicon**. For widest compatibility, you create favicons with the .ico format using the name favicon.ico. You can specify a favicon for a web page by adding a link element that references the appropriate .ico file. You can also specify additional graphic files to serve as icons for shortcuts that users create on mobile devices. These icons, known as **touch icons**, are displayed on users' home screens when users save shortcuts. TABLE G-5 describes the characteristics of the favicons and touch icons used by modern browsers. **CASE** *The art department has created a favicon as well as touch icons for both iOS and Android systems. You add <link> tags to the main and Rooms pages for the Lakeland Reeds website for all three icons.*

STEPS

1. **Return to** index.html **in your editor, insert a blank line before the closing </head> tag, then indent**

QUICK TIP
The .ico format can contain multiple images, so you can create icons at all sizes listed in **TABLE G-5** and include them all in the same .ico file.

2. **Type** `<link rel="shortcut icon" href="images/favicon.ico">`, **then press [Enter]**

   The `rel` value of `shortcut icon` is used to link to a favicon, which appears on the browser tab.

3. **Type** `<link rel="apple-touch-icon" href="images/apple-touch-icon.png">`, **then press [Enter]**

   The `rel` value of "apple-touch-icon" is used to link to a touch icon for iOS devices.

TROUBLE
Note that some browsers show favicons only for websites accessed over the Internet and don't look for the icons for local files. If you don't see the favicon, open the web page from a web server.

4. **Type** `<link rel="icon" sizes="192x192" href="images/android.png">`, **then save your changes**

   The `rel` value of "icon" is used to link to a touch icon for Android devices. Note that this link element should include the `sizes` attribute for maximum compatibility. **FIGURE G-24** shows the code for the link elements inserted in the document.

5. **Reload** index.html **in your browser, then examine the browser tab for the Lakeland Reeds favicon, which resembles the stylized reeds in the logo image**

   FIGURE G-25 shows the favicon in a browser tab. Note that some browsers may display one of the touch icons instead, showing a dark brown background.

TROUBLE
If you're using a different smartphone or browser, follow your usual steps for adding an icon to your home screen.

6. **Open** index.html **on a smartphone or tablet, tap the Menu button ⋮ (Chrome for Android) or the Share button 🔝 (Safari for iOS), tap Add to Home Screen, tap Add, then examine the icon on your home screen**

   FIGURE G-26 shows the touch icon on the home screens of Android and iOS devices. Note that the two icons are almost identical, and simply have slightly different dimensions as described in **TABLE G-5**.

7. **Repeat Steps 2–6 for** rooms.html

8. **Validate the code for your web pages and your style sheet, then make changes as necessary to fix any errors**

FIGURE G-24: link elements for favicon and touch icons added

```
18          <link rel="stylesheet" href="styles.css">
19          <link rel="shortcut icon" href="images/favicon.ico">
20          <link rel="apple-touch-icon" href="images/apple-touch-icon.png">
21          <link rel="icon" sizes="192x192" href="images/android.png">
22      </head>
```

FIGURE G-25: Favicon displayed on desktop browser tab

Customized favicon from favicon.ico file

FIGURE G-26: Touch icons displayed on home screens of mobile devices

Touch icon on Android home screen

Touch icon on iOS home screen

TABLE G-5: Characteristics of favicons and touch icons

platform	format	dimensions	link tag
desktop (all)	.ico (all browsers) .png (all browsers except IE10 and earlier)	16px × 16px (standard resolution) 32px × 32px (high resolution) 48px × 48px (Taskbar)	`<link rel="shortcut icon" href="images/favicon.ico">`
Apple iOS	.png	180px × 180px	`<link rel="apple-touch-icon" href="images/apple-touch-icon.png">`
Google Android	.png	192px × 192px	`<link rel="icon" sizes="192x192" href="images/android.png">`

Practice

Concepts Review

Refer to FIGURE G-27 **to answer the following questions.**

FIGURE G-27

1. Which item is an inline image?
2. Which item is styled by providing a url value for the background **property**?
3. Which item is created using the link **element**?
4. Which item is created using the figcaption **element**?

Match each term with the statement that best describes it.

5. **pixel**
6. **image map**
7. **native**
8. **resolution**
9. **tile**
10. **hotspot**

a. a term for the original dimensions of a bitmap image
b. to display a background image repeatedly both across and down an element to fill it up
c. a shape within an image that has its own link target
d. specifies how close the dots in a bitmap should appear on the output
e. one of the dots that make up a bitmap image
f. HTML code associated with an image that specifies one or more shapes using sets of coordinates and provides a link target for each shape

Inserting and Working with Images

Select the best answer from the list of choices.

11. Which type of image is represented as a grid of dots and their colors?

    a. vector   **c.** SVG

    b. native   **d.** bitmap

12. Which type of image encodes the appearance of a graphic as geometric shapes?

    a. bitmap   **c.** GIF

    b. vector   **d.** JPEG

13. Which image type is best for photographs?

    a. SVG   **c.** PNG

    b. JPEG   **d.** GIF

14. Which attribute do you use to specify text to display in case an image is unavailable or to be read in user agents by programs such as screen readers?

    a. `title`   **c.** `figcaption`

    b. `alt`   **d.** `href`

15. Which element specifies information about an image map and contains all of its hotspots?

    a. `map`   **c.** `img`

    b. `area`   **d.** `link`

16. The `usemap` attribute specifies the value of what attribute for the image map?

    a. `id`   **c.** `name`

    b. `class`   **d.** `map`

17. For widest compatibility, you create favicons using which format?

    a. .svg   **c.** .png

    b. .jpg   **d.** .ico

Skills Review

1. Insert images.

    a. In your editor, open HTM_G-4.html from the SR folder where you store your Data Files for this unit, save it as **index.html**, then repeat to save HTM_G-5.html as **events.html** and HTM_G-6.css as **styles.css**.

    b. In the comment at the top of each file, enter your name and today's date where indicated, then save the files.

    c. Return to events.html in your editor, add a p element below the h2 element in the `article` element with the `class` value `decorative-image`, then within the p element add an `img` element with a `src` value of images/bigjs.gif, a width of 280, a height of 280, and alt text of Big J's Deep Dish Pizza.

    d. Save your changes, then open events.html in a desktop browser and on a handheld device.

    e. Return to styles.css in your editor, create a new style rule for the `img` element at the end of the reset styles section, then add the declarations `max-width: 100%;`, `height: auto;`, and `width: auto;`.

    f. Scroll to the reset styles section, then add the `img` selector to the list of selectors in the style rule that sets border, padding, and margin to 0.

    g. In the main content section and below the h3 style rule, create a style rule with the selector `p.decorative-image` with the declarations `max-width: 35%;` and `float: right;`, then create another style rule with the selector `p.introtext` and the declaration `width: 72%;`.

    h. In the h3 style rule, add the declaration `clear: both;`.

    i. Save your changes, refresh or reload events.html on your handheld device, then verify that the logo image is scaled down.

2. Insert a background image.

    a. In your browser, open the file brick.jpg from the images folder.

    b. Return to styles.css in your editor.

    c. Scroll to the `body` style rule in the body and container section, insert a blank line before the closing `}`, then indent and type `background: url("images/brick.jpg");`.

d. In the background-color declaration above the code you just entered, change the property name background-color to background.

e. Scroll to the print styles section at the bottom of the style sheet, then, in the body, h2, article style rule, replace the background-color property with the background property.

f. Save your work, open index.html in your browser, then verify that the background of the body element is the tiled brick.jpg image.

3. Mark images as figures.

a. Return to events.html in your editor, then, on a new line below the opening tag for the h3 element with the id value queen, add a figure element.

b. Within the figure element, add an img element with a source of images/party.jpg, a width of 450, a height of 238, and alt text of **a long room with a high ceiling, hardwood floor, tables set for 2 and 4 people with tablecloths, and a small raised dais**.

c. Add a figure element below the opening tag for the h3 element with the id value stclair, then within the figure element add an img element with a source of images/gazebo.jpg, a width of 450, a height of 300, and alt text of **an outdoor brick patio containing several tables with chairs, interspersed with poles supporting a translucent covering, and surrounded by trees**.

d. Add a figure element below the opening tag for the h3 element with the id value dundas, then within the figure element add an img element with a source of images/special.jpg, a width of 450, a height of 300, and alt text of **a bright room with a high ceiling and tall windows, a hardwood floor, tables set with chairs, and lamps hanging from the ceiling**.

e. Save your changes, return to styles.css in your editor, scroll to the main content section, then below the h3 style rule, add a rule that uses the figure selector with the declarations max-width: 50%; and float:right;.

f. In the style rule that sets border, padding, and margin to 0 in the reset styles section, add the figure selector to the list of selectors.

g. In the main content section, add the declaration overflow: auto; to the article style rule.

h. Save your changes, then refresh or reload events.html in your browser.

4. Create a figure caption.

a. Return to events.html in your editor, then, within the figure element and below the h3 element with the id value queen, insert a figcaption element containing the text **The Party Room** below the img element.

b. Repeat Step a to add a figcaption element containing the text **The Gazebo** for the figure element below the h3 element with the id value stclair, and a figcaption element containing the text **The Special Events Room** for the figure element below the h3 element with the id value dundas.

c. Save your changes, then return to styles.css in your editor.

d. Within the main content section and below the figure style rule, add a style rule that uses the figcaption selector with the declarations font-size: 1.6em; and text-align: center;.

e. Scroll to the reset styles section, then add the figcaption selector to the list of selectors in the style rule that sets border, padding, and margin to 0.

f. Save your changes, then refresh or reload events.html in your browser.

5. Use images as links.

a. Return to events.html in your editor.

b. Scroll to the opening tag for the article element, then, within the p element with the class value decorative-image, add an a element enclosing the img element and set the href value for the a element to index.html. (*Hint*: Be sure to include the closing </a> tag after the <img> tag.)

c. Save your changes, then refresh or reload events.html in your browser.

d. Move the mouse pointer over the logo image, then verify the mouse pointer becomes a pointing hand.

e. Click the logo image, then verify that index.html opens.

Skills Review (continued)

6. Create an image map and define additional hotspots.

a. In your browser, open the file imagemap.png from the images folder in the SR folder where you store your Data Files for Unit G.

b. Return to events.html in your editor, in the `article` element add a blank line above the h3 element with the id value `queen`, then add a p element with the `class` value `imagemap`.

c. Within the p element you just created, add an `img` element with a source of images/imagemap.png, width of 480, height of 240, and empty alt text.

d. Add a blank line below the closing `</p>` tag you created in Step b, then add a `map` element with a `name` value of `eventsmap`.

e. Within the `map` element, add an `area` element with a `shape` value of `rect`, `coords` of 22,15,137,204, an `href` value of #queen, and alt text of **Party Room**.

f. Below the `area` element you created in the previous step, add another `area` element with a `shape` value of circle, `coords` of 235,114,63, an `href` value of #stclair, and alt text of **Gazebo**.

FIGURE G-28

g. Below the `area` element you created in the previous step, add another `area` element with a shape value of poly, `coords` of 328,25,422,25, 422,75,470,75,470,202,328,202, an `href` value of #dundas, and alt text of **Special Events Room**.

h. In the `<img>` tag for the imagemap.png file, add a `usemap` attribute with a value of #eventsmap, then save your changes.

i. Return to styles.css in your editor, scroll to the main content section, then, in the style rule with the selector `p.introtext`, add the selector `p.imagemap`.

j. Below the style rule you just edited, create a new style rule using the selector `p.imagemap img` with the declaration `max-width:none;`, then save your changes.

k. Refresh or reload events.html in your browser. Your document should match **FIGURE G-28**.

l. Move the mouse pointer over each shape in the map graphic, then verify that the mouse pointer becomes a pointing hand only when it is over each shape.

m. Click each shape, then verify that the page scrolls to the correct section, decreasing the height of your browser window if necessary for testing.

Skills Review (continued)

7. Add a favicon and touch icons.

a. Return to events.html in your editor, then before the closing `</head>` tag, enter a `link` element with a `rel` value of `shortcut icon` and an `href` value of `images/favicon.ico`.

b. Below the `link` element you created in the previous step, add another `link` element with a `rel` value of `apple-touch-icon` and an `href` value of `images/apple-touch-icon.png`.

c. Below the `link` element you created in the previous step, add another `link` element with a `rel` value of `icon`, a `sizes` value of `192x192`, and an `href` value of `images/android.png`.

d. Save events.html, then reload events.html in your browser and verify that the Big J's favicon is displayed in the browser tab.

e. Open index.html on a smartphone or tablet, tap the Menu button ⋮ (Chrome for Android) or the Share button (Safari for iOS), tap Add to Home Screen, tap Add, then examine the icon on your home screen. (*Hint*: If you use a different browser or operating system, follow the steps you normally use.) **FIGURE G-29** shows the icon on the Android home screen.

f. Repeat Steps a-e for index.html

g. Validate the code for your web pages and your style sheet, then make changes as necessary to fix any errors

FIGURE G-29

Independent Challenge 1

Sarah Nguyen, the owner of the Spotted Wren Garden Center, has provided you with a version of the company logo for the website, as well as related photos and a favicon. You add these images to the company's website.

a. In your editor, open HTM_G-7.html from the IC1 folder where you store your Data Files for this unit, save it as **index.html**, then repeat to save HTM_G-8.html as **hours.html** and HTM_G-9.css as **styles.css**. In the comment at the top of each file, enter your name and today's date where indicated, then save the files.

b. In index.html, replace the text of the h1 element with an `img` element referencing the file spotwren.gif in the images folder. Specify a width of 864 and a height of 184, and add **Spotted Wren Garden Center** as the alt text. Save your work, then repeat for hours.html.

c. In styles.css, create a new style rule for the `img` element at the end of the reset styles section, then add the declarations `max-width: 100%;`, `height: auto;`, `width: auto;`, and `display: block;`. In the style rule that sets border, padding, and margin to 0 in the reset styles section, add the `img` selector to the list of selectors. Save your changes, then preview index.html and hours.html in a browser.

d. Return to hours.html in your editor, then link the logo `img` element to index.html. Save your changes, refresh or reload hours.html in a browser, click the logo, then verify that index.html opens.

e. Return to index.html in your editor, then within the `article` element and before the `div` element, add a `figure` element. Within the `figure` element, add an `img` element that references the file cone.jpg in the images folder. Specify a width of 200 and a height of 301, and enter **a monarch butterfly on a purple coneflower** as alt text. Save your changes.

Independent Challenge 1 (continued)

f. Return to styles.css, then add the `figcaption` and `figure` selectors to the list of selectors in the style rule that sets border, padding, and margin to 0 in the reset styles section. At the bottom of the main content section, add a style rule based on the `figure` selector that specifies a width of 25% and floats the element to the right. Save your changes, then refresh or reload index.html in your browser.

g. Return to hours.html in your editor, then within the `article` element and before the `div` element, add a `figure` element. Within the `figure` element, add an `img` element that references the file quince.jpg in the images folder. Specify a width of 200 and a height of 301, and enter **the red blossom of a flowering quince** as alt text. Save your work, then refresh or reload hours.html in your browser.

h. Return to styles.css in your editor, then in the `.container` style rule in the body and page container section, change the existing `background-color` declaration to use the `background` shorthand property, then add a second `background` property that sets the grass.jpg file located in the images folder as the background. In the print styles section at the bottom of the style sheet, replace the `background-color` property with the `background` property in the `.container`, `h1`, `h2`, `p` style rule. Save your changes, then refresh or reload index.html and hours.html in your browser.

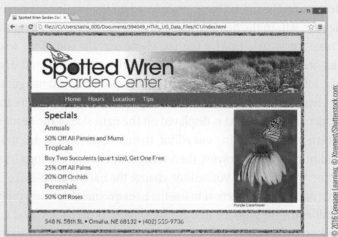

i. Return to index.html in your editor, then in the head section add a `link` element that specifies the file favicon.ico in the images folder as the favicon. Add a second `link` element that specifies the file apple-touch-icon.png in the images folder as an Apple touch icon. Add a third `link` element that specifies the android.jpg file in the images folder as an icon and specifies its dimensions as 192x192. Save your changes, refresh or reload index.html in your browser, then verify that the favicon is displayed as shown in **FIGURE G-30**. Open index.html on a mobile device, save a link to the page on the home screen, then verify that the touch icon is displayed. **FIGURE G-31** shows the touch icon on an iOS device.

j. Repeat Step i for hours.html.

k. Validate all your HTML and CSS documents.

FIGURE G-31

HTML5 & CSS3

© 2016 Cengage Learning; © Xtremest/Shutterstock.com;
© Maxim Tupikov/Shutterstock.com; © Jessica Bethke/Shutterstock.com

© 2016 Cengage Learning; Source: 2015 Apple Inc.

Independent Challenge 2

You incorporate the logo for the Murfreesboro Regional Soccer League into the organizational website that you are creating. You also use an image map to link the parts of a soccer field to explanations of their functions.

a. In your editor, open HTM_G-10.html from the IC2 folder where you store your Data Files for this unit, save it as **index.html**, then repeat to save HTM_G-11.html as **field.html** and HTM_G-12.css as **styles.css**. In the comment at the top of each file, enter your name and today's date where indicated, then save the files.

b. In index.html, within the `header` element and beneath the `h1` element insert a `div` element, then within the `div` element add an `img` element that references the file mrsl.png in the images folder. Specify a width of 224, a height of 105, and a blank `alt` value. Save your changes, then repeat for field.html.

c. In styles.css, within the header section, add declarations to the `h1` style rule to set the width to 61% and float the element on the right. Create a rule based on the `header div` selector that sets the width to 33% and floats the element left. In the `header` style rule, add the declaration `overflow: auto;`.

d. Create a new style rule for the `img` element at the end of the reset styles section, then add the declarations `max-width: 100%;`, `height: auto;`, `width: auto;`, and `display: block;`. Add the `img` selector to the list of selectors in the style rule that sets border, padding, and margin to 0 in the reset styles section. Save your work, preview index.html and field.html in your browser, then verify that the logo graphic is displayed on the left side of the header and the h1 text is displayed on the right side of the header.

e. Return to field.html in your editor, then link the logo image to index.html. Save your changes, refresh or reload field.html in your browser, then verify that clicking the logo image opens index.html.

f. Return to styles.css in your editor, change the `background-color` declaration in the `.container` style rule in the body and page container section to use the `background` shorthand property, then add a second `background` property that specifies the file grass.jpg in the images folder as the background image. In the print styles section, replace the `background-color` property with the `background` property in the `aside, body, .container, footer, header` style rule. Save your changes, refresh or reload index.html in your browser, then verify that a background image of grass is displayed. (*Hint*: The `header` and `article` elements have their own background colors, so the background image should be visible only behind the nav bar.)

g. In your browser, open the file field.jpg from the images folder in the IC2 folder where you store your Data Files for this unit. Return to field.html in your editor, in the `article` element add a blank line above the h3 element containing the text Goal, then add a p element. Within the p element, add an `img` element that references field.jpg in the images folder, with a width of 450, a height of 293, alt text of **diagram of a soccer field**, and `class` value of `imagemap`.

FIGURE G-32

h. Below the p element you just created, add a `map` element with a `name` value of `fieldmap`. In your editor, open the file areas.txt from the IC2 folder, then within the map element add `area` elements for the 9 shapes described in the file.

i. In the `<img>` tag for the field.jpg file, add a `usemap` attribute with a value of `#fieldmap`, then save your changes.

j. In styles.css, at the bottom of the main content section, add a style rule with the `.imagemap` selector and the declaration `max-width: none;`, then save your changes.

k. Refresh or reload events.html in your browser. Your document should match **FIGURE G-32**.

Independent Challenge 2 (continued)

l. Test each shape in the image map, decreasing the height of your browser window if necessary for testing.

m. In index.html, add a `link` element that references favicon.ico in the images folder as a favicon. Add another link element that references apple-touch-icon.png in the images folder as an Apple touch icon. Add a third link element that references android.png in the images folder as a touch icon, specifying its dimensions as 192x192. Save your changes, then repeat for field.html.

n. Refresh or reload index.html in your browser, then verify that the favicon is displayed on the browser tab. Open index.html on a mobile device, save a link to the page on the home screen, then verify that the touch icon is displayed. **FIGURE G-33** shows the touch icon on an Android device.

o. Validate all your HTML and CSS documents.

Independent Challenge 3

Diego Merckx, the manager of Hotel Natoma, has provided you with a web-ready version of the facility's logo as well as photos of a few local attractions. You incorporate these into the hotel's website.

a. In your editor, open HTM_G-13.html from the IC3 folder where you store your Data Files for this unit, save it as **index.html**, then repeat to save HTM_G-14.html as **nearby.html** and HTM_G-15.css as **styles.css**. In the comment at the top of each file, enter your name and today's date where indicated, then save the files.

b. In index.html, replace the text of the h1 element with an `img` element referencing the file logo.gif in the images folder. Specify a width of 368 and a height of 65, and add Hotel Natoma as the alt text. Save your work, then repeat for nearby.html.

c. In styles.css, create a new style rule for the `img` element at the end of the reset styles section, then add the declarations `max-width: 100%;`, `height: auto;`, `width: auto;`, and `display: block;`. Add the img selector to the list of selectors in the style rule that sets border, padding, and margin to 0 in the reset styles section. In the header section, create a new style rule using the h1 img selector with the declarations `margin: 0 auto;` and `display: block;`. Save your changes, then preview index.html and nearby.html in a browser.

d. Return to nearby.html in your editor, then link the logo `img` element to index.html. Save your changes, refresh or reload nearby.html in a browser, click the logo, then verify that index.html opens.

e. Return to index.html in your editor, then within the `article` element, before the p element, add a `figure` element. Within the `figure` element, add an `img` element that references the file bridge.jpg in the images folder. Specify a width of 350 and a height of 232, and enter **the Golden Gate Bridge, looking south from the Marin Headlands toward the Presidio, with downtown San Francisco on the left** as alt text. After the img element, add a `figcaption` element containing the text **Golden Gate Bridge**. Save your changes.

Independent Challenge 3 (continued)

f. Return to styles.css, then in the style rule that sets border, padding, and margin to 0 in the reset styles section, add the `figcaption` and `figure` selectors to the list of selectors. In the main content section and below the `article h3` rule, add a style rule based on the `article figure` selector that specifies a maximum width of 100%, a left margin of 1em, and floats the element to the right. Below the rule you just added, add a style rule based on the `article figcaption` selector that center-aligns text and sets the font weight to bold. In the `article` style rule, add the declaration `overflow: auto;`. Save your changes, then refresh or reload index.html in your browser. Your document should match **FIGURE G-34**.

FIGURE G-34

g. Return to nearby.html in your editor, then within the `article` element and below the h3 element with the text Asian Art Museum, add a `figure` element. Within the `figure` element, add an `img` element that references the file aam.jpg in the images folder. Specify a width of 450 and a height of 337, and enter **the San Francisco Asian Art Museum, a beaux arts building composed of large granite bricks with columns above the entry doors** as alt text. Below the `img` element, add a `figcaption` element containing the same text as the preceding h3 element, **Asian Art Museum**. Repeat for the remaining four h3 elements using the details in **TABLE G-6**, then save your changes.

TABLE G-6

h3/figcaption Text	Filename	Width	Height	Alt Text
City Hall	cityhall.jpg	450	299	San Francisco City Hall, a beaux arts building with columns across the whole front and a gray dome over the center, illuminated from within at dusk
Civic Center Plaza	ccplaza.jpg	334	449	a bronze statue of Abraham Lincoln sitting in a chair, with the word Lincoln and an inscription on the stone base
United Nations Plaza	unplaza.jpg	300	450	a fountain shooting out from within granite slabs, with buildings rising up behind
Cable Car Turnaround	cablecar.jpg	450	300	a cable car on a circular platform made of wood planks, with people lined up in the background

Independent Challenge 3 (continued)

h. In styles.css, scroll to the main content section, then add the declaration `clear: right;` to the `article h3` style rule. Save your changes, then refresh or reload hours.html in your browser.

i. In your browser, open the file map.png from the images folder. Return to nearby.html in your editor, scroll as needed to the `article` element, add a `p` element above the `h3` element containing the text Asian Art Museum. Within the `p` element, add an `img` element that references map.jpg in the images folder, with a width of 465, a height of 347, alt text of **map of the area around Hotel Natoma**, and `class` value of `imagemap`.

j. Below the `p` element you just created, add a `map` element with a `name` value of `nearby`. In your editor, open the file areas.txt from the IC3 folder, then within the `map` element add `area` elements for the 5 shapes described in the file.

k. In the `<img>` tag for the map.png file, add a `usemap` attribute to use the `map` element as an image map, then save your changes.

l. In styles.css, at the bottom of the main content section, add a style rule with the `.imagemap` selector and the declarations `border: 2px solid black;`, `margin: 0 auto;` and `max-width: none;`. Below this style rule, add a style rule with the `.imagemap img` selector that sets `max-width` to `none`. Save your changes.

m. Refresh or reload nearby.html in your browser. Your document should match **FIGURE G-35**.

n. Return to index.html in your editor, then add `link` elements for a favicon, an Apple touch icon, and an Android touch icon with a size of 192x192. Save your changes, refresh or reload index. html in your browser, then verify that the favicon is displayed on the browser tab. Open index.html on a mobile device, save a link to the page on the home screen, then verify that the touch icon is displayed. **FIGURE G-36** shows the touch icon on an iOS device.

o. Repeat Step n for nearby.html.

p. Validate all your HTML and CSS documents.

FIGURE G-35

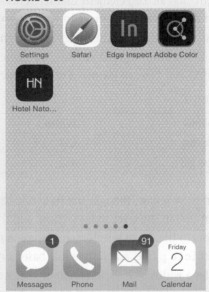

FIGURE G-36

Independent Challenge 4 – Explore

You continue your work building the website for Eating Well in Season by incorporating the company logo, a few marketing images, and an image map.

a. In your editor, open HTM_G-16.html from the IC4 folder where you store your Data Files for this unit, save it as **index.html**, then repeat to save HTM_G-17.html as **farms.html** and HTM_G-18.css as **styles.css**. In the comment at the top of each file, enter your name and today's date where indicated, then save the files.

b. In index.html, within the header element and below the h1 element, add a div element containing an img element that references the file logo.png in the images folder. Specify a width of 216 and a height of 146, and specify an alt attribute with no value. Repeat for farms.html, then save your changes to both files.

c. In styles.css, create a new style rule for the img element at the end of the reset styles section, then add the declarations `max-width: 100%;`, `height: auto;`, `width: auto;`, and `display: block;`. Add the img selector to the list of selectors in the style rule that sets border, padding, and margin to 0 in the reset styles section. In the header section of the style sheet, create a new style rule for the div element within the header element, setting the width to 26%, margins to 2% 4% 1%, and floating the element left. In the header h1 style rule, add a declaration to float the element right. In the header style rule, add the declaration `overflow: auto;`. Save your changes, then preview index.html and farms.html in a browser.

d. Return to farms.html in your editor, then link the logo img element to index.html. Save your changes, refresh or reload farms.html in a browser, click the logo, then verify that index.html opens.

e. Return to index.html in your editor, then, within the article element, add a figure element. Within the figure element, add an img element that references the file meal.jpg in the images folder. Specify a width of 450 and a height of 299. View the image in your browser, then add alt text to index.html that describes the image. (*Hint*: Your alt text should describe the image in enough detail to convey its contents to someone accessing the page who cannot view the image.) After the img element, add a figcaption element containing the text **Healthy Meals.** Repeat to add figure elements using the details in **TABLE G-7**. Save your changes.

TABLE G-7

Filename	Width	Height	figcaption **Text**
veggies.jpg	450	298	Local sources.
delivery.jpg	450	299	Your schedule.

f. Return to styles.css, then, in the style rule that sets border, padding, and margin to 0 in the reset styles section, add the figcaption and figure selectors to the list of selectors. In the main content section and below the article p rule, add a style rule based on the figure selector that specifies a width of 75%, a margin of 1em auto, and a 2px solid black border. Below the rule you just added, add a style rule based on the figcaption selector that sets padding to 0.25em, font size to 2em, font weight to bold, center-aligns text, and sets the background color to white. In the body and page container section, add the declaration `overflow: auto;` in the .article-aside-inner-container style rule. Save your changes, then refresh or reload index.html in your browser. Your document should match **FIGURE G-37**.

FIGURE G-37

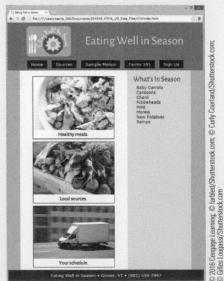

Independent Challenge 4 – Explore (continued)

g. In your browser, open the file farm.jpg from the images folder. Return to farms.html in your editor, in the article element add a p element with a class value of imagemap above the h3 element containing the text Silo. Within the p element, add an img element that references farm.jpg in the images folder, with a width of 456, a height of 221, and empty alt text.

FIGURE G-38

© 2016 Cengage Learning

h. Below the p element you just created, add a map element. Decide on a name for the map and specify it with the name attribute. Using an application or a web service, create area elements for the 3 shapes on the map—one circle and two rectangles. (*Hint*: Use a search engine and the terms *image map coordinate generator* to locate free online services.)

i. Add the area elements you created within the map element, making sure to specify values for the shape, alt, coords, and href attributes. (*Hint*: The href values should be hash links to the corresponding h3 headings within the article element.)

j. In the <img> tag for the farm.png file, add an attribute to use the map element as an image map, then save your changes.

k. In styles.css, at the bottom of the main content section, add a style rule with the .imagemap selector with declarations that center-align text and create a 2px dashed black border. Below the style rule you just added, add a style rule with the .imagemap img selector that sets max-width to none. Save your changes.

FIGURE G-39

© 2016 Cengage Learning; Source: Android

l. Refresh or reload farms.html in your browser. Your document should match **FIGURE G-38**. Test the image map and verify that all three hotspots work, decreasing the height of your browser window if necessary for testing.

m. Return to index.html in your editor, then add link elements for a favicon, an Apple touch icon, and an Android touch icon with a size of 192x192, using the relevant files in the images folder. Save your changes, refresh or reload index.html in your browser, then verify that the favicon is displayed on the browser tab. Open indcx.html on a mobile device, save a link to the page on the home screen, then verify that the touch icon is displayed. **FIGURE G-39** shows the touch icon on an Android device.

n. Repeat Step m for farms.html.

o. Validate all your HTML and CSS documents.

Visual Workshop

In your editor, open the file HTM_G-19.html from the VW folder where you store your Data Files for this unit and save it as **releases.html**. Repeat to save HTM_G-20.css as **styles.css**. Add your first and last names and today's date to the comment section at the top of each file, then save your changes. Use the files in the images folder to style the web page to match the one shown in **FIGURE G-40**, changing and adding to the style sheet as necessary. The logo graphic is logo.gif, the background image is books.png, and the photo of the girl reading a book is browsing.jpg. Specify favicon.ico as the favicon, android.png as the touch icon for Android devices (using dimensions of 192x192), and apple-touch-icon.png as the touch icon for iOS devices. Validate your HTML and CSS code.

FIGURE G-40

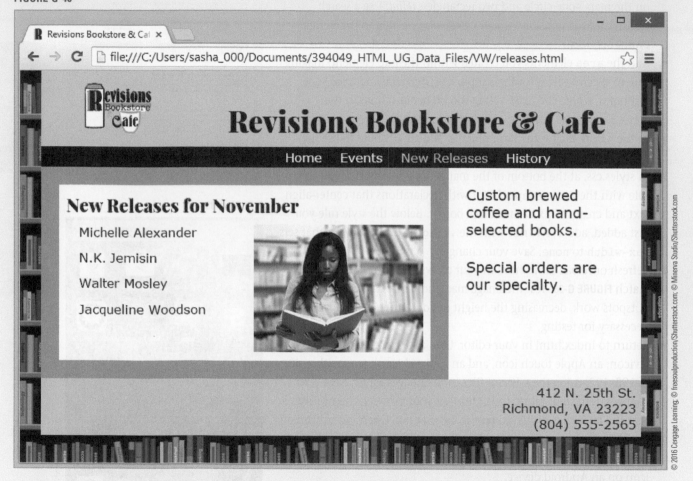

Organizing Content with Lists and Tables

CASE ▷ As you continue your work on the website for the Lakeland Reeds Bed & Breakfast, you format content using lists and tables.

Unit Objectives

After completing this unit, you will be able to:

- Create an ordered list
- Create an unordered list
- Create a description list
- Create a nav bar using a list
- Insert a table
- Debug tables
- Span columns and rows
- Format a table with CSS
- Apply a table-like structure to other elements

Files You Will Need

 L   10 files   IC3   12 files

 SR   10 files   IC4   9 files

 IC1   10 files   VW   7 files

 IC2   9 files

For specific filenames, see Filenames_H.pdf in the Unit H Data Files folder.

Create an Ordered List

You use the HTML ol element to create a list in which items are numbered or lettered sequentially. This type of list is known as an **ordered list** because the order in which the items are listed is important. You create each item in an ordered list with the li element. All the li elements for a list are nested within the opening and closing ol tags. The default marker for each list item is determined by the user agent rendering the web page but it is most often an Arabic numeral (1, 2, 3, . . .). You can use the values of the CSS list-style-type property shown in **TABLE H-1** to change the markers to letters or to a different numbering style. **CASE** ▶ *Phillip Blaine, the owner of Lakeland Reeds Bed & Breakfast, has provided additional information that he'd like you to incorporate into the Reservations web page. You start by adding a list of the most popular weekends at Lakeland Reeds.*

STEPS

1. **In your editor, open HTM_H-1.html from the Lessons folder where you store your Data Files for this unit, save it as reserve.html, then repeat to save HTM_H-2.css as styles.css**

2. **In the comment at the top of each file, enter your name and today's date where indicated, then save the files**

3. **Return to reserve.html, insert a blank line beneath the paragraph *Our most sought-after weekends*, indent to the same level as the paragraph, type `<ol>`, press [Enter], indent to the same level, then type `</ol>`**
   All items in an ordered list are contained between the opening and closing tags for the ol element.

4. **Insert a blank line beneath `<ol>`, indent 3 additional spaces, then type**
   `<li>Independence Day (Jul. 4)</li>`
   The content of each list item is contained between the opening and closing tags for the li element.

5. **Press [Enter], indent as needed to the same level, then type `<li>Memorial Day (last Monday in May)</li>`**

6. **Press [Enter], indent as needed to the same level, type `<li>Labor Day (first Monday in Sep.)</li>`, then save your changes**
   FIGURE H-1 shows the completed HTML code for the ordered list.

7. **Return to styles.css in your editor, create a new style rule for the ol element at the end of the reset styles section, then add the declaration `list-style-type: none;`**
   This declaration removes the default numbering assigned by browsers from ol elements you create. Because you removed the default numbering, you are required to specify the list-style-type for each ordered list in your document.

8. **In the style rule that sets border, padding, and margin to 0 in the reset styles section, add the ol and li selectors to the list of selectors**

9. **Scroll down to the `/* footer section */` comment and, above this comment, add the comment `/* main content lists */`, then, below this comment, create a style rule with the `article ol` selector and the declarations `margin: 1em 0 1em 2em;`, `font-size: 1.3em;`, and `list-style-type: decimal;`**
   FIGURE H-2 shows the changes to the style sheet.

10. **Save your changes, then open reserve.html in a browser**
    As **FIGURE H-3** shows, the list is displayed with each list item numbered sequentially starting at the number 1. Note that the list markers for an ordered list are always displayed outside the content box and on the left. If the list has left padding or margin (as in this example), the markers are displayed within the padding or margin area. If not, the markers are displayed outside the element on the left side.

FIGURE H-1: HTML code for ordered list

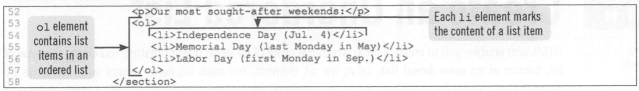

```
52                  <p>Our most sought-after weekends:</p>
53                  <ol>
54                      <li>Independence Day (Jul. 4)</li>
55                      <li>Memorial Day (last Monday in May)</li>
56                      <li>Labor Day (first Monday in Sep.)</li>
57                  </ol>
58              </section>
```

ol element contains list items in an ordered list

Each li element marks the content of a list item

FIGURE H-2: CSS code for ordered list

```
10      /* reset styles */
11      html {
12          font-size: 16px;
13      }
14      a, article, body, div, figcaption, figure, footer, header, h1,
15      h2, h3, img, li, nav, ol, p, section {
16          border: 0;
17          padding: 0;
18          margin: 0;
19      }
20      img {
21          max-width: 100%;
22          height: auto;
23          width: auto;
24      }
25      ol {
26          list-style-type: none;
27      }
```

li and ol selectors added to rule for border, padding, and margin in the reset styles section

list-style-type of none removes the default numbering assigned by browsers to ordered lists

```
137     /* main content lists */
138     article ol {
139         margin: 1em 0 1em 2em;
140         font-size: 1.3em;
141         list-style-type: decimal;
142     }
143
144     /* footer section */
```

list-style-type of decimal uses sequential numbers starting at 1

FIGURE H-3: Ordered list in Reservations web page

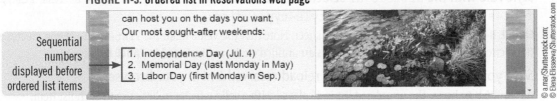

can host you on the days you want.
Our most sought-after weekends:

1. Independence Day (Jul. 4)
2. Memorial Day (last Monday in May)
3. Labor Day (first Monday in Sep.)

Sequential numbers displayed before ordered list items

© a.mar/Shutterstock.com;
© Elena Elisseeva/Shutterstock.com

TABLE H-1: Widely supported values for the CSS list-style-type property for the ol element

value	result	value	result
decimal	1. first item 2. second item	lower-latin lower-roman	i. first item ii. second item
decimal-leading-zero	01. first item 02. second item	none	first item second item
	... 10. tenth item 11. eleventh item	upper-alpha	A. first item B. second item
lower-alpha	a. first item b. second item	upper-latin upper-roman	I. first item II. second item

© 2016 Cengage Learning

Create an Unordered List

HTML also enables you to create a list in which the order of list items doesn't matter. You create this type of list, known as an **unordered list**, using the ul element. You mark list item content with the same li element that you use for an ordered list. In an unordered list, list items are displayed with a bullet at the start of each line. The default bullet character is a solid circle, but you can use the CSS list-style-type property with one of the values shown in **TABLE H-2** to specify a different bullet shape. **CASE** ▶ *Visitors sometimes reserve the entire facility for special events. You add Phillip's list of special events to the Reservations web page as an unordered list.*

STEPS

1. **Return to** reserve.html **in your editor, insert a blank line beneath the paragraph that begins** *Lakeland Reeds is also available*, **indent to the same level as the paragraph, type** <ul>, **press [Enter], indent to the same level, then type** </ul>

   All items in an unordered list are contained between the opening and closing tags for the ul element.

2. **Insert a blank line beneath** <ul>, **indent 3 additional spaces, then type**
   <li>Weddings</li>

   While the containing element is specific to the type of list you're creating, you use the li element for list items when creating either ordered or unordered lists.

3. **Press [Enter], indent as needed to the same level, type** <li>Birthdays</li>, **then repeat to enter the code** <li>Family Reunions</li>

   FIGURE H-4 shows the completed HTML code for the unordered list.

4. **Save your changes, then return to** styles.css **in your editor**

5. **In the style rule that sets border, padding, and margin to 0 in the reset styles section, add the** ul **selector to the list of selectors, then add the** ul **selector to the** ol **style rule in the reset styles section**

6. **Scroll down to the main content lists section, then, below the** article ol **rule, add a new style rule with the** article ul **selector and the declarations** margin: 1em 0 1em 2em;, font-size: 1.3em;, **and** list-style-type: disc;

   FIGURE H-5 shows the changes to the style sheet. Note that the value disc for list-style-type creates a filled circle, while the value circle creates an unfilled circle, as illustrated in **TABLE H-2**.

7. **Save your changes, then refresh or reload** reserve.html **in your browser**

   As **FIGURE H-6** shows, the unordered list is displayed with a solid circular bullet next to each list item.

TABLE H-2: Values for the CSS list-style-type property for the ul element

value	description	example
circle	unfilled circle	o list item
disc	filled circle (default)	• list item
square	filled square	■ list item
none	no character	list item

FIGURE H-4: HTML code for unordered list

```
60                  <section>
61                      <h3>Special Events</h3>
62                      <figure class="alternate">
63                          <img src="images/frolic.jpg" width="350" height="209" alt="people
64                          swimming with a raft in the lake">
65                      </figure>
66                      <p>Lakeland Reeds is also available for booking group special events,
67                      including</p>
68                      <ul>
69                          <li>Weddings</li>
70                          <li>Birthdays</li>
71                          <li>Family Reunions</li>
72                      </ul>
73                      <p><a href="weddings.pdf">Guidelines and reservation form for a special
74                      event at Lakeland Reeds.</a> (PDF)</p>
75                  </section>
```

`ul` element contains list items in an unordered list

Each `li` element marks the content of a list item

FIGURE H-5: CSS code for unordered list

```
10      /* reset styles */
11      html {
12          font-size: 16px;
13      }
14      a, article, body, div, figcaption, figure, footer, header, h1,
15      h2, h3, img, li, nav, ol, p, section, ul {
16          border: 0;
17          padding: 0;
18          margin: 0;
19      }
20      img {
21          max-width: 100%;
22          height: auto;
23          width: auto;
24      }
25      ol, ul {
26          list-style-type: none;
27      }
```

`ul` selector added to two rules in the reset styles section

```
137     /* main content lists */
138       article ol {
139           margin: 1em 0 1em 2em;
140           font-size: 1.3em;
141           list-style-type: decimal;
142       }
143       article ul {
144           margin: 1em 0 1em 2em;
145           font-size: 1.3em;
146           list-style-type: disc;
147       }
```

`list-style-type` of disc uses a filled circle

FIGURE H-6: Unordered list in Reservations web page

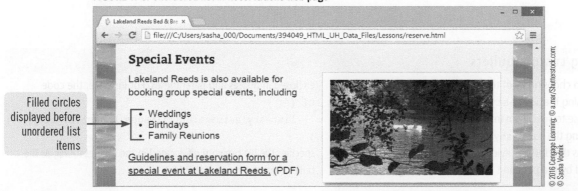

Filled circles displayed before unordered list items

Create a Description List

The dl element creates a **description list**, which enables you to specify a set of items and descriptions. A description list was known in previous versions of HTML as a **definition list**. Unlike ol and ul, dl does not use the li element to specify list items. Instead, a list item uses two elements: dt marks the term or item being described, and dd marks the description. **CASE** ▶ *The contact information for Phillip Blaine on the Reservations page is a set of items and their descriptions. You change the markup for this section to a definition list.*

STEPS

1. **Return to reserve.html in your editor, locate the div element with the class value contact, then in the opening and closing tags, replace div with dl**
   This changes the div element to a description list element.

2. **In the next line, replace the code <p><span> with <dt>, replace the code </span> with </dt>, move the insertion point after the closing </dt> tag, then press [Enter]**

3. **Indent to match the previous line, type <dd>, then replace the closing </p> tag with </dd>**
   Your changes in Steps 2 and 3 have marked the Proprietor label as a dt element and the name Phillip Blaine as a dd element.

4. **Repeat Steps 2 and 3 to convert each of the remaining 3 p elements to a dt and a dd element**
   FIGURE H-7 shows the completed HTML code for the description list.

5. **Save your changes, then return to styles.css in your editor**

6. **In the style rule that sets border, padding, and margin to 0 in the reset styles section, add the dd, dl, and dt selectors to the list of selectors**

7. **Scroll down to the main content lists section, then below the article ul rule, add a new style rule with the article dl selector and the declarations margin: 1em 0; and font-size: 1.3em;**

8. **Below the rule you created in the previous step, add a new style rule with the article dt selector and the declaration font-weight: bold;, then create a new style rule with the article dd selector and the declaration margin-left: 2em;**
   FIGURE H-8 shows the changes. The article dt style rule bolds the item in each set, and the article dd selector indents its description.

9. **Save your changes, then refresh or reload reserve.html in your browser**
   As **FIGURE H-9** shows, each dt element is displayed in bold and each dd element is indented.

Specifying custom bullets

In addition to choosing from the standard selection of bullet characters using the list-style-type property, you can instead choose to specify an image to display as the bullet character using the list-style-image property. The syntax is the same as that for specifying a background image: the text url followed by the path and filename of the image file, enclosed in quotes and parentheses. For instance, the code

```
ul {
    list-style-image:url("images/browntri.gif");
}
```

specifies the file browntri.gif, located in the images folder, as the bullet character for unordered lists.

FIGURE H-7: HTML code for description list

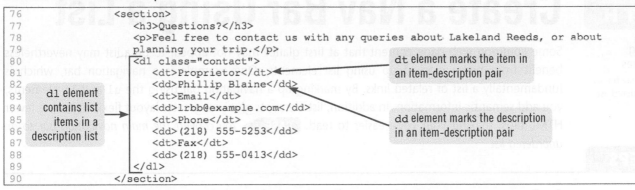

```
76          <section>
77              <h3>Questions?</h3>
78              <p>Feel free to contact us with any queries about Lakeland Reeds, or about
79              planning your trip.</p>
80              <dl class="contact">
81                  <dt>Proprietor</dt>
82                  <dd>Phillip Blaine</dd>
83                  <dt>Email</dt>
84                  <dd>lrbb@example.com</dd>
85                  <dt>Phone</dt>
86                  <dd>(218) 555-5253</dd>
87                  <dt>Fax</dt>
88                  <dd>(218) 555-0413</dd>
89              </dl>
90          </section>
```

dt element marks the item in an item-description pair

dd element marks the description in an item-description pair

dl element contains list items in a description list

FIGURE H-8: CSS code for description list

```
10      /* reset styles */
11      html {
12          font-size: 16px;
13      }
14      a, article, body, dd, div, dl, dt, figcaption, figure, footer, header, h1,
15      h2, h3, img, li, nav, ol, p, section, ul {
16          border: 0;
17          padding: 0;
18          margin: 0;
19      }
```

dd, dl, and dt selectors added to rule for border, padding, and margin in the reset styles section

```
142     article ul {
143         margin: 1em 0 1em 2em;
144         font-size: 1.3em;
145         list-style-type: disc;
146     }
147     article dl {
148         margin: 1em 0;
149         font-size: 1.3em;
150     }
151     article dt {
152         font-weight: bold;
153     }
154     article dd {
155         margin-left: 2em;
156     }
```

Style rule bolds the item in each item-description pair

Style rule indents the description in each item-description pair

FIGURE H-9: Description list in Reservations web page

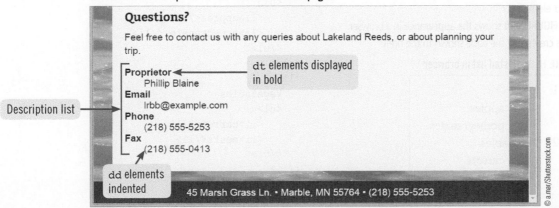

Questions?

Feel free to contact us with any queries about Lakeland Reeds, or about planning your trip.

dt elements displayed in bold

Proprietor
  Phillip Blaine
Email
  lrbb@example.com
Phone
  (218) 555-5253
Fax
  (218) 555-0413

Description list

dd elements indented

45 Marsh Grass Ln. • Marble, MN 55764 • (218) 555-5253

© a.mar/Shutterstock.com

Organizing Content with Lists and Tables

Create a Nav Bar Using a List

Learning
Outcomes
• Mark a nav bar as
an unordered list

Some common web page content that at first glance may not appear to be a list may nevertheless benefit from being marked up using list elements. One example is a navigation bar, which is fundamentally a list of related links. By marking up a navigation bar using the ul and li elements, you add semantic information. In addition, list elements give you greater layout flexibility using fewer HTML tags, making your code easier to read. **CASE** ▶ *You convert the main navigation bar to an unordered list.*

STEPS

1. **Return to reserve.html in your editor, locate the opening <nav> tag with the class value sitenavigation, add a new line below it, indent an additional 3 spaces, then type <ul>**

2. **Add a new line above the closing </nav> tag for the main nav bar, indent an additional 3 spaces, then type </ul>**

TROUBLE
This is the <ul>
tag you entered in
step 1.

3. **In the line below the opening <ul> tag, indent an additional 3 spaces, replace the opening <p> tag with <li>, then replace the closing </p> tag with </li>**

4. **Repeat Step 3 to convert the remaining p elements in the nav bar to li elements**
   Your code should match **FIGURE H-11**.

5. **Save your changes, return to styles.css in your editor, then scroll up to the site navigation bar section**

6. **In the nav.sitenavigation p style rule, change the selector to nav.sitenavigation li, then add the declarations font-size: 1.3em; and line-height: 1.4em;, as shown in FIGURE H-12**

7. **Save your work, then reload reserve.html in your browser**
   As **FIGURE H-13** shows, there is no change in the appearance of the nav bar.

8. **Move the mouse pointer over the Weather link and verify that it still changes color, click the Weather link and verify that a weather page opens, then click your browser's Back button to return to reserve.html**

Creating nested lists

Sometimes nesting a list within another list is the clearest way to present information. It's easy to nest lists in HTML: you simply insert valid code for a list within the content of an li, dt, or dd element.

For instance, **FIGURE H-10** shows the appearance in a browser of the nested lists created by the code shown to the right:

FIGURE H-10: Nested list in browser

```
1. Fruits
     o  apples
     o  pomegranates
2. Vegetables
     o  carrots
     o  beets
```

```
<ol>
   <li>
      Fruits
      <ul>
         <li>apples</li>
         <li>pomegranates</li>
      </ul>
   </li>
   <li>
      Vegetables
      <ul>
         <li>carrots</li>
         <li>beets</li>
      </ul>
   </li>
</ol>
```

FIGURE H-11: HTML code for nav bar using `ul` and `li` elements

```
29          <nav class="sitenavigation">
30              <ul>
31                  <li><a href="index.html">Home</a></li>
                    <li><a href="aboutus.html">About Us</a></li>
                    <li><a href="reserve.html">Reservations</a></li>
                    <li><a href="events.html">Events</a></li>
                    <li><a href="http://wxug.us/1hn14">Weather</a></li>
                    <li><a href="https://goo.gl/maps/bwf5R">Directions</a></li>
37              </ul>
38          </nav>
```

Nav bar links nested within a `ul` element

Each `li` element marks a nav bar link

FIGURE H-12: Updated CSS code for nav bar

```
69      /* site navigation bar */
70      nav.sitenavigation {
71          color: #34180f;
72          text-align: center;
73          background-color: #B8944D;
74      }
75      nav.sitenavigation li {
76          margin: 0.3em 0.5em;
77          display: inline-block;
78          font-size: 1.3em;
79          line-height: 1.4em;
80      }
```

`nav.sitenavigation li` replaces `nav.sitenavigation p` selector

FIGURE H-13: Modified nav bar in browser

Nav bar appearance unchanged, but code now includes additional semantic meaning

© 2016 Cengage Learning; © Unholy Vault Designs/Shutterstock.com; © a.nar/Shutterstock.com; © Elena Elisseeva/Shutterstock.com

Organizing Content with Lists and Tables

209

Insert a Table

Learning Outcomes
• Create a table

In addition to a simple list of items or items and descriptions, HTML enables you to present a larger set of information as a table, which organizes data in horizontal **rows** and vertical **columns**. Each item in a table is displayed in a **cell**, which is the intersection of a row and a column. To create a table in HTML, you use the elements described in **TABLE H-3**. **CASE** ▷ *Phillip would like a table showing a breakdown of room rates. You add this table on the Reservations page.*

STEPS

> **QUICK TIP**
> Table content is placed between opening and closing table tags.

1. Return to reserve.html in your editor, insert a blank line below the h3 element containing the text *Rates*, indent to match the <h3> tag, type <table>, press [Enter], indent as needed, then type </table>

2. Insert a blank line beneath the opening <table> tag, indent 3 spaces more than the previous line, type <thead>, press [Enter], indent to match the previous line, then type </thead>

> **QUICK TIP**
> The thead and tbody elements group table rows into sections.

3. Press [Enter], indent to match the previous line, type <tbody>, press [Enter], indent as needed, then type </tbody>

4. Insert a blank line below the <thead> tag, indent 3 spaces more than the previous line, type <tr>, press [Enter], type </tr>, then repeat twice to add two more tr elements in the tbody section

> **QUICK TIP**
> The number of cells in each row is sufficient for a browser to calculate the number of columns; therefore, no element is required to specify the number or arrangement of columns.

5. Insert a blank line below the first <tr> tag in the thead section, indent 3 spaces more than the previous line, type <th>Period</th>, then enter the following additional th elements on separate lines: <th>Sun Room</th>, <th>Reed Room</th>, and <th>Treehouse</th>

6. Within the first tr element in the tbody section, enter the following td elements: <td>May 1 - Sep. 15</td>, <td>$110</td>, <td>$125</td>, and <td>$150</td>

7. Within the second tr element in the tbody section, enter the td elements <td>Sep. 16 - Apr. 30</td>, <td>$100</td>, <td>$110</td>, and <td>$150</td>, then save your changes

   Your HTML code should match **FIGURE H-14**.

8. Return to styles.css in your editor, in the reset styles section and in the rule that sets border, padding, and margin to 0, add table, tbody, td, tfoot, th, thead, and tr to the list of selectors

> **QUICK TIP**
> Specifying a border for the table element creates a border around the outside of a table, but not around individual cells within it.

9. Type /* main content tables */ above the /* footer section */ comment, then below the new comment create a new style rule with the selectors td, th and the declarations border: 1px solid black; and font-size: 1.3em;, as shown in **FIGURE H-15**

   Because browsers render tables without gridlines by default, you added a border declaration to create a line around each cell.

10. Save your changes, reload reserve.html in your browser, then scroll as necessary to the Rates section

    As **FIGURE H-16** shows, the table content you entered is displayed in a grid, with a border around each cell.

FIGURE H-14: HTML code for table

```
59      <section>
60         <h3>Rates</h3>          The thead element
61         <table>                marks the header rows
62            <thead>
63               <tr>
64                  <th>Period</th>
65                  <th>Sun Room</th>
66                  <th>Reed Room</th>
67                  <th>Treehouse</th>
68               </tr>
69            </thead>
```

The entire contents of a table are enclosed within a table element

Each th element marks the content of a header cell

Code continued with line 70 in figure to the right

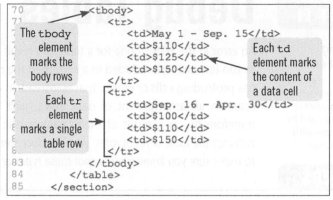

```
70            <tbody>
71               <tr>
                    <td>May 1 - Sep. 15</td>
                    <td>$110</td>
                    <td>$125</td>
                    <td>$150</td>
                 </tr>
                 <tr>
                    <td>Sep. 16 - Apr. 30</td>
                    <td>$100</td>
                    <td>$110</td>
                    <td>$150</td>
                 </tr>
83            </tbody>
84         </table>
85      </section>
```

The tbody element marks the body rows

Each tr element marks a single table row

Each td element marks the content of a data cell

Code continued from figure on the left

FIGURE H-15: CSS code for table

```
14   a, article, body, div, dd, dl, dt, figcaption, figure, footer, header, h1,
15   h2, h3, img, nav, ol, p, section, table, tbody, td, tfoot, th, thead, tr, ul {
16      border: 0;
17      padding: 0;
18      margin: 0;
19   }
```

Selectors added to rule for border, padding, and margin in the reset styles section

```
160   /* main content tables */
161   td, th {
162      border: 1px solid black;
163      font-size: 1.3em;
164   }
165
166   /* footer section */
```

border property for td and th elements adds a line around each cell

FIGURE H-16: Table in Reservations web page

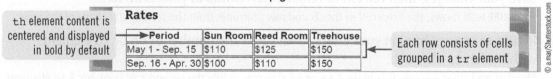

th element content is centered and displayed in bold by default

Each row consists of cells grouped in a tr element

© a.nar/Shutterstock.com

TABLE H-3 HTML Table Structuring Elements

element	content	description
table	entire table	start and end of table content
thead		group of one or more rows that contain column headers; when printed, this content is displayed at the top of each page
tbody	group of rows	group of one or more rows that contain the main body of the table
tfoot		group of one or more rows that contain column footers; when printed, this content is displayed at the bottom of each page
tr	row	start and end of a row
th	cell	content of a table header cell
td		content of a standard table cell

© 2016 Cengage Learning

Debug Tables

Learning
Outcomes
• Recognize and fix
a table row with
missing content
• Recognize and fix
a table row with
extra content

An error in the HTML code for a table can result in unique issues when rendered by a browser. If too many or too few cells are included in a row, then the result is a table that is not a rectangular grid, but one that has protruding cells or empty spaces instead. In addition, omitting or improperly placing a closing tag can result in an arrangement of data that's hard to understand. Some errors are easy to recognize, and therefore fix, as a result of their characteristic appearance in a browser. **CASE** ▸ *As you prepare to enhance the table of room rates, you introduce some errors into your code and examine the result in the browser to make sure you know how to spot these types of errors when you work with tables in the future.*

STEPS

1. **Return to reserve.html in your editor, locate the code `<td>$150</td>` within the second `tr` element, type `<!--` before the `<td>` tag, then type `-->` after the `</td>` tag**

   In order for a table to appear as a rectangular grid, each row must have the same amount of content. By commenting out this `td` element, you create a row that is missing a cell. **FIGURE H-17** shows the edited code.

QUICK TIP
You can visualize the role of each element in a table by opening your browser's developer tools, then mousing over each element to highlight it on the page.

2. **Save your changes, then refresh or reload reserve.html in your browser**

   As **FIGURE H-18** shows, the missing cell in the second row is reflected as an empty spot in the table.

3. **Return to reserve.html in your editor, then count the number of `th` or `td` elements that are not commented out within each `tr` element**

   The first and third rows each contain 4 `th` or `td` elements, while the second row contains only 3 `td` elements that are not commented out. This difference in the number of cells in each row results in the gap displayed in the browser.

4. **Remove the `<!--` and `-->` tags you added in Step 1**

5. **Below the final `td` element and within the second `tr` element, add a new line, indent to match the previous line, then type `<td>$150</td>`**

   When entering the code for a table manually, it's also possible to enter too much content in a single row. Adding an extra cell to this row creates such a row. **FIGURE H-19** shows the edited code.

QUICK TIP
The extra cell is narrower than the other cells because by default, browsers set width to fit the content in the widest cell of a column.

6. **Save your changes, then refresh or reload reserve.html in your browser**

   As **FIGURE H-20** shows, the extra cell in the second row protrudes from the rectangular shape of the table.

7. **Return to reserve.html in your editor, then count the number of `th` or `td` elements within each `tr` element**

   The first and third rows each contain 4 `th` or `td` elements, while the second row contains 5 `td` elements. This difference in the number of cells in each row results in the protruding cell displayed in the browser.

TROUBLE
If your table does not appear as expected, use **FIGURE H-14**, which shows the completed code for the table, to correct any errors.

8. **Remove the `td` element you added in Step 5, save your changes, then refresh or reload reserve.html in your browser**

   Your table once again appears as a rectangle with no protruding or missing cells.

FIGURE H-17: Table code to remove a cell

```
70              <tbody>
71                  <tr>
72                      <td>May 1 - Sep. 15</td>
73                      <td>$110</td>
74                      <td>$125</td>
75                      <!--<td>$150</td>-->
76                  </tr>
```

Commented out td element means this cell will not be displayed, so it creates a row with one fewer cells than other rows

FIGURE H-18: Table with a missing cell in a browser

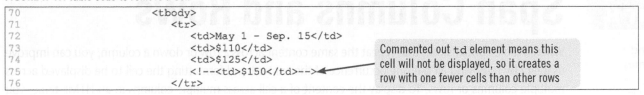

Rates

Period	Sun Room	Reed Room	Treehouse
May 1 - Sep. 15	$110	$125	
Sep. 16 - Apr. 30	$100	$110	$150

© a.mar/Shutterstock.com

Gap in table indicates that one row has less content than other rows; this results from commented out td element

FIGURE H-19: Table code to create a row with an extra cell

```
70              <tbody>
71                  <tr>
72                      <td>May 1 - Sep. 15</td>
73                      <td>$110</td>
74                      <td>$125</td>
75                      <td>$150</td>
76                      <td>$150</td>
77                  </tr>
```

Added td element results in a row with one more cell than other rows

FIGURE H-20: Table with an extra cell in a browser

Rates

Period	Sun Room	Reed Room	Treehouse	
May 1 - Sep. 15	$110	$125	$150	$150
Sep. 16 - Apr. 30	$100	$110	$150	

© a.mar/Shutterstock.com

Protruding cell indicates that row has more content than other rows

Resisting the temptation to use tables for layout

You can style table borders with all the properties that are available for other web page elements, including removing borders completely. In the early days of the web, many developers combined spanned rows and columns with invisible borders to enable the positioning of text, images, and other elements side by side, and in specific areas of a web page. However, as CSS grew and user agent support for it matured, the CSS position and float properties became the preferred method for creating visual layouts. While you can place elements in arbitrary locations by manipulating the number and sizes of rows and columns in a table, doing so erroneously assigns semantic meaning to your web page content; this suggests that user agents should attempt to understand it as a table of related data. In addition, this use of a table creates particularly strong challenges for non-visual user agents such as screen readers in conveying the relationships between web page elements. For these reasons, you should restrict your use of tables only to data whose meaning can be best understood in a grid layout.

Span Columns and Rows

Learning Outcomes
- Display cell content in multiple columns
- Display cell content in multiple rows

When a table contains cells that repeat the same content across a row or down a column, you can improve usability by removing all but one occurrence of the content and formatting the cell to be displayed across multiple columns or rows. To display the content of a cell across multiple columns in an HTML table, you use the colspan attribute in the opening th or td tag for the cell in order to specify the number of columns in which the content should be displayed. Likewise, you use the rowspan attribute to specify the number of rows for cell content to span. **CASE** ▶ *Your plans for the Rates table include an additional row at the top labeling the room listings, as shown in the sketch in* **FIGURE H-21**. *Once the new row is added, you plan to have Period span two rows in order to adjust for the space created by adding the new top row. You add* colspan *and* rowspan *attributes to make the Rates table easier to read while incorporating this new content.*

STEPS

1. **Return to reserve.html in your editor, insert a new line beneath the <thead> tag, indent 3 additional spaces, type <tr>, press [Enter], indent as needed, then type </tr>**

2. **Between the opening and closing tr tags you just entered, indent two additional spaces, type <th>Period</th>, press [Enter], indent as needed, then type <th colspan="3">Room</th>**

   Although the new header row includes only two cells, the colspan attribute marks the second cell to be displayed in 3 columns, so the second cell will span the second, third, and fourth columns. As a result of the cell spanning multiple columns, the new row occupies the same number of columns as the other rows in the table, as shown in **FIGURE H-21**.

3. **Save your work, then reload reserve.html in your browser**

   As **FIGURE H-22** shows, the text *Room* appears in a cell that spans three columns. However, the heading *Period* is now duplicated in the two heading rows.

4. **Return to reserve.html in your editor, within the first tr element, click before the closing > in the opening tag for the th element containing the text *Period*, press [Spacebar], then type rowspan="2"**

5. **Within the second tr element, delete the th element containing the text *Period***

   Even though the second heading row contains code for only three cells, the cell that use the rowspan attribute in the previous row provides the additional content that keeps the row the same length as the other rows in the table. **FIGURE H-23** shows the completed HTML code for the table.

6. **Save your changes, then refresh reserve.html in your browser**

   As **FIGURE H-24** shows, the cell containing the text *Period* spans two rows.

FIGURE H-21: Sketch of table with cells spanning rows and columns

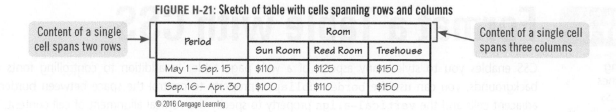

Content of a single cell spans two rows

Content of a single cell spans three columns

© 2016 Cengage Learning

FIGURE H-22: Table cell spanning multiple columns

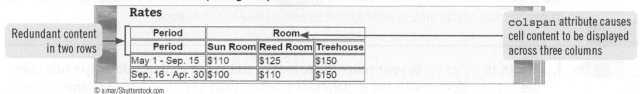

Redundant content in two rows

colspan attribute causes cell content to be displayed across three columns

© a.mar/Shutterstock.com

FIGURE H-23: Code containing `colspan` and `rowspan` attributes

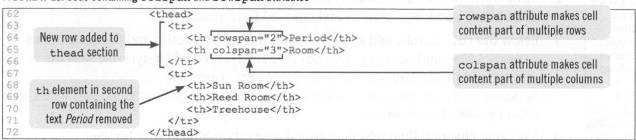

```
62      <thead>
63       ┌ <tr>
64       │    <th rowspan="2">Period</th>
65       │    <th colspan="3">Room</th>
66       └ </tr>
67         <tr>
68          <th>Sun Room</th>
69          <th>Reed Room</th>
70          <th>Treehouse</th>
71         </tr>
72      </thead>
```

New row added to thead section

th element in second row containing the text *Period* removed

rowspan attribute makes cell content part of multiple rows

colspan attribute makes cell content part of multiple columns

FIGURE H-24: Table cell spanning multiple rows

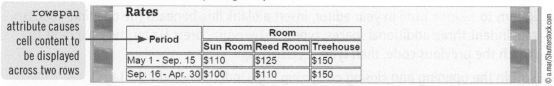

rowspan attribute causes cell content to be displayed across two rows

© a.mar/Shutterstock.com

Calculating the number of columns in a row

When you use `colspan` and `rowspan` attributes, you still need to confirm that your content fits the table dimensions. To do so, start by adding the values for all `colspan` attributes used in the row. Next, add the number of `th` or `td` elements in the row without `colspan` attributes. Finally, add the number of `th` or `td` cells in earlier rows whose content is part of the current row due to `rowspan` values. In short:

   current row `colspan` total
   + cells in current row without `colspan`
   + cells spanning from previous rows with `rowspan`
   = total columns

Running this calculation on any row of your table should produce the same value as for any other row.

If one or more rows appear to be shorter or longer than the surrounding rows, it can be helpful to preview your web page in a browser and inspect the table to identify the cell where the content of one row no longer corresponds to the content above or below it. You may simply need to adjust a `rowspan` or `colspan` value, or add or remove a cell.

In a table that doesn't use colspan or rowspan attributes, you can verify that each row includes content for every column simply by ensuring that each row contains the same number of th or td elements.

Format a Table with CSS

CSS enables you to style many aspects of a web page table. In addition to controlling fonts and backgrounds, you can use the `border-collapse` property to control the space between borders of adjacent cells and the `vertical-align` property to specify the vertical alignment of cell content. You can use these and other CSS properties to style an entire table, a table section (such as `thead` or `tbody`), or individual rows or cells. In addition, you can use the HTML `col` and `colgroup` elements to assign styles to a single column or to a group of columns. **CASE** ▶ *You style the borders and add background colors to different sections of your table to make it easier for users to read and understand.*

STEPS

QUICK TIP
The border-spacing property has no effect when border-collapse is set to collapse, but specifying a value of 0 ensures that browsers do not create extra space between the table's outermost cells and the border of the table element.

1. **Return to** styles.css **in your editor, then, in the reset styles section, add a style rule using the** `table` **selector with the declarations** `border-collapse: collapse;` **and** `border-spacing: 0;`

   Setting `border-collapse` to `collapse` eliminates the default space between the borders of adjacent cells.

2. **Scroll down to the main content tables section, then in the** `td, th` **style rule, add the declarations** `padding: 0.4em;` **and** `text-align: center;`

3. **Below the** `td, th` **rule, add a style rule with the** `table` **selector and the declarations** `width: 100%;` **and** `border: 2px solid black;`, **then add a style rule with the** `th` **selector and the declaration** `background-color: #aecdf4;`

   By default, a table occupies only the width necessary to display its content. At increased widths, each column is widened proportionally.

QUICK TIP
Browsers render only the background (and related), border (and related), visibility, and width CSS properties applied to colgroup and col elements.

4. **Save your changes, then refresh or reload reservation.html in your browser**

   The content of all cells is centered and the cells have increased padding. The table occupies the entire width of the parent element and has a thicker outer border than the cell borders. In addition, the th cells have a light blue background.

5. **Return to** reserve.html **in your editor, insert a blank line beneath the opening** `<table>` **tag, indent three additional spaces, type** `<colgroup>`, **press [Enter] twice, indent to match the previous code, then type** `</colgroup>`

QUICK TIP
Whenever you add col elements, they must cover all the columns in the table. Unless all columns are accounted for in col elements, your code won't validate.

6. **Within the opening and closing** `colgroup` **tags, indent and add the tags** `<col class="table-heading-column">` **and** `<col class="table-data-columns" span="3">` **on separate lines**

   FIGURE H-25 shows the HTML code. By default, each `col` element applies to a single column, starting from the left side of the table. However, you can group consecutive columns into a single `col` element by specifying the number of columns to include as the value of the `span` attribute. All `col` elements must be contained in a colgroup element.

7. **Save your work, return to** styles.css **in your editor, in the main content tables section, below the** `th` **rule, add a rule with the** `.table-heading-column` **selector and the declaration** `background-color: #f1eace;`, **then add a rule with the** `.table-data-columns` **selector and the declaration** `background-color: white;`

   Note that the second character in the color value is a number 1, not a letter l. **FIGURE H-26** shows the completed CSS code.

8. **Save your changes, then refresh or reload reserve.html in your browser**

   As **FIGURE H-27** shows, different background colors are applied to the columns based on the styling of the corresponding `col` elements. Styles specified for table cells, rows, or sections have a higher level of specificity than those applied to a `col` element; for this reason, the heading cells are rendered with the background color from the `th` rule rather than those specified for the col elements.

FIGURE H-25: col and colgroup elements added to HTML code for table

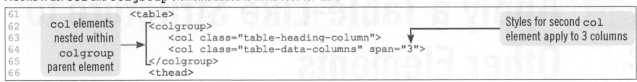

```
61                        <table>
62    col elements        <colgroup>
63    nested within          <col class="table-heading-column">
64    colgroup              <col class="table-data-columns" span="3">     Styles for second col
65    parent element      </colgroup>                                     element apply to 3 columns
66                        <thead>
```

FIGURE H-26: Completed CSS code for table

```
28    table {
29        border-collapse: collapse;
30        border-spacing: 0;
31    }
32
33    /* document-wide styles */
```

```
164    /* main content tables */
165    td, th {
166        border: 1px solid black;
167        padding: 0.4em;
168        font-size: 1.3em;
169        text-align: center;
170    }
171    table {
172        width: 100%;
173        border: 2px solid black;
174    }
175    th {
176        background-color: #aecdf4;
177    }
178    .table-heading-column {
179        background-color: #f1eace;
180    }
181    .table-data-columns {
182        background-color: white;
183    }
```

Applies a background color to the first col element, which encompasses the leftmost column of the table

Applies a different background color to the second col element, which encompasses the remaining 3 columns

FIGURE H-27: Table with background color and other styles applied

Beige background applied to first column based on styling for first col element

Blue background applied to first two rows based on th style rule

White background applied to right three columns based on styling for second col element

Apply a Table-Like Structure to Other Elements

Sometimes you may want to arrange web page elements so they appear visually in a grid, even if these elements would not normally belong in a table. To implement this layout, you first use block-level elements, such as div elements, to create a structure that parallels the nesting of table, tr, th, and td elements in an HTML table. You then set the CSS display property to table-cell for the elements containing the table content, table-row for the container elements for each row, and table for the main parent element. **CASE** *You duplicate the description list containing contact information for making reservations and convert the copy to a table-like layout using CSS.*

STEPS

1. Return to reserve.html in your editor, scroll down to the h3 element that contains the text *Questions?*, select the entire dl element including the opening and closing dl tags, then copy it to the Clipboard

2. Insert a new line before the opening <dl> tag, type <!--, insert a blank line after the closing </dl> tag, then type -->

3. Insert a new line before the opening <!-- tag, paste the content of the Clipboard, then in the opening and closing tags for the pasted description list, replace dl with div, preserving the class value in the opening tag

4. Insert a new line above the first dt element, indent to the same level as the dt element, type <div class="row">, insert a new line below the first dd element, indent to the same level as the dd element, then type </div>

   The new div element serves the role of a tr element in a table.

5. Indent the dt and dd elements within the new div element an additional 3 spaces, replace the opening <dt> tag with <div class="category">, replace the closing </dt> tag with </div>, then, in the opening and closing dd tags, replace dd with div

6. Repeat Steps 4 and 5 for the remaining three sets of dt and dd elements, then compare your code to FIGURE H-28

7. Save your changes, return to styles.css in your editor, add a new line above the /* footer section */ comment, then type /* main content CSS tables */

8. Below the new comment, add a style rule with the .contact selector and the declarations margin: 1em 0;, display: table;, and font-size: 1.3em;, add a style rule with the .row selector and the declaration display: table-row;, add a style rule with the .row div selector and the declarations display: table-cell; and padding: 0.25em 0.5em;, then add a style rule with the .category selector and the declaration font-weight: bold;, as shown in FIGURE H-29

9. Save your changes, refresh or reload reserve.html in your browser, then scroll down to the Questions? section

   As FIGURE H-30 shows, the contact information is now arranged in a grid without borders.

10. Validate the code for your web page and your style sheet, and make changes as necessary to fix any errors

FIGURE H-28: Completed HTML code for displaying contact information in a table-like layout

```
110         <h3>Questions?</h3>
111         <p>Feel free to contact us with any queries about Lakeland Reeds, or about
112         planning your trip.</p>
113       <div class="contact">
114          <div class="row">
115             <div class="category">Proprietor</div>
116             <div>Phillip Blaine</div>
          </div>
          <div class="row">
             <div class="category">Email</div>
             <div>lrbb@example.com</div>
          </div>
          <div class="row">
124             <div class="category">Phone</div>
125             <div>(218) 555-5253</div>
126          </div>
127          <div class="row">
128             <div class="category">Fax</div>
129             <div>(218) 555-0413</div>
130          </div>
       </div>
```

Outermost div element serves the role of a table element

div elements nested within outermost div element serve the role of tr elements

Most deeply nested div elements serve the role of th or td elements

FIGURE H-29: Completed CSS code for displaying contact information in a table-like layout

```
185   /* main content CSS tables */
186   .contact {
187      margin: 1em 0;
188      display: table;
189      font-size: 1.3em;
190   }
191   .row {
192      display: table-row;
193   }
194   .row div {
195      display: table-cell;
196      padding: 0.25em 0.5em;
197   }
198   .category {
199      font-weight: bold;
200   }
201
202   /* footer section */
```

Element with the table value for the display property serves the role of a table element

Element with the table-row value for the display property serves the role of a tr element

Element with the table-cell value for the display property serves the role of a th or td element

FIGURE H-30: Contact information displayed in a table-like layout

Content displayed in a grid with two columns

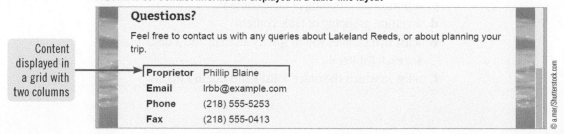

Questions?

Feel free to contact us with any queries about Lakeland Reeds, or about planning your trip.

Proprietor	Phillip Blaine
Email	lrbb@example.com
Phone	(218) 555-5253
Fax	(218) 555-0413

© a.nar/Shutterstock.com

Practice

Concepts Review

Refer to FIGURE H-31 **to answer the following questions.**

FIGURE H-31

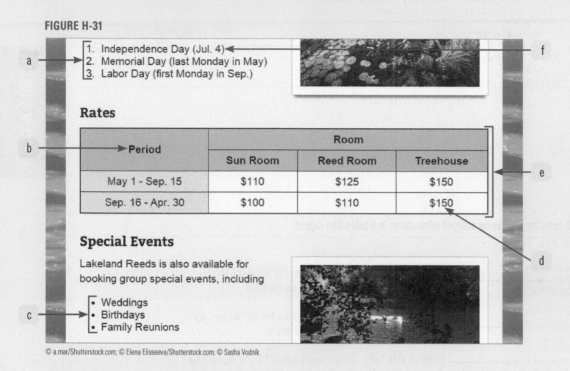

© a.mar/Shutterstock.com; © Elena Elisseeva/Shutterstock.com; © Sasha Vodnik

1. Which item is created using the td element?
2. Which item is created using the ul element?
3. Which item is created using the ol element?
4. Which item is created using the th element?
5. Which item is created using the table element?
6. Which item is created using the li element?

Match each term with the statement that best describes it.

7. **column**
8. **description list**
9. **ordered list**
10. **unordered list**
11. **row**
12. **cell**

   a. a table component that displays a single item of data
   b. a list in which items are numbered or lettered sequentially
   c. a horizontal grouping of table content
   d. a vertical grouping of table content
   e. a list that enables you to specify an item and a description
     for each list item
   f. a list in which the order of list items doesn't matter

Select the best answer from the list of choices.

13. Which element do you use to create a list that is usually displayed with bullet characters?

    a. dd

    b. ul

    c. dl

    d. ol

14. What is a common cause of a protruding cell in a table?

    a. a missing thead element

    b. a missing tbody element

    c. a missing th or td element in one row

    d. an extra th or td element in one row

15. What is a common cause of an empty space in a table?

    a. a missing thead element

    b. a missing tbody element

    c. a missing th or td element in one row

    d. an extra th or td element in one row

Skills Review

1. **Create an ordered list.**

    a. In your editor, open the file HTM_H-3.html from the SR folder where you store your Data Files for this unit, save it as **index.html**, then repeat to save the file HTM_H_4.html as **history.html**, HTM_H_5.html as **location.html**, and HTM_H_6.css as **styles.css**.

    b. Within the comment section at the top of each file, enter your first and last names and today's date, then save.

    c. Return to index.html in your editor, then below the p element containing the text *Eat in, carry out, or call for delivery*, insert a p element with the class value accent containing the text **Enjoy award winning pizza in your home in just three steps:**.

    d. Below the p element, insert starting and ending tags for an ordered list on separate lines at the same indent level.

    e. On a new line and between the tags you just entered, indent three additional spaces, add a list item element containing the text **Call the location nearest you.**, then repeat to insert two additional list items containing the text **Place your order and listen for your doorbell.** and **Open the box and dig in!**

    f. Save your changes, return to styles.css in your editor, then, in the reset styles section, add the ol and li selectors to the list of selectors in the style rule that sets border, padding, and margin to 0.

    g. At the end of the reset styles section, add a rule for the ol element that sets list-style-type to none.

    h. Scroll down as necessary to the /* footer section */ comment, then above it add the text **main content lists** as a new comment.

    i. Below the new comment you entered, create a style rule with the article ol selector that sets the width to 70%, the margin to 1em auto, the padding to 1em, left-aligns text, precedes each list item with a decimal number, and sets the background color to #ddd.

    j. Below the rule you created in the previous step, create a style rule with the article ol li selector that sets the left margin to 2em.

    k. Save your changes, open index.html in your browser, then verify that the three list items you entered are displayed in a list numbered 1, 2, and 3.

2. **Create an unordered list.**

    a. Return to history.html in your editor, locate the p element with the class value contrastbox, then edit the opening and closing tags for the element to make it an unordered list without a class value.

    b. Edit the opening and closing tags for each p element within the unordered list to make each a list item.

    c. Save your changes, return to styles.css in your editor, in the reset styles section add the ul selector to the list of selectors in the style rule that sets border, padding, and margin to 0, then add the ul selector to the style rule for ol elements that sets list-style-type to none.

    d. Scroll down to the /* main content lists */ comment, then in the two style rules above the comment, change the selector article div.contrastbox to article ul and change the selector article div.contrastbox p to article ul li.

    e. Cut and paste the /* main content lists */ comment so it is above the article ul style rule.

f. Save your changes, open history.html in your browser, then verify that the three words *flavor*, *aroma*, and *fresh* in the middle of the article are bold, centered, and displayed in a gray box and without bullet characters.

3. Create a description list.

a. Return to index.html in your editor, then within the `footer` element, add a blank line below the opening `<footer>` tag, indent an additional three spaces, enter the opening tag for a description list, add a blank line above the closing `</footer>` tag, indent an additional 3 spaces, then enter the closing tag for a description list.

b. For each p element within the `footer` element, increase the indent by three spaces, then remove the opening and closing p tags.

c. Mark the address *150 St. Joseph St.* as a description list term, move the `span` element and its content onto its own line at the same indent level, then mark the content of the new line as a description list description. (*Hint*: Include the `span` element within the code for the description item.) Repeat for the remaining two locations.

d. Save your changes, return to styles.css in your editor, then in the reset styles section add the `dl`, `dt`, and `dd` selectors to the list of selectors in the style rule that sets border, padding, and margin to 0.

e. Save your changes, reload index.html in your browser, then verify that each address and phone number is displayed on a separate line, and that each phone number is displayed in bold and indented in the contact information.

f. Return to index.html in your editor, copy the description list element to the Clipboard, including its opening and closing tags, return to history.html in your editor, replace the content of the `footer` element with the content of the Clipboard, save your changes, then repeat for location.html.

g. Reload history.html in your browser, verify that the footer content matches index.html, then repeat for location.html.

4. Create a navigation bar using a list.

a. Return to index.html in your editor, then within the nav element, add a blank line below the opening `<nav>` tag, indent an additional three spaces, enter the opening tag for an unordered list, add a blank line above the closing `</nav>` tag, indent an additional 3 spaces, then enter the closing tag for an unordered list.

b. For each p element within the nav element, increase the indent by three spaces, then replace the opening and closing p tags with tags that mark each element as a list item.

c. Save your changes, return to styles.css in your editor, scroll as necessary to the site navigation section, change the selector `nav.sitenavigation p` to `nav.sitenavigation li`, then change the selector `nav.sitenavigation p a` to `nav.sitenavigation li a`.

d. Save your changes, reload index.html in your browser, verify that the nav bar is displayed as shown in **FIGURE H-32**, click the History link, then verify that the History page is displayed. Note that the appearance of the nav bar on the History page will not match **FIGURE H-32**; you'll fix this in the following steps.

e. Return to index.html in your editor, then within the nav element, copy the unordered list tags and their content to the Clipboard.

f. Return to history.html in your editor, paste the content of the Clipboard to replace the content of the nav element, save your work, then repeat for location.html.

g. Refresh or reload history.html in your web browser, verify that the appearance of the nav bar matches that of index.html, click the Locations link, verify that the appearance of the nav bar matches the other pages, click the Home link, then verify that the index.html page is displayed.

FIGURE H-32

5. Insert a table.

a. Return to location.html in your editor, locate the h3 heading containing the text *Queen’s Park/UT*, insert a blank line beneath the p element containing the phone number, indent as needed to match the previous line, then insert opening and closing tags for a `table` element on separate lines at the same indent level.

b. Between the opening and closing tags you just entered, add opening and closing tags for table head and table body sections with each tag on its own line and indented three spaces more than the `table` tags.

c. Within the table head tags, add opening and closing tags for a table row, with each tag on its own line and indented three spaces more than the table head tags. Repeat to add opening and closing tags for three table rows in the table body section.

d. Within the table row element for the table head section, add table head cell elements containing the text **Day**, **Open**, and **Close** on separate lines, indented three spaces more than the opening table row tag. Repeat to add the following content to table data cell elements in the three table body rows:

Row 1: **Mon-Thu, 11am, 10pm**   Row 2: **Fri-Sat, 11am, 11pm**   Row 3: **Sun, Noon, 10pm**

e. Repeat Steps a–d to insert two more tables using the same content for the header row and the following content for the table body:

h3 heading *St. Clair*:

Row 1: **Mon-Thu, 11am, 9:30pm**   Row 2: **Fri-Sat, 11am, 11pm**   Row 3: **Sun, Noon, 9:30pm**

h3 heading *Dundas*:

Row 1: **Mon-Thu, 11am, 11pm**   Row 2: **Fri-Sat, 11am, Midnight**   Row 3: **Sun, Noon, 11pm**

f. Save your changes, return to styles.css in your editor, then in the reset styles section add the `table`, `thead`, `tbody`, `th`, and `td` selectors to the list of selectors in the style rule that sets border, padding, and margin to 0.

g. At the end of the reset styles section, create a style rule using the `table` selector that collapses borders and sets border spacing to 0.

h. Scroll down as necessary to the `/* footer section */` comment, then above it add the text **main content tables** as a new comment.

i. Below the new comment you entered, create a style rule with the `table` selector that sets the width to 50% and the margin to `0 auto`, create a rule with the `th` and `td` selectors that creates a 1px solid black border, create a rule with the `th` selector that sets padding to 0.1em 0.3em and background color to `#ffcc66`, then create a rule with the `td` selector that sets padding to 0.3em and left-aligns text.

j. Save your changes, reload location.html in your browser, then verify that each table makes sense and contains all the information specified in the previous steps.

6. Debug tables.

a. Return to location.html in your editor.

b. In the table below the h3 heading *Queen’s Park/UT*, add a table data cell containing the text **10pm** below the code for the final cell in the first row of the table body section.

c. Save your changes, refresh or reload location.html in your browser, then notice the effect of the extra cell.

d. Return to location.html in your editor, then comment out the line of code you added in Step b.

e. Comment out the code for the first table data cell in the second row of the table body section, save your changes, refresh or reload location.html in your browser, then notice the gap created by the missing cell.

f. Return to location.html in your editor, remove the comment tags from the first table data cell in the second row of the table body section, save your changes, refresh or reload location.html in your browser, then verify that all tables are displayed without extra or missing cells.

7. Span columns and rows.

a. Return to location.html in your editor, locate the table you inserted beneath the h3 heading *Queen’s Park/UT*, then insert opening and closing tags for a new row element just above the closing tag for the table head section.

b. In the first table row, select the code for the cells containing the text *Open* and *Close*, cut the text to the Clipboard, then paste it within the table row element for the second row in the table head section.

c. In the first table row, below the code for the table header cell containing the text *Day*, add code for a second table head element containing the text **Hours**.

d. In the table header cell containing the text *Day* in the first row of the table header section, add an attribute that indicates that the cell content should span 2 rows.

Skills Review (continued)

e. In the table header cell containing the text *Hours* in the first row of the table header section, add an attribute that indicates that the cell content should span 2 columns.

f. Copy the table head section including the opening and closing tags to the Clipboard, then paste it to replace the table head section in each of the remaining 2 tables in the document.

g. Save your changes, reload location.html in your browser, then verify that the table structure matches that shown in **FIGURE H-33**. Note that the table formatting will not match the figure; you'll fix this in Step 8.

FIGURE H-33

© 2016 Cengage Learning; © Xtremest/Shutterstock.com

8. Format a table with CSS.

a. Return to location.html in your editor, insert a blank line beneath the opening `<table>` tag for the first table you created, indent three additional spaces, then add a container element for column groups.

b. Within the container element, add an element that applies the `class` value `table-heading-column` to the first column, add another element that applies the `class` value `table-data-columns` and spans the last two columns. Repeat Steps a and b for the other two tables.

c. Save your changes, return to styles.css in your editor, scroll as necessary to the main content tables section, then at the bottom of the section add a style rule for the `class` value `table-heading-column` that sets the background color to `#ccc`.

d. Save your changes, open location.html in your browser, then verify that the days of the week in each table have a gray background, as shown in **FIGURE H-33**.

9. Apply a table-like structure to other elements.

a. Return to index.html in your editor, scroll down to the `footer` element, select the entire description list including the opening and closing tags, then copy it to the Clipboard.

b. Comment out the description list element, then above the comment out code, paste the Clipboard content.

c. In the opening and closing tags for the pasted description list, replace `dl` with `div`, specifying the `class` value `contact` in the opening tag.

d. Insert a new line above the first `dt` element, indent to the same level as the `dt` element, enter an opening `<div>` tag with the `class` value `row`, insert a new line below the first `dd` element, indent to the same level as the `dd` element, then insert a closing `</div>` tag.

e. Indent the `dt` and `dd` elements within the new `div` element an additional three spaces, in the opening and closing `dt` tags replace `dt` with `div`, then in the opening and closing `dd` tags, replace `dd` with `div`, specifying the `class` value `phone` in the opening tag.

f. Repeat Steps d and e for the remaining two sets of `dt` and `dd` elements.

g. Save your changes, copy the CSS table you created to the Clipboard, including its opening and closing tags, return to history.html in your editor, replace the content of the `footer` element with the content of the Clipboard, save your changes, then repeat for location.html.

h. Return to styles.css in your editor, add a new line above the `/* print styles */` comment, then add a comment containing the text **footer CSS table**.

i. Below the new comment, add a style rule with the `.contact` selector and declarations that set margins to `0 auto` and `display` to `table`, add a style rule with the `.row` selector and a declaration that sets `display` to `table-row`, add a style rule with the `.row div` selector and declarations that set `display` to `table-cell` and padding to 0.25em 0.5em;, then add a style rule with the `.phone` selector and a declaration that bolds text.

j. Save your changes, refresh or reload location.html in your browser, verify that the contact information in the page footer uses a table-like structure.

k. Validate the code for your web pages and your style sheet, and make changes as necessary to fix any errors.

Independent Challenge 1

Sarah Nguyen, the owner of the Spotted Wren Garden Center, has given you additional content to add to the website you've been creating for her. You add this information using lists and tables.

a. In your editor, open HTM_H-7.html from the IC1 folder where you store your Data Files for this unit, save it as **hours.html**, then repeat to save HTM_H-8.html as **resource.html** and HTM_H-9.css as **styles.css**. In the comment at the top of each file, enter your name and today's date where indicated, then save the files.

b. Return to resource.html in your editor. Beneath the h3 heading *Omaha area plant hardiness zone information*, insert the following table. (*Hint*: Use `rowspan` attributes for the cells containing the text *Zone, Last frost, First frost, May 1,* and *Oct 15*. Use a `colspan` attribute for the cell containing the text *Average annual minimum temp*. The HTML character code for the degree symbol is `&deg;`).

TABLE H-4

Zone	Average annual minimum temp		Last frost	First frost
	Fahrenheit	**Celsius**		
4b	–25°F to –20°F	–28.9°C to –31.6°C		
5a	–20°F to –15°F	–26.2°C to –28.8°C	May 1	Oct 15
5b	–15°F to –10°F	–23.4°C to –26.1°C		

c. Save your changes, return to styles.css in your editor, in the reset styles section add the `table`, `thead`, `tbody`, `th`, and `td` selectors to the list of selectors in the style rule that sets border, padding, and margin to 0. At the end of the reset styles section, create a style rule using the `table` selector that collapses borders and sets border spacing to 0.

d. Above the `/* footer section */` comment, add a comment containing the text **main content table**. Below the comment, add a style rule for `th` and `td` elements that creates a 1px solid black border and sets the padding to 0.5em, then add a rule for `th` elements that sets the background color to `yellow`. Save your changes.

e. Return to resource.html in your editor, then, in the code for the table, add a `colgroup` element that contains a child element with the `class` name `zone` for styling the first column, a child element with `class` name `temps` for styling the second and third columns, and a child element with the `class` name `frost` for styling the fourth and fifth columns. Save your changes, return to styles.css, in the main content table section add a style rule for the element with the `class` value `temps` that sets the background color to `#87f547`, then add a style rule for the element with the `class` value `frost` that sets the background color to `#f5a88c`. Save your changes, reload resource.html in your browser, then verify that the table appears as shown in **FIGURE H-34**.

FIGURE H-34

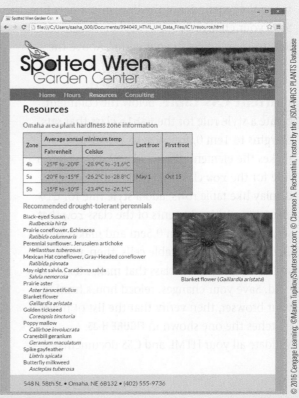

Independent Challenge 1 (continued)

f. Return to resource.html in your editor. Below the h3 element containing the text *Recommended drought-tolerant perennials* and the figure that follows it, mark up the list of plant names as a description list with the common names as terms and the Latin names that follow as descriptions. Save your changes, return to styles.css in your editor, then, above the /* footer section */ comment, add a comment containing the text **main content description list.** Below the comment, create a style rule to style the content of all description elements in a description list in italic and with a 1em left margin. Scroll up as necessary to the reset styles section, then add the dd, dl, and dt selectors to the list of selectors in the style rule that sets border, padding, and margin to 0. Save your changes, reload resource.html in your browser, then verify that the definition list matches the one shown in **FIGURE H-34**.

g. Return to resource.html in your editor. Convert the code for the nav bar to an unordered list by changing the p element that encloses each link to an li element, then enclosing the code for all the links within a ul element. Repeat for hours.html, then save your changes to both documents. Return to styles.css in your editor, scroll as necessary to the site navigation section, then change the selector for the nav.sitenavigation p rule to nav.sitenavigation li. Scroll up as necessary to the reset styles section, then add the ul and li selectors to the list of selectors in the style rule that sets border, padding, and margin to 0. At the end of the reset styles section, create a style rule using the ul selector that sets list-style-type to none. Save your changes, refresh or reload resource.html in your browser, then verify that the appearance of the navigation bar is unchanged. Click the Hours link, verify that the Hours page opens, then verify that the nav bar on that page is unchanged.

h. Return to hours.html in your editor. Beneath the h2 heading, insert a new line containing a div element with the class value table at the same indent level as the previous line. Add a closing tag for the div element below the last line of store hours information. Enclose each line of code containing store hours information in a div element with the class value row, then delete the opening and closing p tags from each line. For each line, enclose the abbreviation of the day of the week within a div element, delete the colon (:) that follows it, move the remainder of the line onto a new line, then enclose the content of the new line in a div element. Save your changes.

i. Return to styles.css in your editor. Above the /* footer section */ comment, add a comment containing the text **main content CSS table**. Below the comment, create a style rule for the table class that sets margins to 1em 0, font size to 1.3em, and makes the element display like a table, create a rule for the row class that makes the elements display like table rows, add a style rule for div elements within elements of the class row that sets padding to 0.25em 0.5em and makes the elements display like table cells, then add a style rule for the day class that makes text bold. Save your changes, reload hours.html in your browser, then verify that the list of hours matches the one shown in **FIGURE H-35**.

FIGURE H-35

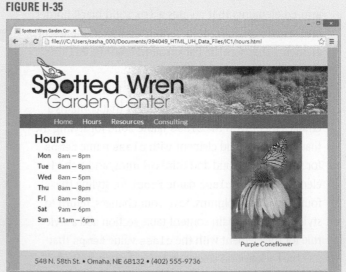

j. Validate all your HTML and CSS documents.

Independent Challenge 2

You add new information about the Murfreesboro Regional Soccer League to the website that you are creating. You mark up the new information using an unordered list and several tables. You also change the markup for the nav bar to an unordered list.

a. In your editor, open HTM_H-10.html from the IC2 folder where you store your Data Files for this unit, save it as **started.html**, then repeat to save HTM_H-11.html as **schedule.html** and HTM_H-12.css as **styles.css**. In the comment at the top of each file, enter your name and today's date where indicated, then save the files.

b. In started.html, locate the paragraph that begins *If you're interested in joining up*, then insert a blank line below it. Add an unordered list containing the following four list items: **Child/Teen (6–18): $50, Student (19–24): $50, Adult (25–59): $65**, and **Senior (60+): $40**. Save your changes, then return to styles.css in your editor. In the reset styles section, add the ul and li selectors to the list of selectors in the style rule that sets border, padding, and margin to 0. At the end of the reset styles section, create a style rule using the ul selector that sets list-style-type to none. Above the /* footer section */ comment, add a comment containing the text **main content unordered list**. Below the comment, create a style rule for unordered lists within the article element that sets margins to 0 0 1em 3em, adds 7% padding on the left side, uses filled circles for list item markers, and sets the font size to 1.2em. Save your changes, open started.html in a browser, then verify that the bulleted list you created matches **FIGURE H-36**.

c. Return to started.html in your editor. Convert the code for the nav bar to an unordered list by enclosing the p elements that mark nav bar items within an element that marks an unordered list, then changing each p element that encloses a nav bar item to a list item element. Repeat for schedule.html, then save your changes to both documents. Return to styles.css in your editor. In the site navigation section, below the nav.sitenavigation rule, create a style rule that applies only to list item elements within the nav element with the class value sitenavigation that sets the font size to 1.2em. Save your work, reload started.html in your browser, then verify that the appearance of the nav bar matches **FIGURE H-36**. Click the Schedules link, ensure that the Schedules page opens, then verify the appearance of the nav bar also matches **FIGURE H-36**.

FIGURE H-36

Independent Challenge 2 (continued)

d. Return to schedule.html in your editor, then convert the four lists of game dates and times into tables. Create a heading row for each table with heading cells containing the text **Date** and **Time**. Split the information for each game into two cells, the first containing the date and the second containing the start time. Set the `class` value for the first table to `red-team-schedule`, the second table to `blue-team-schedule`, the third table to `green-team-schedule`, and the fourth table to `yellow-team-schedule`. Save your changes, then return to styles.css in your editor. Above the comment `/* main content unordered list */`, add a comment containing the text **main content tables**, then below the new comment add a style rule for `table` elements that sets the width to 90% and sets margins to 0 auto. Add a style rule for table header cells and table data cells that creates 1px solid black borders and sets padding to 0.5em. Add a style rule for table header cell elements that sets the background color to `#ddd`. Create a rule for the element with the class value `red-team-schedule` that creates a 5px solid red border, then create a rule that adds a 5px solid red bottom border to header cells within this element Create a rule for the element with the class value `blue-team-schedule` that creates a 5px solid blue border, then create a rule that adds a 5px solid blue bottom border to header cells within this element and sets their text color to `blue`. Create a rule for the element with the class value `green-team-schedule` that creates a 5px solid green border, then create a rule that adds a 5px solid green bottom border to header cells within this element and sets their text color to `green`. Create a rule for the element with the class value `yellow-team-schedule` that creates a 5px solid border using the color `#e6da57`, then create a rule that adds a 5px solid bottom border using the color `#e6da57` to header cells within this element and sets their text color to `yellow`. Save your changes, refresh or reload schedule.html in your browser, then verify that all four tables are displayed correctly. Fix any missing or extra cells.

e. Using **FIGURE H-37** as a guide, add a third column to each table that displays the field letter where each game will be played. (*Hint*: To add a column, add a new cell at the end of each row element.) Save your work, refresh or reload schedule.html in your browser, then verify that your tables match those shown in **FIGURE H-37**.

f. Validate all your HTML and CSS documents.

FIGURE H-37

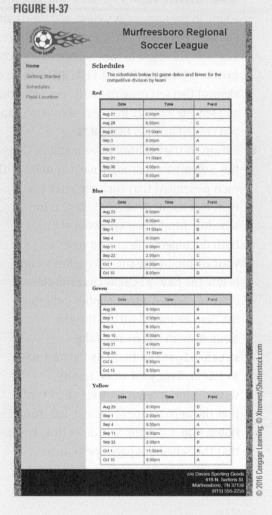

Independent Challenge 3

As you continue your work on the website for Hotel Natoma, you incorporate additional information about the hotel and local attractions using some of the techniques for organizing content that you learned in this unit.

FIGURE H-38

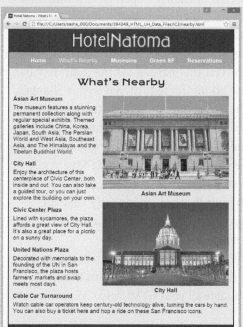

a. In your editor, open HTM_H-13.html from the IC3 folder where you store your Data Files for this unit, save it as **nearby.html**, then repeat to save HTM_H-14.html as **museums.html**, HTM_H-15.html as **greensf.html**, and HTM_H-16.css as **styles.css**. In the comment at the top of each file, enter your name and today's date where indicated, then save the files.

b. In nearby.html, mark the list of nearby locations and descriptions as a description list. Save your changes, then in styles.css, above the comment /* footer section */, create a comment containing the text **main content description list**. Add a style rule that bolds the text of description list term items, then add a rule that sets margins of 0.4em 0 1em for description list description items. In the reset styles section, add the dd, dl, and dt selectors to the list of selectors in the style rule that sets border, padding, and margin to 0. Save your changes, open nearby.html in a browser, then verify that it matches **FIGURE H-38**.

c. In museums.html, mark the list of museums as an unordered list. Save your changes, then in styles.css, above the comment /* main content description list */, create a comment containing the text **main content unordered lists**. Create a style rule for unordered lists that sets the left margin to 5%, displays a filled circle next to each list item, and sets the line height to 1.4em. In the reset styles section, add the ul and li selectors to the list of selectors in the style rule that sets border, padding, and margin to 0. At the end of the reset styles section, create a style rule using the ul selector that sets list-style-type to none. Save your changes, open museums.html in a browser, then verify that it matches **FIGURE H-39**.

FIGURE H-39

d. In greensf.html, mark the list of destinations as an ordered list. Save your changes, then in styles.css, above the comment /* footer section */, create a comment containing the text **main content ordered list**. Create a style rule for ordered lists that sets left and right margins to 5% and uses decimal numbering, then create a style rule for list items within an ordered list that creates 0.6em padding on the left. In the reset styles section, add the ol selector to the list of selectors in the style rule that sets border, padding, and margin to 0 and in the style rule that sets list-style-type to none.

Independent Challenge 3 (continued)

e. Save your changes, open greensf.html in a browser, then verify that it matches **FIGURE H-40**.

f. Return to greensf.html in your editor, then convert the markup for the main nav bar to use an unordered list. Save your changes, then in styles.css, in the site navigation section, change the selector for the `nav.sitenavigation p` rule to `nav.sitenavigation li`. Save your changes, refresh or reload greensf.html in your browser, then verify that the appearance of the nav bar remains unchanged.

g. Return to your editor, then repeat Step d for nearby.html and for museums.html.

h. Validate all your HTML and CSS documents.

FIGURE H-40

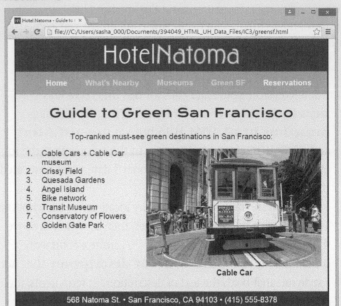

Independent Challenge 4 – Explore

As you continue your work on the website for Eating Well In Season, a provider of locally-sourced, healthy meals, you mark existing information using lists and you incorporate new information in a table.

a. In your editor, open HTM_H-17.html from the IC3 folder where you store your Data Files for this unit, save it as **menus.html**, then repeat to save HTM_H-18.html as **pricing.html**, and HTM_H-19.css as **styles.css**. In the comment at the top of each file, enter your name and today's date where indicated, then save the files.

b. In menus.html, mark the list of meals and menu items under the *Sample Menus* h2 heading as a description list. (*Hint*: More than one `dd` element can follow each `dt` element.) Save your changes, then in styles. css, below the last rule in the main content section, create a comment containing the text **main content description list**. Add a style rule for the description list that sets the font family to the font stack Verdana, Geneva, sans-serif and sets margins to 0 1em 1em, then create a rule for description list term items that formats text in bold and sets a top margin of 1em. In the reset styles section, add the `dd`, `dl`, and `dt` selectors to the list of selectors in the style rule that sets border, padding, and margin to 0. Save your changes, open menus.html in a browser, then verify that the display of the description list matches the one in **FIGURE H-41**.

FIGURE H-41

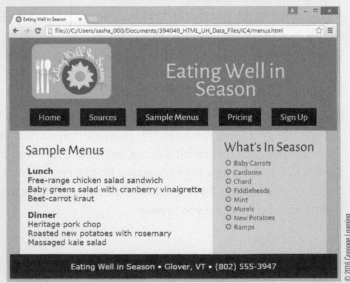

Independent Challenge 4 – Explore (continued)

c. In menus.html, mark the content of the sidebar below the h2 element as an unordered list. Save your changes, then in styles.css, below the last rule in the sidebar section, create a comment containing the text **sidebar unordered lists**. Create a style rule for unordered lists within `aside` elements that sets the left margin to 2em and uses the image bullet.png from the images folder as the item marker (*Hint*: Use the `list-style-image` property with the syntax `url("path/filename")`). In the reset styles section, add the ul and li selectors to the list of selectors in the style rule that sets border, padding, and margin to 0. At the end of the reset styles section, create a style rule using the ul selector that sets `list-style-type` to none. Save your changes, refresh or reload menus. html in your browser, then verify that it matches **FIGURE H-41**.

d. Return to menus.html in your editor, then convert the markup for the main nav bar to use an unordered list. Save your changes, then in styles.css, in the site navigation section, change the selector for the `nav.sitenavigation` p rule to `nav.sitenavigation li`. Save your changes, refresh or reload menus.html in your browser, then verify that the appearance of the nav bar remains unchanged.

e. Return to menus.html in your editor, copy the unordered list from the sidebar, switch to pricing.html in your editor, then paste the unordered list in the code for the sidebar, replacing the existing content below the h2 element. Repeat to copy the ordered list in the nav bar for menus.html and paste it in pricing.html.

f. In the `article` element in pricing.html, create the table shown in **TABLE H-5**. Specify the `class` value `specific-headers` for the second row of the header section. Save your changes.

TABLE H-5

Meal	Monthly Cost	
	once a week	daily
Lunch	$60	$390
Dinner	$80	$520
Both	$125	$800

© 2016 Cengage Learning

g. Return to styles.css in your editor, above the main content description list section, create a comment containing the text **main content table**. Create a style rule for the `table` element that sets a width of 90% and margins to 1em auto. Create a rule for table header cells and table data cells that sets width to 33.3%, creates a 1px solid black border, sets padding to 0.3em 1em, and sets the font family to `Verdana, Geneva, sans-serif`. Create a rule for table header cells that sets the background color to `#98c13d`. Create a rule for table header cells nested in the element with the `class` value `.specific-headers` that sets the background color to `rgb(246,224,65)`. Save your changes, open pricing.html in a browser, then verify that it matches **FIGURE H-42**.

h. Validate all of your HTML and CSS documents and make any edits necessary to address any issues.

FIGURE H-42

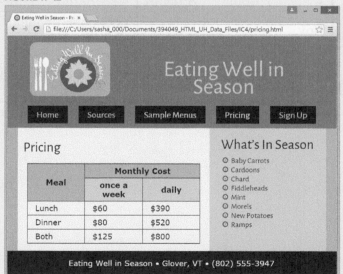

© 2016 Cengage Learning

Visual Workshop

In your editor, open the file HTM_H-20.html from the VW folder where you store your Data Files for this unit and save it as **events.html**. Repeat to save HTM_H-21.css as **styles.css**. Add your first and last names and today's date to the comment section at the top of each file, then save your changes. Add the table shown in **FIGURE H-43**, within the div element nested in the article element. (*Hint*: Use the title class to italicize the book title, and use the color rgb(253,245,230) for the table header background.) Convert the code for the nav bar to an unordered list, changing and adding to the style sheet as necessary. Validate your HTML and CSS code.

FIGURE H-43

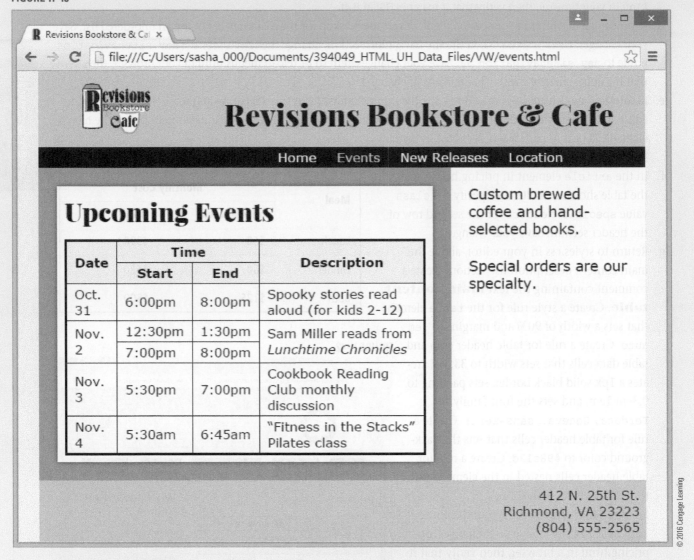

Organizing Content with Lists and Tables

HTML Elements

CASE ▶ This table includes all HTML elements covered in this text, along with selected attributes.

element	content/function
global attributes that apply to all HTML elements	
id="*id*"	a unique identifier for the current element
lang="*keyword*"	the primary language of the element contents, from a standard list of abbreviations
class="*class*"	one or more classes that the element is part of, separated by spaces
style="*style*"	one or more CSS declarations that apply only to the current element
!	contains comment text within the <!-- --> tag pair
a	links enclosed text or elements to another web page or other resource
href="*filename* | *url*"	address of web page or other resource that opens when the link is clicked or activated
target="_blank | _self"	a keyword for the window or tab in which the linked resource opens
area	creates a shape within an image map
alt="*text*"	text to display or be read aloud in place of the shape
coords="*x1,y1,…*"	a comma-separated list of coordinates for the specified shape value measured from the top and left edges of the image
href="*filename* | *url*"	a URL, local filename, or hash link to the target document or location opened by the hotspot
shape="circle | poly | rect"	the type of shape to create
article	contains a stand-alone piece of work, such as a single entry in a blog
aside	contains a part of a page that's tangential to the main page content
body	contains the contents visible in the main window of a web browser
br	inserts a line break
col	encloses one or more table columns to treat as a unit
span="*value*"	specifies the number of columns to include in the element
colgroup	encloses the col elements for a table
span="*value*"	specifies the number of columns to include in the element when no col elements are specified
dd	marks a description associated with a dt element in a description list
div	marks block-level content with no specific semantic meaning
dl	marks a description list, in which each item is comprised of a term and its description
dt	marks a term or an item being described in a description list
figcaption	marks caption text associated with an img element; always enclosed within a figure element
figure	contains an image that adds information to a web page; a user agent should be able to link the content of a figure element and move it to another location without affecting the information conveyed by the web page
footer	contains information about a section or document that usually appears at the end of a web page, such as attributions and/or footnotes
h1, h2, h3, h4, h5, h6	mark heading text; h1 is the highest level heading on a web page and h6 is the lowest

element	content/function
head	contains information about a web page, including elements that are not visible within the browser window
header	contains information about a section or document that usually appears at the beginning, such as a heading, logo, and/or table of contents
html	encloses all the code for a web page

img
    alt="*text*"
    src="*url
	filename*"
	    width="*value*"
	    height="*value*"
	    usemap="*name*"
		inserts an image
		text to display or be read aloud in place of the image
		path and filename for the image file to display
		native width of the image in pixels
		native height of the image in pixels
		name attribute value of map element to use as image map

li	marks list item content in an ordered list or an unordered list

link
    href="*filename
	url*"
	    rel="keyword"
	    media="*media*"
	    type="*type*"
		makes the content of an external file available in an HTML document
		specifies the destination
		keyword specifying the type of link
		media for which the linked resource is intended (default: all)
		MIME type of the linked resource

map name="*name*"	parent element for area elements that make up an image map name value referenced by usemap attribute in img element

meta
    name="*name*"
    http-equiv="*keyword*"
    content="*content*"
    charset="*charset*"
	enables you to pass information about a web page to user agents that open it
	the type of metadata being provided, from list of standard metadata names
	directions to the user agent on handling the web page
	the content of the metadata described by the name value
	the character encoding that the document uses

nav	contains site or page navigation elements
ol	marks an ordered list, in which items are numbered or lettered sequentially
p	marks a paragraph of text

script
    src="*filename*"
    type="*type*"
	contains script code or a link to an external file containing script code
	path and filename for the external script file
	the script language or data format

section	encloses a section of content focused on a common theme, such as a chapter of a larger work
span	contains inline text or elements; enables you to style inline elements
style type="*type*"	encloses style sheet code a MIME value indicating the language of the style sheet code
table	marks content to present as a table
tbody	encloses table body rows

td
    colspan="*value*"
    rowspan="*value*"
	marks the content of a table data cell
	the number of columns that the cell spans
	the number of rows that the cell spans

tfoot	encloses table footer rows

th
    colspan="*value*"
    rowspan="*value*"
	marks the content of a table header cell
	the number of columns that the cell spans
	the number of rows that the cell spans

thead	encloses table header rows
title	specifies text that appears on the title bar or tab of a web browser opening the page
tr	encloses table cell elements that make up a single table row
ul	marks an unordered list, in which the order of items doesn't matter

CSS Properties

CASE ▶ This table includes all CSS properties covered in this text, along with selected values.

property	values	specifies
@media	all; print; screen; or speech	style rules that apply only to indicated media
@page	(none)	style rules for a limited set of properties that apply only to paged output (such as printed output)
background	*background-image background-position [/background-size] background-repeat background-attachment background-clip background-color*	one or more properties related to background listed in a specific order (shorthand property)
background-attachment	scroll; local; or fixed	whether a background image scrolls with document content (scroll, the default), scrolls only with element content (local), or does not scroll (fixed)
background-blend-mode	normal; multiply; screen; overlay; darken; lighten; color-dodge; color-burn; hard-light; soft-light; difference; exclusion; hue; saturation; color; or luminosity	how overlapping background images blend with each other and with background color
background-clip	content-box; padding-box; or border-box (default)	whether a background image extends only behind element content (content-box), up to the inner edge of the border (padding-box), or to the outer edge of the border (border-box, the default)
background-color	color name from list of supported colors; rgb triplet in the format rgb(*rrr,ggg,bbb*); rgba value in the format rgba(*rrr,ggg,bbb,a*); hsl value in the format hsl(*hhh,sss,lll*); hsla value in the format hsla(*hhh,sss,lll,a*); or hexadecimal triplet in the format #*rrggbb*	an element's fill color, behind any content such as text
background-image	url("*path/filename*")	an image file to use as the background for an element
background-origin	content-box; padding-box; or border-box (default)	whether a background image starts only behind element content (content-box), at the inner edge of the border (padding-box), or at the outer edge of the border (border-box, the default)
background-position	one to four values from the keywords static; relative; absolute; sticky; or fixed, or values in CSS units	the position within an element of the edges of a background image
background-repeat	one or two values from the keywords repeat; repeat-x; repeat-y; space, round; or no-repeat	whether a background image is repeated horizontally, vertically, both, or neither, using one or two keywords

property	values	specifies
background-size	one or two values from the keywords auto; cover; or contain; or values in CSS units	the size of a background image with keywords, lengths, or percentages
border	a space-separated list of a thickness value in a CSS unit, a style keyword, and a CSS color name or value (% values are not supported for thickness), in the format thickness style color	the visible border around an element
border-collapse	collapse or separate (the default)	whether space is displayed between the borders of adjacent table cells (separate) or not (collapse)
border-color border-top-color border-right-color border-bottom-color border-left-color	color name from list of supported colors; rgb triplet in the format rgb(rrr,ggg,bbb); rgba value in the format rgba(rrr,ggg,bbb,a); hsl value in the format hsl(hhh,sss,lll); hsla value in the format hsla(hhh,sss,lll,a); or hexadecimal triplet in the format #rrggbb	the color of an element border on one or more sides
border-spacing	1 or 2 values in CSS units	the distance between the borders of adjacent table cells if the value of border-collapse is separate
border-style border-top-style border-right-style border-bottom-style border-left-style	dashed; dotted; double; groove; hidden; inset; none; ridge; outset; or solid	the style of an element border on one or more sides
border-width border-top-width border-right-width border-bottom-width border-left-width	thin; medium; thick; or a value in a CSS unit (% values not supported)	the thickness of an element border on one or more sides
bottom	value in ems, pixels, or another supported unit; or percent of the height of the browser window	the distance the element is moved up from the bottom edge of the browser window (fixed positioning) or positioned ancestor element (relative or absolute positioning); the default value, 0, leaves the element in its original vertical position
box-shadow	a horizontal offset in pixels; a vertical offset in pixels; a blur radius in pixels (optional); a shadow color (optional); a spread distance in pixels (optional); and the inset keyword (optional)	the shadow to create behind a block-level element
clear	left; right; both; or none	floated elements are not displayed to the left, right, or on either side of another element
color	color name from list of supported colors; rgb triplet in the format rgb(rrr,ggg,bbb); rgba value in the format rgba(rrr,ggg,bbb,a); hsl value in the format hsl(hhh,sss,lll); hsla value in the format hsla(hhh,sss,lll,a); or hexadecimal triplet in the format #rrggbb	an element's foreground color; for elements containing text, this is the text color
display	block; inline; inline-block; none; table; table-cell; table-row	how an element is rendered
float	left; right; or none	horizontal alignment of an element with the left or right edge of the parent element, and allows elements that follow to fill in the remaining horizontal space

property	values	specifies
font	[font-style] [font-variant] [font-weight] font-size [/line-height] font-family; at minimum, both font-size and font-family values must be specified, and all values within square brackets are optional	multiple font-related properties listed in a specific order (shorthand property)
font-family	font family name or font stack	the font family in which the text of an element is displayed
font-size	a value in a CSS unit	the relative or absolute size of text
font-style	italic; oblique; or normal	whether characters are displayed slanted or in standard orientation
font-variant	small-caps; other language-specific and font-specific keywords	a variant of the default font to use, including a font family's small caps style or other language-specific and font-specific styles
font-weight	normal; bold; 100; 200; 300; 400; 500; 600; 700; 800; or 900	the weight of text
height	a value in a CSS unit; % value based on width of parent element	the vertical size of an element's content, excluding border, padding, and margin
left	value in ems, pixels, or another supported unit; or percent of the width of the browser window	the distance the element is moved from the left toward the right edge of the browser window (fixed positioning) or positioned ancestor element (relative or absolute positioning); the default value, 0, leaves the element in its original horizontal position
line-height	a value in a CSS unit; or a value without units to specify a multiple of the default line height	the amount of blank space above and below each line of text
list-style-image	url("path/filename")	the image used as a list item marker
list-style-type	ordered list: decimal; decimal-leading-zero; lower-alpha; lower-latin; lower-roman; none; upper-alpha; upper-latin; upper-roman; or language-specific values unordered list: circle; disc; square; or none	the list item marker for an ordered or an unordered list
margin margin-top margin-right margin-bottom margin-left	a value in a CSS unit; % value based on width of parent element	the space outside a border between the border and adjacent or parent elements
max-height	a value in a CSS unit; % value based on width of parent element	the maximum vertical size of an element's content, excluding border, padding, and margin
max-width	a value in a CSS unit; % value based on width of parent element	the maximum horizontal size of an element's content, excluding border, padding, and margin
min-height	a value in a CSS unit; % value based on width of parent element	the minimum vertical size of an element's content, excluding border, padding, and margin
min-width	a value in a CSS unit; % value based on width of parent element	the minimum horizontal size of an element's content, excluding border, padding, and margin
opacity	a decimal value from 0 (fully transparent) to 1 (fully opaque)	how transparent an element is
padding padding-top padding-right padding-bottom padding-left	a value in a CSS unit; % value based on width of parent element	the space inside a border between the border and the element content

property	values	specifies
position	absolute; fixed; relative; static (default)	precisely where an element should be positioned on the web page
right	value in ems, pixels, or another supported unit; or percent of the width of the browser window	the distance the element is moved from the right toward the left edge of the browser window (fixed positioning) or positioned ancestor element (relative or absolute positioning); the default value, 0, leaves the element in its original horizontal position
text-align	left; right; center; justify; inherit (same value as enclosing element)	the horizontal alignment of text and other inline or inline-block elements within a parent element
text-shadow	a horizontal offset in pixels; a vertical offset in pixels; a blur radius in pixels (optional); and a shadow color (optional)	the shadow created behind text
top	value in ems, pixels, or another supported unit; or percent of the height of the browser window	the distance the element is moved down from the top edge of the browser window (fixed positioning) or positioned ancestor element (relative or absolute positioning); the default value, 0, leaves the element in its original vertical position
vertical-align	top; middle (the default); or bottom	the vertical alignment of table cell contents
width	a value in a CSS unit; % value based on width of parent element	the horizontal size of an element's content, excluding border, padding, and margin
z-index	positive or negative integer, or 0	the position of an element in the stacking order; an element with a larger value is displayed on top of an element with a smaller value

Uploading Files to a Web Server

CASE You are ready to upload a web page that you've created for Lakeland Reeds Bed & Breakfast. In this appendix, you will configure your FTP client to connect to your web server and you will upload the web page.

Appendix Objectives

After completing this unit, you will be able to:

- Prepare to go live with your website
- Configure your FTP client
- Upload website files

NOTE: To complete the steps in this appendix, you need the login name, password, configuration information, and public address for a web host to which you're permitted to publish files. This may be available free through your school or through your home Internet service provider, or you may choose to purchase a plan from a commercial web host.

File You Will Need

index.html

Prepare to Go Live with Your Website

Once you and your client, if relevant, are satisfied with the appearance and functionality of a website you've created, the final step is to publish it to a web server in order to make it available to anyone with web access, a step sometimes known as *going live*. Before you publish a website, though, it can be useful to perform a few final checks and optimizations to maximize the site's performance and to ensure that the code is as intelligible as possible, both for future revisions and for anyone who wants to understand how your design works. **CASE** ▸ *As you prepare to publish a web page you have created for Lakeland Reeds B&B, you review some common techniques for testing and finalizing a website.*

DETAILS

The process of testing and finalizing a website may include the following:

- **Publishing to a testing server**

  Viewing pages directly from your local computer is sometimes the easiest way to quickly test and make changes while developing a website. However, it's important to transfer all the files in your website to a web server and test them from a published location in order to catch any server-related problems before the site goes live. Because you don't want potential users to stumble upon the unfinished site and be frustrated by any remaining glitches, you should use a testing server, which is a web server that's available only to you, not to all web users, as illustrated in **FIGURE APP C-1**. Some large organizations have web servers set aside for this purpose; however, for smaller-scale development, creating a password-protected folder on your main web server can suffice. You can then publish your site to this folder and view the pages in your browser after entering the password; once you've worked out any remaining issues, you can simply transfer the files to the main directory.

- **Performing browser tests and usability tests**

  Just as you've done at each stage of development, it's important to test your final website using the browsers that are most common among your target audience. Browser use can vary widely by geography; differences can also show up based on many other factors, so it's important to identify your target audience and research which browsers potential clients are most likely to be using to access your site. In addition, it's important to verify that each aspect of the site is functioning by testing all links to ensure that they open the correct targets or pages and by testing any interactive content, such as scripts and CSS pseudo-classes, to verify that it works as expected.

  In addition to doing your own testing, it can be invaluable to bring members of your target audience into the testing process. Conducting usability tests in which you ask potential users to complete common tasks and locate information on a prototype of your website can give you important insight into the structure and function of your site, and help you understand what, if anything, could use tweaking before you publish the site.

- **Checking for errors using web development tools**

  A number of software tools are available to help you identify and fix errors in your web pages. Major browsers include features that let you view the HTML and CSS code for any element in a page, as well as debug scripts. Utilities, both downloadable and online, can also help you clean up your HTML and CSS code.

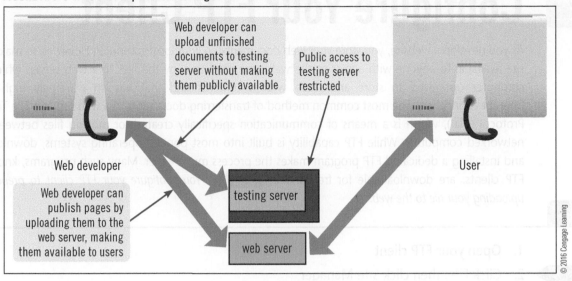

© 2016 Cengage Learning

Publishing with a Domain Name

Even for small businesses and personal pages, it's common to publish websites using domain names. Obtaining and publishing with a domain name requires three different services. First, you reserve a domain name through a domain name registrar. You pay a registrar for the rights to use a domain name for a specified period of time, which can be extended as needed to ensure the website has the same domain name over its lifetime. Any changes you wish to make in your domain name registration, including changing your contact info or transferring the domain to another party, must be done through this registrar. Next, to make your pages available on the web, they need to be located on a web server, which is a computer that's always connected to the Internet and is running software to listen for and respond to requests for web pages. While it's possible to run a web server over a home broadband connection, the vast majority of websites are hosted on machines in facilities known as server farms that are specially designed to provide a constant flow of electricity and uninterrupted Internet access. For a monthly or yearly fee, you can rent space on a server through a web host, which is one of thousands of companies worldwide that provide access to these machines. The final step is to ensure that your domain name and your web server are connected in the domain name service (DNS), which is a central directory for the web, similar to a phone book. Once you rent space on a web server, your web hosting provider will give you an IP address that points to your web space. Many registrars offer DNS hosting for free as part of their registry services; likewise, web hosts generally offer this service as well. You can pick one of these organizations, but not both, to be your DNS host, thereby finalizing the link between your hosted website and your domain name.

Configure Your FTP Client

As you develop a website, you store your web documents on your local computer. However, to make your site available to anyone with access to the web, you need to copy the files to a web server, which is a computer optimized to store and share web documents and that has an extremely high-speed Internet connection. The most common method of transferring documents to a web server is File Transfer Protocol (FTP), which is a means of communication specifically created for moving files between two networked computers. While FTP capability is built into most popular operating systems, downloading and installing a dedicated FTP program makes the process much easier. Many such programs, known as FTP clients, are downloadable for free online. **CASE** *You configure your FTP client to prepare for uploading your file to the web.*

STEPS

1. **Open your FTP client**

2. **Click** File, **then click** Site Manager

   TROUBLE
   These steps are for FileZilla, a free FTP client available at filezilla-project.org. If you are using a different FTP client, obtain configuration instructions from your instructor or technical support person, or from the documentation that came with the program.

   FileZilla opens the Site Manager dialog box, which provides options for setting up a new connection to a web server.

3. **Click** New Site, **type a descriptive name for the web server you are configuring, such as the name or abbreviation of your school or web hosting company, then press** [Enter]

4. **Click the** Host **box, then type the FTP address provided by your instructor, technical support person, or web host**

5. **Click the** Logon Type **arrow, then click** Ask for password

6. **Click the** User **box, then type the user name provided by your instructor or technical support person**

   FIGURE APP C-2 shows the completed Site Manager dialog box.

7. **Click** Connect, **type your password, click the** Remember password ... **check box to uncheck it, then click** OK

   TROUBLE
   If you aren't able to connect to your web server, ask your instructor or technical support person about other configuration options you might need to select.

   FileZilla saves the new configuration and tests your connection to the FTP server. **FIGURE APP C-3** shows a successful connection in FileZilla.

8. **Click** Server **on the Menu Bar, then click** Disconnect **to end your FTP connection**

FIGURE APP C-2: Site Manager dialog box

List of web servers configured for this FTP client (yours will differ)

Descriptive name for the web server

Saves configuration information and tests connection

FTP address of web server (your Host will differ)

"Ask for password" prompts for password each time you connect; "Normal" stores password for this site

Login name for your account on your web server (your username will differ)

Source: FileZilla

FIGURE APP C-3: View of connected web server

Navigation area for directories on local computer

List of files and folders in current directory on local computer

Navigation area for directories on web server

List of files and folders in current directory on web server

Source: FileZilla

Configuring a testing server

As part of the web development process, it's useful to upload your pages to your web server for testing purposes before actually making them available to the public. The final upload location for pages on your web server is not a good location for this purpose because all pages you upload to that location are immediately available to the entire World Wide Web—even pages that still contain errors or don't display properly. Instead, web developers often maintain a separate testing server for their projects, which is a location available on a local network or on the web that is non-publicized and may even require a password for access. When using an FTP client to access a testing server, you use the same local source folder as for final files. The target location, however, may be a different folder on the same web server, or a different web host altogether.

Upload Website Files

Once your FTP client is configured to access your web server and your files have been tested and validated, you can upload these final files for your website, which makes them available to anyone using the web. **CASE** *You upload the web page for the Lakeland Reeds website to the web host and verify that it was uploaded correctly.*

STEPS

1. **Open your FTP client and connect to your web server**

2. **Use the Local site directory tree on the left side of the FileZilla window to navigate to the drive and folder where you store your Data Files for this appendix**
   The index.html file is displayed in the Local site file list below the directory tree.

3. **Use the Remote site directory tree on the right side of the FileZilla window to navigate to the folder designated for your web pages on the web server**
   Any web documents that you copy to this directory are available on the web.

4. **In the Local site file list, drag index.html to the Remote site file list and release the mouse button**

5. **If necessary, enter your password, click the Remember password ... check box to uncheck it, then click OK**
   The file is copied to your web server, as shown in **FIGURE APP C-4**.

6. **Click Server on the Menu Bar, then click Disconnect to end your FTP connection**

TROUBLE
If you do not see the web page shown in Figure C-5, verify that the web address open in your browser exactly matches the web publishing address you were provided.

7. **Open your web browser, then navigate to the web publishing address provided by your instructor or technical support person**
   The Lakeland Reeds web page is displayed, as shown in **FIGURE APP C-5**.

FIGURE APP C-4: Website file copied to web server

File selected and dragged to Remote site file list →

File copied to web server →

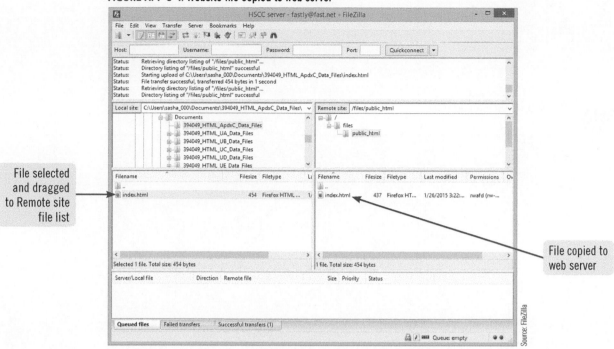

Source: FileZilla

FIGURE APP C-5: Web page opened from remote web server

Contents of published web page displayed in browser window →

Address bar displays URL of web server (yours will differ) →

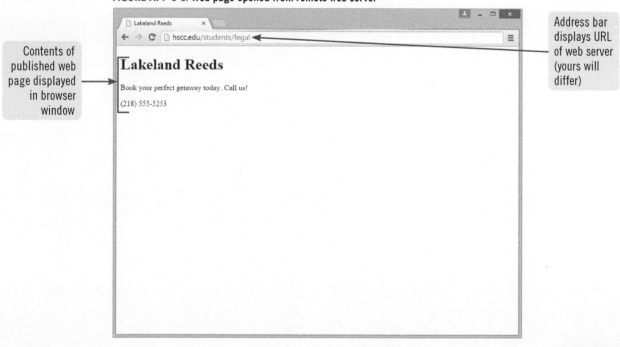

Glossary

@font-face rule A variation of a style rule that indicates the name of a downloadable font and the location of the necessary files.

Absolute link A link that specifies the full and complete address for a target document on the web.

absolute positioning A positioning technique that takes an element out of the normal flow and positions it in a location you specify.

absolute units Units such as pixels that represent a specific length or height that doesn't change.

alt text Text to display in case an image is unavailable or needs to be read in user agents by software such as screen readers; created with the alt attribute of the img element.

attribute Additional code within an opening element tag that specifies information about that element.

Bitmap image An electronic representation of an image as a grid of dots, with a color specified for each dot.

block-level element An element rendered as a box occupying the full length of its parent element, with a line break before and after.

body section A web page section whose contents include elements that are visible in the main window of a web browser, such as paragraphs and headings.

border In the box model, a line around an element formatted with a width, style, and color.

box model The model CSS uses to represent the characteristics of every web page element as a rectangular box with several global properties.

browser history The log your browser maintains of URLs that you've visited.

bug A problem that results from incorrectly written code.

Cascading Style Sheets (CSS) A companion language to HTML designed for describing the appearance of web page elements.

cell The intersection of a row and a column in a table, in which each item of data is displayed.

character encoding The system user agents should employ to translate the electronic information representing a web page into human-recognizable symbols, such as letters and numbers.

character reference A specially formatted code that represents characters in the HTML document character set.

child element An element nested within another element.

class selector A selector that creates a style rule based on values assigned to elements using the HTML class attribute.

clients Computers that access web documents over a network from a web server.

code editor A text editor that is optimized for writing code in a programming language.

collapse The term for what happens in the box model when adjacent top and bottom margins combine into a single margin equal to the greater of the two values.

column A vertical set of data in a table.

comment A text element in your web page code that is not rendered by user agents and is viewable only by people who examine the HTML code of your web pages.

commenting out Enclosing a declaration within comment characters so user agents won't apply it to your documents while preserving it in your style sheet.

CSS See Cascading Style Sheets (CSS).

CSS3 The most recent version of CSS.

custom font A font that is not installed on a user's computer but that a user agent can download and apply.

Debugging The process of finding and removing bugs from code.

declaration The basic building block of CSS code, which is a combination of a property name and a value.

definition list The name for a description list in previous versions of HTML.

description list A list that enables you to specify a set of items and descriptions.

design document See project plan.

developer tools Utilities that are built into all modern browsers that you can use to debug your code.

dots per inch (DPI) The unit of measurement for image resolution, which specifies how close the dots in the bitmap image should appear on the output.

downloadable font See custom font.

DPI See dots per inch (DPI).

Em A CSS unit that represents a multiple of the computed font size for the current element, where 1em represents 100% of this size.

email harvester A program that continually explores web pages looking for email addresses that in turn receive spam emails.

embedded style sheet CSS style rules entered in the head element of an HTML document.

Extensible Hypertext Markup Language (XHTML) A version of HTML that conforms to the rules of Extensible Markup Language (XML).

Extensible Markup Language (XML) A markup language whose rules are combined with those of HTML to create XHTML.

extension A small application that changes the way web pages are rendered in a browser or integrates features with the content of a web page.

external style sheet A separate file containing style information that multiple web pages can link to.

Favicon A custom graphic file for a website, displayed on the browser tab or bookmarks list in a desktop browser.

fixed positioning A visual effect that involves an element remaining in the same position in the browser window while a user scrolls the remaining page content.

fluid layout A layout in which content size is constrained with the min-width and max-width properties and the columns are sized using percentages.

font family A collection of a single typeface and its variants.

font stack A list of font families in order of preference, separated by commas.

Generic font family A grouping of font families according to shared characteristics.

GIF An older graphics format that works best for art that contains limited numbers of colors and areas with defined borders between areas; short for Graphics Interchange Format.

grandchild element The child element of an element's child element.

grandparent element The parent element of an element's parent element.

Hand-coding Creating a web page by entering HTML directly.

hash link A link to an id property value.

head section The section of an HTML document containing elements that are not part of the main web page, such as the title element.

hex system *See* hexadecimal system.

hexadecimal system A system for specifying colors that uses a pound sign (#) followed by six digits, which may include the numbers 0–9 and the letters a–f; the first two digits specify the red value, the middle two digits indicate the green value, and the final pair of digits represents the blue value.

hotspot A linked shape in an image map.

HTML *See* Hypertext Markup Language (HTML).

HTML5 The most recent version of HTML.

http *See* Hypertext Transfer Protocol (http).

https *See* Hypertext Transfer Protocol Secure (https).

hyperlink *See* link.

Hypertext Markup Language (HTML) The language in which web pages are written, which provides a standardized format for specifying the structure of a web page.

Hypertext Transfer Protocol (http) One of the schemes that web servers use to make documents available.

Hypertext Transfer Protocol Secure (https) One of the schemes that web servers use to make documents available.

ID selector A CSS selector that applies code in its associated style rule to the element with the specified id attribute value.

image map HTML code associated with an image that specifies one or more shapes using sets of coordinates and provides a link target for each shape.

inheritance The process of applying an element's declarations to all of its descendant elements.

inline element An element that does not expand to fill the space of its parent and that is not rendered with line breaks before or after.

inline style A style rule inserted into the opening tag of an element using the style attribute.

JPEG An image format optimized for images that contain many colors, such as photographs; *also called* JPG; short for Joint Photographic Experts Group, the organization that created it.

JPG *See* JPEG.

Layer A new level displayed on top of the normal flow, into which a positioned element is placed.

link Text or another web page element that users can select to move to related content in the same page or in another document.

liquid layout *See* fluid layout.

lorem ipsum Text from an essay by the Roman philosopher Cicero that has been standard filler for print layouts since the 1500s.

Mailto link A link that creates a new email to a specified recipient.

margin In the box model, the space outside the border between the border and adjacent or parent elements.

media query A variation of a style rule that you use to create a group of rules for a specific device.

multi-line comment A comment that occupies multiple lines, with the opening and closing tags often on their own lines.

Named character reference A character reference that uses an abbreviation-based code.

native For a bitmap image, the native dimensions are the original width and height at which the image was saved.

nav bar *See* navigation bar.

navigation bar A set of links for moving between web pages in a website.

nested The state of being located within; when a tag pair occurs within another tag pair, the inner pair is said to be nested within the outer pair.

normal flow The default arrangement of elements in a web document, in which elements are displayed in the order they appear, with most elements displayed below the element that precedes them.

numeric character reference A character reference that uses a number code.

One-sided tag An HTML tag that is used by itself, rather than in a pair.

ordered list A list in which items are numbered or lettered sequentially.

Padding In the box model, the space inside a border between the border and the element content.

parent element An element with another element nested within it.

path The part of a URL composed of the sequence of folders in which the target document is stored on the server.

percent A CSS unit that represents a percentage of another value for the current element or an ancestor element; each CSS property that takes a value in % specifies what value the % calculation is based on.

pixel A CSS unit that represents a unit equal to approximately 1/96 inch or 0.26 millimeter.

pixels The individual dots that make up an image, used to measure the size of a bitmap image.

PNG A graphics format that works best for art that contains limited numbers of colors and areas with defined borders between areas; short for Portable Network Graphics.

preview To open a web page in one or more browsers and examine the result.

project plan A summary of a client's parameters for a web site, including audience, budget, and timeline. *Also called* design document.

property An aspect of the appearance of a web page element that can be modified.

pseudo-class A categorization of a web page element based on a relationship or condition of the element at a given moment, rather than on a static attribute value.

pseudo-element A selector that identifies a specific part of an element and lets you style the selection as if it were its own element.

Relative link A link that gives only the path and filename information necessary to locate the target document based on the location of the current web page.

relative positioning A positioning technique that lets you make adjustments to the default position of an element while preserving the space allotted to the element in the normal flow.

relative units Units such as ems, percent, and rems that are calculated based on the sizes of other elements on a web page.

rem A CSS unit that represents a multiple of the computed font size for the html element, where 1rem represents 100% of this size; term is short for *root em*.

rendering engine Software that translates web page elements into visual, auditory, or tactile representations based on web standards.

reset rule A style rule that resets one or more common properties of multiple elements to a common baseline, ensuring that default values that may be different between browsers do not cause a web page to be displayed inconsistently.

resolution Specifies how close the dots in a bitmap image should appear on the output; measured in dots per inch (DPI).

rgb system A system that uses rgb triplets to specify colors.

rgb triplet A set of comma-separated values, each ranging from 0–255 or 0–100%, which represent the amounts of red, green, and blue in a color.

row A horizontal set of data in a table.

Sans-serif font A font that does not incorporate serifs.

Scalable Vector Graphics (SVG) A graphics format that's optimal for encoding line art and that can be displayed at different dimensions with no decrease in quality.

scheme The way that computers ask for and communicate about a requested document.

screen reader Devices that many people with visual impairments use to access the web, which read aloud web page text and descriptions that a user selects.

selector The part of a style rule that identifies the HTML element or elements to which the declarations apply.

semantic Describes languages such as HTML5, which are intended to indicate the meanings of elements such as headings and paragraphs, but not to tell web browsers how the elements should appear.

semantic element An HTML5 element that indicates the role of its content.

serif A small finishing stroke at the end of a line making up a character in some fonts.

serif font A font that uses serifs.

server name The part of a URL that identifies the general location of a target document on the web.

short link A generated URL that uses an especially short domain name and a specially crafted path to represent a large, unwieldy link as a short, manageable URL.

shortcut property A property that assigns values to multiple other CSS properties with a single declaration.

sibling element When two elements are both children of the same element, they are sibling elements.

single-line comment A comment that includes the opening tag, comment text, and closing tag on a single line.

skip link A link that targets an id value at the start of the main page content and allows users to bypass navigation.

specificity A selector's priority relative to other selectors.

stack To overlap web page elements using positioning.

stacking context The element containing elements to be stacked using the z-index property.

static layout A layout that specifies a fixed width for web page content.

storyboard In website planning, a sketch that shows the links between the pages in the website.

style rule A line or block of CSS code that specifies the presentation of web page elements.

SVG *See* Scalable Vector Graphics (SVG).

Tag An HTML code that specifies how user agents should treat an item in a web document.

target document The location, web page, or other document that a link opens.

template A generic website layout that includes a color scheme and element positions, but which uses placeholder images and text.

touch icon A custom graphic file that serves as the icon for shortcuts that users create on mobile devices.

type selector The name of an HTML element used as a selector, which applies associated declarations to every instance of the specified element in a web document.

Uniform resource locator (URL) A standard format for specifying how and where to access a resource on the Internet.

unordered list A list in which the order of list items doesn't matter.

URL *See* uniform resource locator (URL).

user agents Programs and devices that interpret web documents.

Validation An automated process of comparing code you've written against the coding standards for the language, such as HTML5 or XHTML, in which it's written.

vector graphic An electronic representation of an image using geometric shapes.

viewport The imaginary window through which most mobile browsers display web pages.

viewport meta element A meta element with the name attribute set to a value of viewport, which is used to change a browser's viewport settings.

W3C *See* World Wide Web consortium (W3C).

WCAG *See* Web Content Accessibility Guidelines (WCAG).

web *See* World Wide Web.

web address *See* uniform resource locator (URL).

Web Content Accessibility Guidelines (WCAG) A widely used reference for implementing web accessibility that is maintained by the World Wide Web Consortium (W3C).

web page A document formatted to be accessible on the web.

web server A computer that is running web server software and that is always connected to the Internet.

web server software Software that makes web documents available over a network to other computers.

website A collection of web pages that is available to anyone with web access.

white space Empty space in a layout.

wireframe In website planning, a sketch that outlines the components of each page in a website and their places in the layout.

World Wide Web A vast collection of publicly accessible, linked documents written in Hypertext Markup Language and related languages. *Also called* web.

World Wide Web Consortium (W3C) An organization that helps build consensus around changes and additions to HTML5 and publishes descriptions of the current standards.

XHTML *See* Extensible Hypertext Markup Language (XHTML).

XML *See* Extensible Markup Language (XML).

Index